Early Modern Spain

Early Modern Spain

A Documentary History

Edited by
JON COWANS

PENN

University of Pennsylvania Press

Philadelphia

Publication of this volume was assisted by a grant from the
Program for Cultural Cooperation between Spain's Ministry of
Education and Culture and United States Universities

10 9 8 7 6 5 4 3 2 1

Published by
University of Pennsylvania Press
Philadelphia, Pennsylvania 19104-4011

Library of Congress Cataloging-in-Publication Data

Early modern Spain : a documentary history / edited by Jon Cowans.
    p. cm.
Includes bibliographical references and index.
ISBN 0-8122-3716-1 (cloth : alk. paper) — ISBN 0-8122-1845-0 (pbk. : alk. paper)
    1. Spain—History—Ferdinand and Isabella, 1479–1516—Sources. 2. Spain—History—
House of Austria, 1516–1700—Sources. 3. Spain—History—Bourbons, 1700—Sources.
I. Cowans, Jon.
DP161.5.E27 2003
946—dc21   2002045413

Contents

INTRODUCTION

During most of the nineteenth and twentieth centuries Spain occupied a curiously marginal place in the field of modern European historiography, a former superpower generally neglected by a profession focusing mainly on the history of Britain, France, and Germany. Yet if perceptions of Spain as a "backward," barely European country accounted for these collective attitudes among historians during most of the nineteenth and twentieth centuries, a series of striking changes taking place in the last decades of the twentieth century—including the country's successful transition to democracy following the death of the dictator Francisco Franco in 1975, its rapid socio-economic transformation beginning even before Franco's death, and the freeing of the country's intellectual life from the constraints of dictatorship and poverty—laid the groundwork for the advent of a new wave of excellent studies of Spain's past. Both inside and outside Spain, historians have been rethinking old topics and exploring comparatively new ones such as gender, culture, and memory, furnishing readers of Spanish history with a richer literature than ever before. At the same time, the Spanish language has become far and away the most widely studied foreign language in the United States, among other places, and Spain itself continues to grow as a destination for English speakers traveling abroad, creating even greater interest in Spain's past. Yet despite these encouraging developments, English readers interested in learning Spanish history through the fascinating path of reading primary historical texts have remained without the kind of documents collection that has long been available for other countries. For although there is an invaluable collection of historical documents on Iberia in the Middle Ages—Olivia Remie Constable's *Medieval Iberia*—and several large Spanish-language collections of historical texts, English speakers have long lacked any similar collection of translated historical documents on early-modern and modern Spain. It is that gap in the literature that these two volumes seek to fill.

The starting point for this collection is one of the most important moments in all of Spanish history: the marriage of Ferdinand of Aragon and Isabella of Castile in 1469. The marriage of those two sovereigns involved not a complete fusion of two societies but simply a union of the Crowns—a prospect less likely to provoke resistance among those wary of change and of threats to existing privileges—but the joining of the two largest Iberian kingdoms nonetheless marks the point at which one may begin to speak of Spain as a political entity. That entity itself continued to grow, as Ferdinand and Isabella won the kingdom of Granada by war in 1492—completing the nearly eight-hundred-year "Reconquest" of Iberia from its Muslim rulers—

and (after Isabella's death) also acquired the small northern kingdom of Navarre by force and diplomacy in 1512. Of course the "Catholic kings" also added to their holdings by sponsoring the voyages of Christopher Columbus and others, though few could fully appreciate those discoveries' significance at first. While pursuing this ambitious program, Ferdinand and Isabella generally kept their promise not to tamper with long-standing internal political arrangements in Castile and Aragon (particularly in the latter), but they did take some tentative steps that ended up creating a more unified and homogeneous realm. Some of their actions, such as the establishment of the Inquisition in Spain and the decision to expel Spain's Jews in 1492, may offend modern sensibilities, but they enjoyed strong support at the time, and they certainly served the rulers' overall aims. Establishing increasing control over the nobility and over the Church in Spain were also among their notable accomplishments, and in doing so they helped create the foundations for a powerful modern state.

In spite of all they did to create a powerful Spain, however, Ferdinand and Isabella had no son to inherit the throne, so upon Ferdinand's death in 1516 the throne passed to their daughter, Juana, who was widely deemed mentally incapable of heading a government. In her place, their Flemish grandson Charles of Ghent (known as Charles I of Spain and Charles V of the Holy Roman Empire) became Spain's actual ruler. Charles's accession to power in Spain had immense implications for the country, for the new king also ruled over large European territories, most notably modern-day Belgium and the Netherlands. Many Spaniards resented being ruled by a foreigner—who was widely expected to reside abroad and neglect Spain—but the defeat of two rebellions at the beginning of Charles's reign secured his position in Spain. Charles eventually proved quite devoted to Spain, and in time he won over many skeptics; his vigorous efforts to crush Protestantism throughout Europe were certainly popular in Spain, and it did not hurt that Charles also ruled over what was proving to be a large and lucrative empire in the New World. As a favored son of the Vatican, Spain also played a central role in waging the long-standing war between Christians and Muslims throughout the Mediterranean region.

Spain grew even more powerful under Charles's successor, Philip II (reigned 1556–1598), who added Portugal to his holdings in 1580 and who benefited from an enormous influx of silver from the New World in the second half of the century. Yet Philip also confronted a very serious rebellion in the Low Countries, where Protestants, local nobles, and merchants all had reason to resent Spanish rule. Fighting the Dutch rebels proved very expensive for Spain, and although the American silver seemed to make a military victory in the Low Countries possible, the rebellion dragged on for years. English assistance to the Dutch played a leading role in Philip's decision to send the "Invincible Armada" against England in 1588, but that famous expedition ended in defeat, and in its aftermath many Spaniards began to sense a profound national crisis.

The costs of empire naturally had serious domestic implications, and the Crown continued to seek new sources of revenue at home to supplement the income coming from America. The burden of a series of new forms of taxation fell primarily on Castile and on Spain's commoners (the Church and nobility being exempt from many forms of taxation), but even these new revenues could not rescue the Crown's chronically ill finances. These taxes took their toll on Spain's economy, absorbing capital and adding to the woes of a largely landless peasantry already forced to pay tithes to the Church and rents and fees to the land's owners, and among the many contemporary observers who remarked upon the depopulation of the countryside, discussions of the burdens of taxation loomed large.

By the end of Philip's reign in 1598, more and more reformers, known as *arbitristas*, were analyzing Spain's perceived decline and prescribing a wide range of new policies. Enacting such reforms, however, proved very difficult in a society full of powerful groups determined to guard entrenched privileges, and when reformers denounced cultural attitudes such as a disdain for manual labor (a traditionally noble attitude that many commoners also adopted), they took on extremely intractable problems. The analysis of national decline became a kind of national pastime, but real reforms were far less common than treatises on the subject.

Philip II himself presided over considerable troubles, including the defeat of the Armada and periodic declarations of royal bankruptcy, but matters worsened under his successors, Philip III (1598–1621), Philip IV (1621–1665), and Charles II (1665–1700). In the New World, English, French, and Dutch interlopers made serious inroads into Spanish territory, where they found Spanish subjects eager to ignore the Crown's rules on commerce, and the flow of bullion from the colonies fluctuated and declined. In Europe, Spain gradually abandoned its losing effort against the Dutch rebels, signing a truce in 1609 and a treaty recognizing Dutch independence in 1648, while also fighting periodic wars against the French and facing a rebellion in the Crown's Italian possessions in 1647. And in Iberia a simultaneous revolt of the Catalans and Portuguese in 1640 forced Philip IV and his chief minister, the Count-Duke of Olivares, to devote troops and resources to two fronts at once. Although Philip's troops defeated the Catalans, war with the Portuguese continued for years, and the Crown eventually accepted Portuguese independence in 1668. Also during this period, the Crown decreed the expulsion of the remaining Moriscos, Muslims who had ostensibly converted to Christianity but who remained the object of considerable suspicion and hatred. Their departure in 1609 marked the end of almost a thousand years of Muslim life in Iberia.

Ironically, however, Spain entered a cultural Golden Age at the very time that its economic and military picture looked so bleak. So while the *arbitristas* were analyzing Spain's ills, brilliant artists such as El Greco, Diego Velázquez, Francisco de Zurbarán, and Bartolomé Esteban Murillo were at work, as were writers such as Miguel de Cervantes, Lope de Vega, Tirso de Molina, and Francisco de Quevedo. Moreover, despite the bad news coming in from the many corners of Spain's empire, the country still ruled over vast holdings that were the envy of other European powers. Nonetheless, Spain's fortunes reached their nadir under Charles II, whose reign was marked by a deterioration of royal power and the spectacle of a chronically ill—some even said bewitched—king incapable of fathering a child.

Charles's death in 1700 marked the end of the Habsburg dynasty, touching off a European war won by an alliance favoring the French Bourbon candidate for the Spanish throne. In the diplomatic accords signed at the war's end, Spain lost its last European possessions, reducing the country's overseas possessions to the American territories, the Philippines, Guam, and the Canary Islands. Within Spain, Aragon had opposed the French candidate, Philip of Anjou, out of fears that he would follow the centralizing, absolutist approach that his grandfather, Louis XIV, had pursued in France, but the region's ill-fated decision to fight against Philip merely made it easier for the victorious king to curtail Aragon's traditional political autonomy. Over the course of the eighteenth century, the Bourbons enacted many significant reforms both at home and in the American colonies, reforms that did indeed reflect the influence of French absolutism. But if this was absolutism, it was at least enlightened absolutism, for the ideas of the Enlightenment had also followed the Bourbons to Spain, reinvigorating the country's intellectual life and inspiring a new round of essays on reform. How extensively this new spirit was reflected in policies is open to question, but kings such as Charles III (1759–1788) did take a number of bold steps, from the expulsion of the Jesuits to the reduction of the nobles' political power and the promotion of projects to aid Spain's economy.

With the advent of the French Revolution in 1789, however, fears that Spain might follow France down the path of political violence and chaos damaged the impetus for reform, and the Crown did its best to keep any word of events in France from crossing the Pyrenees. By 1793, growing tensions between France and Spain culminated in a declaration of war, but French advances across the border soon led Spain to seek peace. In the ensuing diplomatic maneuvering, Spain, concerned over British encroachment in its American colonies, chose to change sides and ally with France against Britain. It was that alliance with France that eventually led to the arrival of Napoleon's troops in Spain, and the end of an entire period of Spanish history.

The introductions to the documents seek to provide background information both on their authors and on the relevant historical context. In the hopes of leaving as much space as possible for the documents themselves, however, we have tried to keep the introductions brief, so those desiring lengthy, detailed discussion of historical background should consult one of the many fine histories of Spain listed in the Bibliography. Moreover, the introductions refrain from summarizing each document's content, instead allowing the figures from Spain's past to speak for themselves.

Regarding the translations, which are the work of the editor unless otherwise noted, special care has been taken to make the English texts comprehensible to contemporary readers, including those who may be unfamiliar with Spanish history. In documents translated by others, some changes have been made, bringing language up to date and using contemporary American spellings. Of course modes of expression change over time, and when choices had to be made, we have favored clarity over strict adherence to the linguistic styles of the past. In many passages, discussions of obscure matters have been omitted (indicated by ellipses), while in others brief explanations (in brackets) have been inserted into the text. In the treatment of proper names, we have generally tried to use the Spanish versions, but in those cases where individuals are already well known by their English-language names—Ferdinand and Isabella, for example—we have followed common practice and used the English versions. The order of the documents is generally chronological, but when a document was written years after the events in question, it is the date of the events rather than the writing of the document that has determined its placement.

Those who read Spanish should be aware of several excellent published collections of historical documents to which this work owes a great deal. One is a series of books edited by Fernando Díaz-Plaja, entitled *Historia de España en sus documentos* (see citations in the Bibliography). Also of immense value is the massive collection known as the Biblioteca de autores españoles, which began publication in the nineteenth century, and now runs to over three hundred volumes. Finally, I wish to mention Alfonso García-Gallo's

Manual de historia del derecho español, which presents an enormous number of well-chosen documents in a single volume.

In any collection such as this, one ultimately has to leave out many worthy subjects and documents. The book does not include selections from Spanish literature, not because literature is unimportant for understanding history, but on the contrary, because it is so important that it deserves full treatment elsewhere. The availability of documents also varies greatly by topic, making it difficult to do justice to crucial issues such as the outlook of those at the bottom of Spanish society, though efforts have been made here to include descriptions of their lives recorded by literate contemporaries. We hope that this collection will contribute to people's understanding of the history of one of Europe's most important and fascinating countries.

Acknowledgments

I would like to thank several people who helped make this project a reality. For their careful comments and suggestions on the manuscript, I am indebted to Professors Antonio Feros of New York University, James Boyden of Tulane University, and Victoria Enders of Northern Arizona University. I would also like to express my gratitude for a grant to support publication of this book from the Program for Cultural Cooperation between Spain's Ministry of Education and Culture and United States Universities. Thanks are also due to those publishers and organizations that were kind enough to allow me to reprint material under copyright. I also wish to thank the librarians and staff at the New York Public Library, New York University's Bobst Library, Rutgers University's Alexander and Dana Libraries, Columbia University's Butler Library, and the Instituto Cervantes in New York. I am grateful to the Cultural Office of the Embassy of Spain in Washington, D.C., for answering questions and helping me secure permission to reprint documents. Finally, I would like to thank everyone at the University of Pennsylvania Press for their diligent work on this project. Special thanks go to Alison Anderson for her expert and cheerful responses to my many inquiries during the editing process, and, most of all, to Jerry Singerman, who was so helpful in answering questions, in offering advice, and in seeing this project through from the outset.

1. King Ferdinand,
Marriage Concessions (1469)

As Europe emerged from the Middle Ages, larger states were being formed through war and diplomacy. Castile was the largest kingdom in the Iberian Peninsula in the fifteenth century, but by the second half of that century Castile's rulers were considering further expansion by means of a marriage linking them with the monarchs of another kingdom. In 1469, the eighteen-year-old Isabella, one of the possible heirs to the Castilian throne, was seeking both to strengthen her claims against internal rivals and to advance Castile's position internationally, and she and her supporters understood how crucial a well-chosen marriage would be. After considering her options, she chose not to marry princes from the Portuguese and French royal families, but rather the seventeen-year-old Ferdinand of Aragon. For Ferdinand, strengthening ties with Castile seemed a useful means of bolstering his power internally and protecting his lands against threats from France.

The rulers of Castile and Aragon were already related, and the two kingdoms had extensive cultural and economic ties, but the idea of a formal union of the Crowns of Castile and Aragon still encountered strong resistance in both kingdoms. In issuing this document specifying the political terms of the marriage, Ferdinand hoped to mollify its opponents, and the terms it contains offer a portrait of the power structure of Castile at that time. Those terms also illustrate why historians often refer to the marriage as a "union of the Crowns" rather than a true unification of two nations.

SOURCE: Diego Clemencín, *Elogio de la Reina Católica Doña Isabel*, vol. 6 (Madrid: Imprenta de I. Sancha, 1821), app. 2, 577–81.

Marriage Concessions Granted by Lord Ferdinand, King of Sicily and Crown Prince of Aragon, to Lady Isabella, Crown Princess of Castile (Cervera, January 7, 1469)

I, Lord Ferdinand, by the grace of God, king of Sicily along with His Majesty the King [John II], my very honorable father, with whom I rule and reign jointly in the said kingdom of Sicily; heir of all his kingdoms and lands, governor general, prince of Gerona, duke of Monblanc, count of Ribagorza, lord of the city of Balaguer; for the reason that between me and Her Majesty Lady Isabella, crown princess and heiress of the kingdoms and domains of Castile and León, it is hoped by the grace of our Lord to contract matrimony; . . . I promise and swear to uphold the following clauses. . . .

1. First, that as a Catholic king and lord, I will remain devoted and obedient to the commands and exhortations of the Apostolic Holy See [Vatican] and its supreme pontiffs [popes], and I will place myself at the disposal of the prelates and ecclesiastical and religious persons, with all due honor and respect to the holy Church.

Spain is United w/ please to be loyal to Rome

2. With full filial obedience, devotion, and reverence, I will treat His Highness King Henry, her brother, like a lord and father. . . .

4. I will observe and have proper justice observed and administered in all the said kingdoms and domains of Castile and León, . . . and I will listen to all of those who come to me seeking justice, as a good and proper Catholic king should, and I will see to the assistance of poor and needy persons.

5. To console the peoples and towns in these kingdoms, I will grant them audiences and treat them with love and clemency, as a good king should treat his vassals, in matters of justice and all other things.

6. I will observe and maintain established ways and the laudable customs, laws, *fueros* [charters consisting of traditional rights], and privileges of these kingdoms and domains, in all their cities, towns, and places, as it is customary for kings to do when they come to power.

7. I will treat all the greater and lesser lords and others of the kingdom properly and with due love, affection, and honor, as one may expect of a good king.

8. I will preserve and maintain in the ruling councils of these kingdoms the privileges, honors, and prerogatives of the illustrious and revered lord archbishop of Toledo, primate of the Spains, elder counselor of Castile, and my very dear and beloved uncle; and similarly, the archbishop of Seville and the illustrious and magnificent lord masters of Santiago. . . ; and the bishop of Burgos, and the other grandees, knights, and lords who shall remain in his service and mine; we will not cause them any real or personal affront without cause. . . .

10. I will go personally to these kingdoms [Castile and León] to reside and be in them with Her Highness the princess, and I will not leave them without her will and counsel, and I will not remove her from them without her consent and will.

11. If God should grant us offspring, either sons or daughters, as we may hope, I will never remove them from her, nor will I remove them from those kingdoms. . . .

12. I will not relinquish or give away any city, town, or fortress of these kingdoms . . . or anything else belonging to the royal Crown without the consent and will of Her Highness the princess. . . .

13. All the privileges, letters, and other documents that shall be written, drawn up, or sent, by her or by me, must be signed jointly by both of us. . . .

14. We will not place anyone in the council of these kingdoms who is not Castilian and a native of Castile, without the consent and due deliberation of said princess.

17. Whenever said princess should wish to make a gift of any town or place . . . she may do so freely, and I will respect that gift as if I made it myself. . . .

18. When there shall be vacancies for the position of archbishop, bishop, abbot . . . [and so on], we will act jointly, taking her will into account. . . .

19. I will not deprive any lord or other persons, ecclesiastical or secular, of privileges, including cities, towns, or places and fortresses, granted so far by His Highness, my father the king, or by any other relative of his or mine, or by any servant of these kingdoms and domains; and we will not do this for any reason of any kind without the consent and expressed will of said princess. . . .

21. I will maintain all Her Highness's servants and ladies-in-waiting, of any grade, state, or position in which they are serving, and I will preserve, love, and respect them as she does herself; and I will leave in possession of any city, town, or place those to whom she has entrusted them; and similarly, all the offices of said cities, towns, and places will remain in the possession of those who now hold them, and she will name all successors by her own decree.

22. I will not go anywhere in these kingdoms, under any pretext or reason, without her consent and due counsel.

23. Once we have these kingdoms and domains of Castile and León in our joint power, we will be obliged to wage war on the Moors, enemies of the holy Catholic faith, as the other preceding Catholic monarchs have done; and in succeeding to these kingdoms, I will take on the obligation to pay, and I will pay, the expenses for the fortresses on the frontier with the Moors, as other kings have done.

24. I will undertake no war or peace treaty with any neighboring king or lord of any kind, nor with any knight or lord of said kingdoms, whether ecclesiastical or secular, without the will and knowledge of Her Highness the princess and her counselors.

2. Ferdinand and Isabella, Letter on the Inquisition (1480)

In the thirteenth and fourteenth centuries, the Catholic Church had sought to police the faith by many means, including an institution known as the Inquisition, or Holy Office. As the term "inquisition" suggests, this judicial institution went beyond the passive role of trying those cases of heresy and other religious crimes that people brought to its attention, actively seeking to uncover such crimes on its own initiative. In those centuries, the Inquisition was particularly active in northern Italy and southern France, but also operated in the kingdom of Aragon.

The idea of establishing the Inquisition in Castile arose in the 1470s, when clerics there began urging Ferdinand and Isabella to take vigorous measures against the *conversos*, Jews who had converted to Christianity. (Many Jews had converted during the fifteenth century, in the wake of the great pogrom of 1391 and subsequent religious persecution.) These converts, who retained a separate identity—and some pride in that identity—attracted the resentment of certain Castilians, who soon accused them of being false converts secretly working to spread the Jewish religion. Perhaps believing those accusations, and also seeking to consolidate their own rather tenuous power (or at least to avoid dangerous turmoil in their kingdoms), Ferdinand and Isabella wrote to Pope Sixtus IV, seeking authorization to establish the Inquisition in their domains. On November 1, 1478, the pope granted this request.

At first the Inquisition operated only in Andalusia, but over time it was extended to the rest of Spain. One ongoing issue concerned control over the Inquisition; previously, the papacy had controlled the Inquisition, but Ferdinand and Isabella managed to secure for themselves control over the Inquisition in their kingdoms, so its establishment should be seen as part of their overall efforts to develop royal power in Spain. The establishment of the Inquisition may also be seen within the context of the long-term effort to forge religious and cultural unity in Spain, in a time when Christians were still at war with the Muslim kingdom of Granada (though the Inquisition did not at first focus on converted Muslims). In this letter to the Council of Seville, the king and queen sketch out the basic justification for the Inquisition's existence in addition to giving local authorities instructions about the institution's establishment.

SOURCE: D. Joaquín Guichot Y Parody, *Historia del Excmo. Ayuntamiento de la muy noble, muy leal, muy heróica é invicta Ciudad de Sevilla*, vol. 1 (Seville: Tipografía de la Región, 1896), 182–83.

Letter of Commission to Carry Out Inquiries into Bad Christians

Be advised that we have taken note that in our kingdoms and domains there have been and are certain bad Christians, apostates, heretics, and *confesos*, who, despite receiving the sacrament of baptism and being baptized, and having the name of Christians, have turned and converted, and continue to turn and convert, to the sect, superstition, and faithlessness of the Jews.

Desiring and wishing to resolve this problem, in order to avoid the great evil and harm that could grow out of this were the aforementioned not punished, we decree the following.

We beseeched our very Holy Father to enact some salutary remedy concerning this matter; His Holiness, upon our appeal, granted and conceded to us the power to select two or three persons with the specific qualifications to become Inquisitors, who, through this apostolic power, would proceed against any unfaithful and wicked Christians, and against those who favor and receive them, persecuting and punishing them to the fullest extent that law and custom allow.

By virtue of this power granted to us, and accepting it and using it as we see fit, we name and choose for Inquisitors of said infidelity, apostasy, and heretical depravity the venerable and pious fathers Friar Miguel de Morillo, master in holy theology, and Friar Juan de San Martín, prior of the monastery of San Pablo of the city of Seville and the Order of Preachers. And so it is our will that these Inquisitors should carry out and practice their work of Inquisition without any impediment. And for this purpose, you will grant them any favor and assistance, to uproot from our kingdoms and domains all abomination, apostasy, and heresy.

Therefore we command you that, whenever you are requested by those Inquisitors, you shall place your men and relatives at their disposal; and you shall let them have your jails in which to keep their prisoners; and should they wish to have a separate jail, you shall agree to that; and you shall give them chains and stocks and all the other equipment that may be necessary for the keeping of said prisoners. And you shall adhere to and carry out any sentence, censure, and penalty they give, and you shall denounce the infidels and their supporters and those who help conceal, no matter what their estate, position, or status. And you shall do all this under penalty of the confiscation of all of your property and the loss of your position.

I, the King; I, the Queen

3. Juan de Mariana,
The Conquest of Granada (1601)

Once they had joined forces and consolidated their powers in Castile and Aragon, Ferdinand and Isabella devoted even greater attention to completing the centuries-old effort to reconquer the Iberian lands that Muslims had seized in the eighth century. In 1492, the Catholic armies finally closed in on the last remaining stronghold of Moorish rule in Spain, the city of Granada; rather than fight a seemingly hopeless battle, the Moorish ruler, Boabdil, chose to negotiate terms for surrender. This passage from a chronicle written a little over a century later offers a glimpse of an important moment in Spain's history, while also suggesting the image of "the Catholic monarchs" that endured in Spain long after their death.

SOURCE: *Historia general de España compuesta, enmendada, y añadida por el padre Juan de Mariana*, ed. Don José Sabau y Blanco, vol. 13 (Madrid: Imprenta de D. Leonardo Núñez de Vargas, 1819), 112–17.

[King Ferdinand], dressed in his royal costume and his splendid garments, headed for the castle and the city with his entourage, dressed for war, a wondrous sight to see. Soon after came the queen, their children, the grandees, arrayed in brocades and fine silks. . . . [The Moor] Boabdil, the prince, came out to meet them accompanied by fifty men on horseback. He indicated that he wished to dismount to kiss the victor's hand, but the king would not consent to it. Then, looking gravely at the ground, [Boabdil] said: "Yours we are, invincible king; we deliver this city and kingdom to you, trusting that you will treat us with mercy and moderation." Having said this, he gave him the keys to the castle. . . .

The king, kneeling with great humility, gave thanks to God for the empire of those wicked people having been uprooted in Spain, and for the banner of the cross having been raised in that city, where for so long impiety had prevailed with such force and with such deep roots. He prayed to God that His mercy should allow this victory to endure forever. . . .

The king and queen, Lord Ferdinand and Lady Isabella, with all their personal adornments, which were very rich, and being in their prime and having won that war and having conquered that new kingdom, appeared even more majestic than before.

They distinguished themselves among all, and they were equal among themselves. They were seen as if they were more than human, as if they had been sent from heaven for the good of Spain. In truth it was they who brought about justice, which had been in ruins before them. They proclaimed very good laws for the government of the people and for the punishment of crimes. They defended religion and faith, founded public peace, and calmed discord and disturbance at home and abroad. They extended their realms, not only in Spain, but at the same time to the far corners of the earth.

What really deserves praise is that they distributed prizes and honors, of which there are very great and rich ones in Spain, not based on the nobility of one's ancestors or on some personal favor, but rather based on each person's merits, thus inspiring the talents of their vassals and leading them to devote themselves to the pursuit of virtue and learning. So much good came of all this that one cannot even describe it; the thing is proclaimed by itself and by its effects. To tell the truth, in what part of the world can one find more erudite or holier priests and bishops? Where can one find more prudent or fair judges? So it is that before their time one could find few Spaniards of distinguished learning; from that point on, who could adequately say how many in Spain have excelled in all sorts of letters and erudition?

Each of the two was of average height, with well-proportioned limbs, quite attractive, showing majesty in all his physical movements and of very pleasing and serious expression, of white skin, though somewhat tanned. The king in particular had become darkened through the labors of war, and had long brown hair, and his beard trimmed in the style of the time, with broad eyebrows, balding, with a small mouth, red lips, small and thin teeth, broad shoulders, a straight neck, a clear voice, quick of tongue, a clear mind, of grave and proper judgment, with a gentle and courteous manner, and merciful toward those with whom he negotiated. He was skilled in matters of war and unparalleled in the art of government, so willing to work on these matters that he seemed to rest by working. . . .

The queen was attractive in appearance, with blonde hair and light blue eyes, and she wore no makeup, demonstrating a singular gravity, moderation, and modesty. She was very pious and studious; she loved her husband, but with caution and reserve. She came to know something of the Latin language, making up for the king, Lord Ferdinand, not having learned it as a child; she took pleasure in reading history and speaking with men of letters. . . .

I will conclude by saying that with the entrance of the king and queen in Granada and their taking over of that city, the Moors, by the will of God, fortunately were forever subjected to the lordship of Christians in that part of Spain, in the year of our salvation, 1492, on the sixth of January, a Friday. . . . That date, as it happens, is by ancient custom very happy and solemn for all Christians, being the Festival of the Kings and the Epiphany, and the date is now no less laudable, fortunate, and happy for all of Spain, and ill-fated for the Moors, because of this new victory; for in uprooting and destroying impiety in it, the infamous past of our nation and its damages have been made good, and no small part of Spain was brought back into the fold of the rest of Christendom, receiving the government and the laws that were given to it—a great joy in which the rest of Christian nations shared.

Letters were written to Pope Innocent and to kings, and ambassadors were sent to give them such happy news and to inform them that the war with the Moors was over, with the enemies of Christ now dead and subjected, with the yoke having been placed on Granada, a city formerly built and adorned with the spoils of Christians. Finally with this victory all of Spain belonged to Christ our Lord, whose it had once been. Cities and provinces near and far celebrated the news with great rejoicing and bonfires. . . .

As a sign of his happiness and to recognize the responsibility for that great event, the pope, the cardinals, and the Roman people ordered and made a solemn procession to the Church of Santiago of the Spaniards. There services were celebrated, and in a sermon the preacher praised and exalted, as was fitting, the king and queen and the entire nation of Spain, their accomplishments, their courage, and their remarkable victories.

4. Surrender Treaty of the Kingdom of Granada (1491)

Seven centuries of intermittent efforts by Christians to win back territories lost to the Moors in the eighth century finally culminated in the Christian victory over the Moors in the kingdom of Granada. The Christian armies had been taking pieces of the remaining Moorish lands in a series of sieges and campaigns in the area from 1484 on, and by 1491, the Christians had reduced the Moorish lands to those surrounding the city of Granada itself. Ferdinand and Isabella achieved their victories through a combination of military and diplomatic means, as they exploited bitter divisions between two members of the same Muslim royal family: Boabdil (referred to in this document as Abí Abdilehi) and his uncle, El Zagal. In October 1491, Boabdil, seeing the futility of holding out against the besieging Christians, opened negotiations, and soon the two sides worked out the following terms of surrender. In January 1492, Boabdil formally surrendered, handing the keys to the city personally to Ferdinand.

SOURCE: Florencio Janer, *Condición social de los moriscos de España* (Madrid: Imprenta de la Real Academia de Historia, 1857), 222–28.

First, that the Moorish king and the military chiefs, jurists, judges, religious advisers, governors, learned men, and all of the commanders and men of substance and all of the commoners of the city of Granada, including the Albaicín and its surrounding areas, shall, with love, peace, and goodwill, . . . within the next forty days turn over to Their Highnesses or to their agent the fortress of the Alhambra and the Alhizan, with all their towers and gates, and all the other fortresses, towers, and gates of the city of Granada and of the Albaicín and the surrounding areas extending out into the countryside, so that they may occupy them in their name with their people and at their will. . . .

At the end of the forty days, all the Moors shall surrender to Their Highnesses freely and without coercion, and they shall do what good and loyal vassals are obliged to do for their kings and natural lords. And to assure secure conditions during this surrender, one day ahead of surrendering the fortresses, they shall offer as hostages the minister Jucef Aben Comixa, with five hundred persons, children and siblings of the leading citizens of the city and of the Albaicín and its surrounding areas, so that they may remain under the power of Their Highnesses for ten days, while the fortresses are surrendered and secured, placing people and supplies in them, and during all of this time they shall be given everything they need for their sustenance; and once all is surrendered, they will be freed.

Once the fortresses are surrendered, Their Highnesses and the prince, Don Juan, their son, shall, for themselves and for the monarchs who succeed them, receive as their vassals and natural subjects the King Abí Abdilehi [Boabdil] and the military governors, judges, jurists, religious advisers, learned men, governors, commanders and squires, and all the greater and lesser common people, including men and women, inhabitants of Granada and the Albaicín and its surrounding areas and its fortresses, villages and other places, and also of the Alpujarras [region] and of other places that shall fall under this accord and treaty in any way, and they shall be allowed to stay in their houses, estates, and inherited properties at that time and forever, and they will not allow any harm or damage to be done to them without intervening. . . . Nor shall their goods or their estates be taken away from them, nor even any part of them; but rather they will be revered, honored, and respected by their subjects and vassals, as are all of those who live under their government and rule. . . .

On the day when King Abí Abdilehi shall surrender the fortresses and towers, Their Highnesses shall order that his son shall be returned to him, along with all the hostages, and their wives and children, with the exception of those who have converted to Christianity.

Their Highnesses and their successors forever shall let King Abí Abdilehi and his military chiefs, judges, religious advisers, governors, commanders, and other men of substance and all of the greater and lesser commoners live under their own law, and they shall not allow anyone to take away their mosques or minarets or muezzins, nor shall they take away the endowed properties of their mosques and the rents they receive, nor shall they interfere with their ways and customs.

The Moors shall be judged under their own laws and courts by the Islamic law they are accustomed to observing, under the authority of their judges.

Neither at this time nor at any future time shall [Their Highnesses] take their arms and horses away, or allow these to be taken away, except for their large and small artillery, which they must promptly turn over to agents sent by Their Highnesses.

All of the Moors, great and small, men and women, from Granada and its lands as well as from Alpujarras and all its places, who shall want to go live in the Berber lands or any other place they wish may sell their estates, furniture, and goods in any way they wish and to whomever they wish, and neither Their Highnesses nor their successors shall ever take away or permit to take away these things from those who purchased them. . . .

Their Highnesses shall give free and safe passage to those Moors who may wish to go to the Berber lands or other places, along with their families, movable goods, merchandise, jewels, gold, silver, and all types of weapons except for artillery. And for those who may wish to go, they shall provide ten large ships that will take them where they want to go for seventy days, leaving them free and safe in the ports of the Berber lands where Christian merchant ships are accustomed to going to trade. Moreover, all those who shall wish to go within three years may do so, and Their Highnesses shall send ships wherever they ask to go, giving them safe passage, as long as they are requested fifty days in advance. . . .

Once these three years are up, they may still go to the Berber lands whenever they wish, and they shall be allowed to do so upon payment of one *ducado* per person plus the cost of the passage in the ships in which they travel. . . .

Neither Their Highnesses nor their son, the prince don Juan, nor those who succeed them shall ever order the Moors who are their vassals to wear signs on their clothing, as the Jews wear.

Neither King Abdilehi nor the other Moors of the city of Granada or of the Albaicín and its surrounding areas shall pay the taxes that are levied on houses and possessions for the next three years, and they shall only pay the harvest tax of one-tenth in August and autumn, and the one-tenth on cattle they had, . . . as the Christians are accustomed to paying.

At the time of the surrender of the city and its areas, the Moors are obliged to turn over to Their Highnesses all of the Christian captives, male and female, so that they may be freed without any kind of ransom being asked or given. . . .

Their Highnesses shall order that at no time shall either beasts of burden or servants be taken from King Abdilehi, the military governors, judges [and others] for any reason without their approval and without their being compensated fairly.

They shall not allow any Christians to enter in the mosques of the Moors where they pray, without the consent of their officials, and anyone who enters otherwise shall be punished for it.

Their Highnesses shall not permit Jews to have any power or authority over Moors, nor shall they be allowed to collect any kind of rent from them.

King Abdilehi and his military chiefs, judges, jurists, religious advisers, governors, learned men, commanders and squires, and all the common people of the city of Granada and of the Albaicín and its surrounding areas and of the Alpujarras region and other places shall be respected and treated well by Their Highnesses and their ministers, and their views shall be heard and their customs and rites guaranteed, and all the officials shall be allowed to charge their rents and enjoy the privileges and liberties to which they are accustomed, and it is just that these things be maintained.

Their Highnesses shall order that they shall not be forced to take in boarders, nor shall any clothing, birds, animals, or supplies of any kind be taken from the Moors without their consent.

Legal disputes that arise among Moors shall be judged by their Islamic law . . . and by their judges and jurists, as is their custom, and if a dispute shall arise between a Christian and a Moor, judgment shall be made by one Christian and one Moorish official, so that neither party can complain about the sentence. . . .

The Moors shall not give or pay to Their Highnesses more tribute than that they are accustomed to paying to the Moorish kings. . . .

It shall not be allowed for any person to mistreat, by deed or by word, any Christian man or woman who, previous to this treaty, has converted to Islam; and if any Moor has a wife who is a renegade [a Christian who converted to Islam], that person shall not be forced to become Christian against her will, and she shall be interviewed in the presence of Christians and Moors, and her will shall be followed; and the same will be done with the boys and girls born to a Christian woman and a Moorish man.

No Moor shall be forced to become Christian against his will. And if a woman in love, either married or a widow, should wish to become Christian, she shall not be allowed to convert until she is interviewed. . . .

Neither Their Highnesses nor their successors shall ever ask King Abdilehi or those from Granada and its lands, nor the others who enter into this agreement, to give back horses, property, cattle, gold, silver, jewels, nor any other thing that was won in any way during the war and rebellion, either from Christians or from Moors who are or are not Mudéjares [Muslims who lived under Christian rule]. . . .

If any Moor has injured or killed a Christian man or woman who was his captive, he will not be held accountable for it.

Once the three years are up, the Moors shall not pay any greater amount in rent for estates and lands than it shall appear fair for them to pay in light of their value and quality.

The judges, officials, and governors Their Highnesses shall appoint in the city of Granada and its surrounding areas shall be persons who will honor the Moors and treat them affectionately, and shall observe this treaty; if anyone should do anything improper, Their Highnesses shall order them to be replaced and punished.

Their Highnesses and their successors shall not ask or inquire of King Abdilehi or any other person covered by this agreement about anything they have done, no matter what it is, previous to the day of the surrender of this city and its fortresses.

No military governor, squire, or servant of King [El] Zagal shall have any position or authority at any time over the kings of Granada. . . .

The Moors shall not be compelled or forced into any kind of military service against their will, and if Their Highnesses shall wish to recruit any horsemen, summoning them to any place in Andalusia, they shall order them to be paid from the day they leave until they return to their homes.

Their Highnesses shall order the maintenance of the existing irrigation channels, ditches, and fountains that go into Granada, and they shall neither alter them nor take any part of them; and should anyone do so or should anyone throw any dirty thing into them, they shall be punished for it. . . .

Any contractual and written debts that exist among the Moors must be paid. . . .

Christian slaughterhouses shall be kept separate from those of the Moors, and the supplies from one shall not be mixed together with those of the other. . . .

The Jews who are natives of Granada and the Albaicín and its surrounding areas and all the other places covered by this agreement shall benefit from its contents, provided that those who do not convert to Christianity must leave for the Berber lands within three years, starting from December 8 of this year.

Their Highnesses shall order that all that is contained in this treaty be observed starting from the day when the fortresses of the city of Granada are surrendered. . . .

5. Ferdinand and Isabella, Decree of Expulsion of the Jews (1492)

As Ferdinand of Aragon and Isabella of Castile carried out their project of political union, they faced what they saw as a great obstacle to their dream of a united kingdom: the continuing presence of Muslims and Jews. Jews had been in Spain since the days of the Roman Empire, and they had become quite culturally assimilated; for centuries they had also played crucial economic roles and even served as advisers and physicians to monarchs and nobles. Nevertheless, mistrust, persecution, and conflict often marked the relationship between Jews and Christians, leading many Jews to convert to Christianity, particularly in the fifteenth century. Unsatisfied with conversions they considered insincere and deceptive, zealous and intolerant Spaniards demanded and got the establishment of the Inquisition by 1480, but because the Inquisition only had jurisdiction over Christians, these observers felt that Spain's remaining Jews had to be expelled altogether. Amid the final campaigns against the Moorish kingdom of Granada, which brought the ideal of a purely Catholic Spain within reach, the combination of the pressures of Christian zealots and Ferdinand and Isabella's own prejudices (fueled, perhaps, by suspicions that Ferdinand himself had Jewish ancestry) led them to issue the following decree on March 31, 1492.

SOURCE: "Edicto de los Reyes Católicos (31 marzo 1492) desterrando de sus estados a todos los judíos," *Boletín de la Real Academia de la Historia* 11 (1887): 512–20.

Lord Ferdinand and Lady Isabella, by the grace of God, king and queen of Castile, León, Aragon, Sicily, Granada, Toledo, Valencia, Galicia, the Balearic Islands, Seville, Sardinia, Cordoba, Corsica, Murcia, Jaen, the Algarve, Algeciras, Gibraltar, and the Canary Islands, count and countess of Barcelona, lords of Biscay and Molina, dukes of Athens and Neopatria, counts of Roussillon and Cerdana, marquises of Oristan and Gociano, to Prince Juan, our very dear and beloved son, and to the princes, prelates, dukes, marquises, counts, masters of the orders, priors, grandees, commanders, governors of castles and fortresses of our kingdoms and domains, and to the councils, magistrates, mayors, constables, district judges, knights, squires, officials, and . . . to all the other cities, towns, and places of our kingdoms and domains, and to all the Jews and all Jewish persons in them, including men and women of any age, and to all other persons of any estate, dignity, preeminence, and condition. . . .

You know, or should know, that because we have been informed that in our kingdoms there have been some bad Christians who have been Judaizing and apostasizing from our holy Catholic faith, caused in large part by communication of the Jews with Christians, in the Cortes that we held in the city of Toledo in the past year of 1480 we ordered the separation of those Jews in all the cities, towns, and places in our kingdoms and domains, creating separate places for the Jews to live, hoping that with this separation the problem would be solved. Moreover we had sought and ordered the Inquisition to proceed in our kingdoms and domains, and as you know it has operated for more than twelve years, finding many guilty persons as is well known. We are informed by the Inquisitors and many other religious persons . . . of the great damage that has been done and is being done to Christians by the contact, conversation, and communication they have had and have with Jews; this is proven by the fact that they always seek by all possible means to subvert faithful Christians and take them away from our holy Catholic faith, separating them from it and luring them and perverting them with their flawed beliefs and opinions, teaching them the ceremonies and practices of their law, holding sessions where they read to them and teach them what they are supposed to believe and do according to their law, seeking to circumcise their sons, giving them books from which to pray, and declaring the fasts they are to observe, joining with them in reading and teaching them the history of their law, notifying them of the festivals in advance, advising them of what they must observe and do in them, bringing to their houses and giving them unleavened bread and ceremonially slaughtered meat, instructing them in the things they must avoid, including foods and other things required by their law, and persuading them as much as they can to keep and observe the law of Moses, leading them to believe that there is no other law or truth except that. This is all proved by many statements and confessions, both by the Jews themselves and by those who were perverted and deceived by them, and this has resulted in great damage, harm, and disregard for our holy Catholic faith.

And although we have previously been informed of this, and we knew that the true remedy for all of this damage and disturbance lay in completely prohibiting communication between said Jews and the Christians and expelling them from all of our kingdoms, we tried to content ourselves with ordering them to leave all of the cities and towns and places of Andalusia, where it appeared that they had done the most damage, believing that this would suffice for those in the other cities, towns, and places of our kingdoms and domains to stop doing and committing the things we have said. Yet we are informed that neither that measure nor the sentences that have been passed against some of those Jews who have been found guilty of said crimes and infractions against our holy Catholic faith have provided a complete remedy. In order to resolve this and see to it that such disregard and offense toward our Christian faith and religion stops—for every day it seems that the

Jews increasingly pursue their evil and harmful mission wherever they live and converse—and because there can be no place for offending our holy faith, both among those whom God has so far wished to protect and those who have fallen and mended their ways, returning to the holy mother Church, according to the weakness of our humanity and the cleverness and seduction of the devil, who continues to make war on us, it could easily happen if the principal cause of this is not removed, by expelling the Jews from our kingdoms. For if it is reasonable, when any serious and despicable crime is committed by anyone in a given college or university, that . . . those who pervert the good and honest life of the others be expelled from those places, and even for causes less damaging to the republic, then is it not all the more reasonable concerning much greater and more dangerous and contagious crimes such as this one?

Therefore, on the advice and counsel of several prelates and grandees and knights of our kingdoms, as well as other learned and knowledgeable persons with whom we have consulted, and having deliberated at length on this, we have resolved to order all of the Jews and Jewesses of our kingdoms to leave them, never to return to them, nor to any part of them. And we thus order that this letter be distributed, in which we order all of the Jews and Jewesses of any age who live and reside and are in our kingdoms and domains, including natives as well as those who are not natives and who for whatever reason or purpose may have come here or are here, to leave all of our kingdoms and domains along with their sons and daughters and male and female servants and Jewish family members small and large of any age by the end of this coming July of the present year. And they should not dare to return or to be in any part of them, either residing or passing through or in any other capacity, under the penalty that if they do not . . . comply, and if they should be found in our kingdoms and domains or if they come to them in any way, then they shall incur the penalty of death and the confiscation of all of their property for the benefit of our chamber and treasury; they shall incur this penalty by the mere fact, without any trial, sentence, or declaration.

We also order and prohibit anyone in these kingdoms, of any estate, condition, or dignity whatsoever from daring to receive, take in, shelter, or defend any Jew or Jewess either publicly or secretly, in their houses or in any other place, from the end of July on, forever in these lands, under penalty of the loss of all their property, vassals, castles, and other inheritances, and also to lose anything granted by us and by our chamber and treasury.

And so that the Jews and Jewesses can during the said period of time until the end of July better dispose of their goods and property, by this present decree we take them under our royal protection, shelter, and defense; we guarantee them and their property so that . . . until the end of July they may go about and be secure, and they may enter and sell or exchange or alienate all of their movable and fixed property, disposing of it freely as they wish, and during this period of time no harm or damage shall be done to them, either in their persons or their property, under the penalties that fall upon and are incurred by those who violate our royal justice. And in the same way we authorize the Jews and Jewesses to take their goods and property out of our kingdoms and domains by land or sea, as long as they do not take any gold, silver, or coins, nor anything else prohibited by the laws of our kingdoms, except in the form of merchandise. . . .

And so that this may be brought to the attention of everyone, and so that no one may claim ignorance, we order that this, our letter, be posted in the usual places and sites.

6. The Expulsion of the Jews from Spain (1495)
Translated from Hebrew by Alexander Marx

The decree expelling the Jews from Spain was carried out according to royal instructions in 1492. Although most of the Jews left, some chose to convert to
Christianity in order to remain in Spain; those who converted but continued
to practice Judaism in secret were known as Marranos. The following text, written in Hebrew by an anonymous Jewish observer three years after the expulsion,
gives one contemporary's account of what happened to the Jews.

SOURCE: Alexander Marx, "The Expulsion of the Jews from Spain," *Jewish
Quarterly Review* 20 (1908): 253–56.

And in the year 5252 (1492), in the days of King Ferdinand, the Lord visited
the remnant of his people a second time [the first being the anti-Jewish
pogroms, or mob attacks, of 1391], and exiled them in the days of King Ferdinand. After the king had captured the city of Granada from the Ishmaelites
[Muslims], and it had surrendered to him . . . he ordered the expulsion of all
the Jews in all parts of his kingdom. . . . Even before that the queen had
expelled them from the kingdom of Andalusia.

The king gave them three months in which to leave. It was announced
in public in every city on the first of May. . . . The number of the exiled
was not counted, but, after many inquiries, I found that the most generally
accepted estimate is 50,000 families, or, as others say, 53,000. [Editor's note:
some historians today consider this estimate too high.] They had houses,
fields, vineyards, and cattle, and most of them were artisans. At that time
there existed many academies in Spain. . . . [In Salamanca] there was a great
expert in mathematics, and whenever there was any doubt on mathemati-
cal questions in the Christian academy of that city they referred them to
him. . . .

In the course of the three months' respite granted them they endeavored
to effect an arrangement permitting them to stay on in the country, and they
felt confident of success. Their representatives were the rabbi Don Abraham
Senior, the leader of the Spanish congregations, who was attended by a ret-
inue on thirty mules, and R. Meïr, the secretary to the king, and Don Isaac
Abarbanel, who had fled to Castile from the king of Portugal, and then occupied an equally prominent position at the Spanish royal court. . . . Rabbi Isaac
of León used to call this Don Abraham Senior Soné Or (Hater of Light),
because he was a heretic, and the end proved that he was right, as he was
converted to Christianity at the age of eighty, he and all his family, and
R. Meïr with him. Don Abraham had arranged the nuptials between the king
and the queen. The queen was the heiress to the throne, and the king one of

the Spanish nobility. On account of this, Don Abraham was appointed leader of the Jews, but not with their consent.

The agreement permitting them to remain in the country on the payment of a large sum of money was almost completed when it was frustrated by the interference of an official, who referred to the story of the cross [a reference to Judas betraying Jesus for thirty pieces of silver]. Then the queen gave an answer to the representatives of the Jews, similar to the saying of King Solomon: "The king's heart is in the hand of the Lord, as the rivers of water. He turneth it whithersoever he will." She said furthermore: "Do you believe that this comes upon you from us? The Lord hath put this thing into the heart of the king." Then they saw that there was evil determined against them by the king, and they gave up the hope of remaining. But the time had become short, and they had to hasten their exodus from Spain. They sold their houses, their landed estates, and their cattle for very small prices, to save themselves. The king did not allow them to carry silver and gold out of his country, so that they were compelled to exchange their silver and gold for merchandise of cloths and skins and other things.

One hundred and twenty thousand of them went to Portugal, according to a compact which a prominent man . . . had made with the king of Portugal, and they paid one ducat for every soul, and the fourth part of all the merchandise they had carried thither; and he allowed them to stay in his country six months. This king acted much worse toward them than the king of Spain, and after the six months had elapsed he made slaves of all those who remained in his country, and he banished seven hundred children to a remote island to settle it, and all of them died. Some say that there were double as many. Upon them the scriptural word was fulfilled: "Thy sons and thy daughters shall be given unto another people," etc. He also ordered the congregation of Lisbon, his capital, not to raise their voice in their prayers, that the Lord might not hear their complaining about the violence that was done unto them.

Many of the exiled Spaniards went to Mohammedan [Muslim] countries, to Fez, Tlemcen, and the Berber provinces, under the king of Tunis [in North Africa]. Most of the Muslims did not allow them into their cities, and many of them died in the fields from hunger, thirst, and lack of everything. The lions and bears, which are numerous in this country, killed some of them while they lay starving outside of the cities. A Jew in the kingdom of Tlemcen, named Abraham, the viceroy who ruled the kingdom, made part of them come to his kingdom, and he spent a large amount of money to help them. The Jews of Northern Africa were very charitable toward them. A part of those who went to Northern Africa, as they found no rest and no place that would receive them, returned to Spain, and became converts, and through them the prophecy of Jeremiah was fulfilled: "He hath spread a net for my feet, he hath turned me back." For, originally, they had all fled for the sake of the unity of God; only a very few had become converts throughout all the boundaries of Spain; they did not spare their fortunes, yea, parents escaped without having regard to their children.

When the edict of expulsion became known in the other countries, vessels came from Genoa to carry away the Jews. The crews of these vessels, too, acted maliciously and meanly toward the Jews, robbed them, and delivered some of them to the famous pirate of that time, who was called the Corsair of Genoa. To those who escaped and arrived at Genoa the people of the city showed themselves merciless, and oppressed and robbed them, and the cruelty of their wicked hearts went so far that they took the infants from the mothers' breasts.

Many ships with Jews, especially from Sicily, went to the city of Naples on the coast. The king of this country was friendly to the Jews, received them all, and was merciful toward them, and he helped them with money. The Jews who were in Naples supplied them with food as much as they could, and sent around to the other parts of Italy to collect money to sustain them. The Marranos in this city lent them money on pledges without interest; even the Dominican brotherhood acted mercifully toward them. But all this was not enough to keep them alive. Some of them died by famine, others sold their children to Christians to sustain their life. Finally, a plague broke out among them, spread to Naples, and very many of them died, so that the living wearied of burying the dead.

Part of the exiled Spaniards went over sea to Turkey. Some of them were thrown into the sea and drowned, but those who arrived there the king of Turkey received kindly, as they were artisans. He lent them money to settle many of them on an island, and gave them fields and estates.

A few of the exiles were dispersed in the countries of Italy, in the city of Ferrara, in the counties of Romagna, the Marches, and Patrimonium, and in Rome.

Before the expulsion, the king of Spain had stretched forth his hand against the Marranos and investigated their secrets, because they observed part of the laws secretly, and he had ordered the Jews in every city to proclaim in the synagogues that whoever knew of any Marrano who gave oil to the lighting of the synagogue, or money for any holy purpose, must reveal his name on penalty of excommunication. Thus the preachers made proclamation in the synagogues in the presence of the royal officials. . . . Oh, how that sword of excommunication wrought havoc among the Spanish Jews, who, wherever they turned, found hardship and misfortune! By means of this accusation the Spanish king had many thousands of the Marranos burned and confiscated their fortunes without number. . . . It seems that this was from the Lord to destroy these Marranos, who halted between two opinions, as if they had made a new law for themselves. Their end shows that they did not sanctify the name of the Lord in the hour of their death. When they asked them in which religion they wanted to die, they chose Christianity, in order to die an easier death, and they died with a cross in their hands. Only a few of them died as Jews, and of these few, most were women.

Ottoman Empire, Naples, Sicily

7. Christopher Columbus,
Letter on the New World (1493)

Despite all the momentous events of the time in Spain, including the defeat of the Muslim kingdom of Granada and the expulsion of the Jews from Spain, the news of the discoveries that the Genoese explorer Christopher Columbus reported to his sponsors, Ferdinand and Isabella, in 1493 very quickly began to draw a great deal of attention in Spain and Europe. Just what Columbus had discovered was unclear at first, for the explorer who had set out seeking a new sea route to Asia was firmly convinced that it was Asia he had found. Of course given the skepticism that had surrounded reports by earlier explorers and travelers such as Marco Polo, many Europeans probably doubted at least some of what Columbus said in his initial letter to the Crown (addressed to a royal official named Luis de Santángel). It turns out that a healthy dose of skepticism was indeed in order, for much of the letter's content is factually mistaken and/or highly exaggerated, as Columbus sought to make his rather costly effort appear an overwhelming success. Nevertheless, despite its many errors and fictions, the letter is still extremely valuable for the insights it offers into the discoverers' mental world and their perceptions of the new lands and peoples. Moreover, because the letter was soon widely translated and reprinted throughout Europe, it also reveals the kinds of tales that soon led others to undertake the highly risky voyage across the seas.

Much about this document remains unclear, and scholars have been debating over it for many years. Some of this obscurity derives from the secrecy that national rivalries—particularly that between Spain and Portugal—produced concerning overseas discoveries, and Columbus's own desire to prevent other explorers from intruding on terrain he hoped to govern may also explain why the letter contains so many blatant geographical inaccuracies. Exactly who even wrote the text is also open to question, for there is no known original of the letter Columbus wrote summarizing information from his logbook, and it appears that Spanish officials, perhaps seeking to bolster Spain's claims to possess these lands, subsequently altered the letter. (The letter itself was lost for centuries, turning up again only at the end of the nineteenth century.) The source for this translation is the Spanish language text, though references to terms used in other versions are occasionally added in brackets.

SOURCE: The letter has been published in countless editions, including Carlos Sanz, ed., *La carta de Colón, 15 febrero–14 marzo 1493* (Madrid: Gráficas Yagües, 1961).

Sir, Because I know that you will take pleasure in the great victory that our Lord has granted me on my voyage, I am writing this to you so that you will know how in thirty-three days [another version says twenty, but thirty-three is the correct number] I reached the Indies with the fleet that the most illustrious king and queen, our lords, gave me; in that place I found many islands populated with countless people. I took possession of all of these for Their Highnesses, making my proclamation with the royal banner unfurled, and I was not contradicted. To the first island I found I gave the name San Salvador, in commemoration of His High Majesty, who has marvelously granted all of this; the Indians call it Guanahaní. To the second I gave the name Santa María de Concepción; to the third, Ferrandina [Fernandina]; to the fourth, Isabella [some versions say Isla Bella]; to the fifth, the island Juana [Cuba], and so on for each new one. When I arrived at Juana, I followed its coastline westward, and I found it so large that I thought it must be the mainland, the province of Cathay [China]. I did not find towns and villages along that coast, but only tiny hamlets full of people with whom I could not speak, for they all ran away, so I proceeded along that route, thinking that I could not fail to find great cities or towns. After many leagues, seeing that there was nothing new and that the coast was leading me toward the north, the opposite direction from where I wished to go (for the winter was already approaching and it was my desire to head south, and also because the wind was carrying me along), I decided not to wait for a change in the weather, and I turned around and proceeded to a harbor from which I had sent two men inland to look for kings or great cities. They traveled for three days and found endless tiny hamlets and countless people, but no substantial settlement, so they returned.

At that time I had learned from some other Indians I had already seized that this land was an island, and so I followed its coast eastward for one hundred seven leagues, until it ended; from that cape I saw another island to the east, some eighteen leagues away, which I then named La Española [Hispaniola, now containing Haiti and the Dominican Republic]. I then went there, following the northern coast toward the east, as I had done at Juana, one hundred seventy-eight leagues in a straight line toward the east. . . . This island, like all the others, is very fertile, and this one extremely so. In it there are many harbors along the coast, beyond comparison with all others I know in Christendom, and so many large and good rivers that it is a marvel to behold. Its lands are high, and it contains many mountain ranges and very high peaks. . . . They are all extremely beautiful, in a thousand different shapes, and all accessible and full of trees of a thousand different kinds, so high that they seem to reach the sky; I am told that they never lose their foliage, which is easy to believe since they are so green and so beautiful, like the trees in May in Spain; some were in bloom, and some bore fruit, and so on, according to their type. And a nightingale was singing, and other birds of a thousand kinds in the month of November, which is when I was there. There are palm trees of six or eight kinds, and it is a wonder to see them, given their unusual and beautiful shapes; but the same is true of the other trees, fruits, and grasses. The island also has marvelous pine groves, and there are very large open fields, and there is honey, and many different varieties of birds and fruits. In this land there are many mines of metals, and there are countless people. La Española is a marvel; the mountains and mountain ranges, the meadows and open fields, and the lands are so beautiful and broad for planting and sowing, and for raising cattle of all kinds, and for building towns and settlements. The harbors here must be seen to be believed, and the rivers bring forth great amounts of good water, and most also bring forth gold. The trees and fruits and grasses are very different from those of Juana. In this island there are many spices and great mines of gold and other metals.

The people of this island, and of all the others I have found and been to or heard of, all go naked, men and women alike, just like the day they were born, though some women cover themselves in a single place with a single leaf of grass or a thing made of cotton for that purpose. They have neither iron nor steel nor weapons, nor are they given to using them; not because they are well disposed or of great stature, but rather because they are so timid that it is a wonder. They have no other weapons other than canes cut from young reeds, at the end of which they fasten a sharp stick, but they do not dare to use these; many times it has happened that I have sent two or three men inland to seek out some town and speak with people, but they flee in great numbers, for once they see them coming, they run away, a father not even protecting his child, and this is not because any harm has been done to them. On the contrary, in every place I have gone and asked to converse, I have given them everything I had, including cloth and many other things, without receiving anything in return; yet still they are hopelessly timid. The truth is that after they are reassured and they lose this fear, they are so completely without guile and so generous with all they have that one would not believe it without seeing it. Whenever they are asked for something, they never say no, but rather, they invite the person to take it, and they show so much love that they would give their hearts, and whether it be something valuable or something cheap, they . . . are equally content. I forbade my men to give them such worthless things as pieces of broken cups or broken glass or pieces of leather straps, but when they saw such things they acted like it was the greatest jewel in the world. I have ascertained that a sailor traded a piece of a leather strap for a piece of gold weighing two and half castellanos, and others received even more for things of even less value. . . . They even accepted pieces of broken barrel staves, giving everything they had, like beasts, so that it seemed wrong to me. I forbade it, and I freely gave them a thousand good things that I had brought along, so that they would be won over and, moreover, become Christians inclined toward love and the service of Their Highnesses and the entire Castilian nation, seeking to help give us those things that they have in abundance and that we need.

They know neither religion nor idolatry, except that they believe that all force and all good things come from the heavens. And they believed very firmly that I, along with these ships and people, came from the heavens, with such amazement did they receive me everywhere once they had gotten over their fear. This does not happen because they are ignorant, for they have very sharp minds and are men who navigate all these seas, and the full account they provide of all of it is a marvel, but rather because they had never before seen men wearing clothing, nor ships such as ours.

As soon as I arrived in the Indies at the first island I found, I took some of them by force so that they might learn [our language] and inform me about what there was around here, and so it was that soon they understood us, and we understood them, whether by language or by signs, and they have been very beneficial to us. I still keep them with me these days, and they still believe I come from the heavens, as I have learned from the many conversations they have had with me, and these were the first to say this wherever I went. The others went running from house to house and to the neighboring villages, crying out, "Come, come see the people from the heavens." Thus everyone, men and women, large and small alike, after overcoming their fear of us, came, and all brought things to eat and drink, which they gave us with a love that was a marvel to behold. . . .

In all of these islands I did not see much diversity in the people's appearance or customs or language, for all understand each other, which is a very odd thing, and because of this I hope Their Highnesses shall undertake the conversion of these people to our holy faith, to which they are very much inclined.

I have already said how I had gone one hundred seven leagues along the seacoast of the island Juana on a straight line from west to east, and from that journey I can say that this island is larger than England and Scotland combined, for beyond these one hundred seven leagues there were to the west two provinces I have not visited; one of these they call Auau [or Avan], where people are born with tails; these provinces cannot be less than fifty or sixty leagues long, judging by what one can understand from these Indians I have, who know all of the islands. This other island, La Española, is larger in circumference than Spain, from Colonya [unclear: perhaps Colliure, or Colibre] around to Fuenterrabía in Vizcaya, for on one of its sides I went one hundred eighty-eight great leagues on a straight line from west to east.

[Other versions of the letter give different numbers of leagues.] This is something to be desired, and when seen, not to be let go; in that place, of all that I have taken possession of for Their Highnesses, and all are wealthier than I know and can say; and I hold all of them for Their Highnesses so that they may dispose of them as they will as fully as they do with their kingdoms of Castile. This island of La Española is the place best suited for gold mines and other commerce, either with the mainland on this side or with that of the Great Khan on the other side, where there must be great commerce and profit. I have taken possession of a great town, which I have named La Villa de Navidad. In that town I have built a fortress which by this time must be fully completed, and in it I have left plenty of men for such a task, with arms, artillery, and supplies for more than a year, as well as a small boat and a skilled seaman with knowledge of all the arts required to build others. I have made such a strong friendship with the king of that land that he was proud to call me and consider me his brother, and even if these people should have a change of heart or become offended, neither he nor his people know what arms are, and they go about naked, as I have said. They are the most timid people in the world, so that by themselves, the men I left there could destroy the entire land, and the island presents no danger to those who know how to take care of themselves.

In all those islands it seems to me that all the men are content with one woman, and to their chief or king they give as many as twenty. It seems to me that the women worked more than the men; I have not been able to tell whether they have property of their own, for it seemed to me that that which one person had was shared by all, especially when it came to food. In these islands I have not yet found any human monsters, as many expected. They are instead all people of very pleasing appearance; they are not Negroes as in Guinea, except that their hair flows freely, and they do not live where the sun's rays are too strong. It is true that the sun is very strong there, that place being only twenty-six degrees from the equator [actually twenty]. In these islands where there are mountains, the winter was at times quite cold, but they bear it through the help of their custom of eating food with lots of excessively hot spices. Monsters I did not find or hear of, except for on one island, the second one encountered upon arriving in the Indies; that island is populated by people who are, on all the other islands, considered very ferocious, and who eat human flesh. These people have many canoes, with which they travel throughout all the islands of India, robbing and taking what they want. They are no more deformed than the others, though they have the custom of wearing their hair as long as that of women, and they use bows and arrows as well as the same weapons made of canes with sharpened sticks at the end, lacking iron as they do. They are ferocious among these other people who are so excessively cowardly, but I do not hold them any higher than the others. They are the ones who get together with the women of Matinino [the term is unclear, probably an error in the original], which is the first island one encounters in coming to the Indies from Spain, on which there are no men. These women do not do feminine tasks, but rather wield bows and arrows and the aforementioned canes, and they arm and cover themselves with plates of copper, of which they have much. Another island I am told is larger than Hispaniola, and on it the people have no hair. In another there is gold beyond measure, and about this and the others I bring with me Indians as witnesses.

In conclusion, to speak only of what has happened on this voyage, which was so rapid, Their Highnesses can see that I will give them as much gold as they might need if Their Highnesses should give me even a little assistance; all the spices and cotton Their Highnesses should command to have brought, and as much mastic [an aromatic resin] as they wish to have brought, . . . and as many slaves as they wish to have brought, from among those idolaters. And I believe I have found rhubarb and cinnamon and a thousand other valuable things that the people I left there will have found, for I have not stopped at any point as long as the wind allowed me to sail, other than in La Villa de Navidad, where I left men well stocked and secured. In truth, I would have done much more if my ships had served as they should reasonably have done. This is enough, and eternal God, our Lord, who gives victories in things that seem impossible to all of those who follow His path; and this was most certainly one, for although others may have imagined or written about these lands, it was all just conjecture with no one having come and seen them, and those who . . . heard these things considered them little more than fables.

So it is, then, that our Redeemer granted a victory to our most illustrious king and queen and their kingdoms, bringing fame for such great things, and all of Christendom should take pleasure and celebrate greatly, and give solemn thanks to the Holy Trinity with many solemn prayers for this great exaltation and for converting so many peoples to our holy faith, and also for the temporal goods, as not only Spain but indeed all Christians will derive comfort and profits from it. This is thus a brief account of the facts. Written on the caravel at the Canary Islands on February 15, 1493.

Your servant,

The Admiral

8. The Requirement (1513)
Translated from Spanish by Arthur Helps

This document, probably written by the legal scholar Juan López de Palacios Rubios in 1513, reflects sixteenth-century Spaniards' legalism, as well as their concerns about the morality of the conquest in the New World. It was drafted for the conquistadors to read to the people of the New World before engaging in battle there, but unfortunately it was often read in places where the intended audience could not even hear it, and of course there were rarely interpreters available to read it in the local languages. Moreover, the concepts it contained would have been completely foreign to the locals. Despite its absurdities—which some Spaniards pointed out at the time—it did play some role in assuaging the conquerors' consciences, and it is certainly valuable from a historical point of view in that it illustrates Spanish self-images and the ideology of the conquest of the New World in its early years.

SOURCE: Arthur Helps, *The Spanish Conquest in America*, vol. 1 (London: John Lane, 1900), 264–67.

On the part of the king, Lord Ferdinand, and of Lady Juana, his daughter, queen of Castile and León, subduers of the barbarous nations, we their servants notify and make known to you, as best we can, that the Lord our God, living and eternal, created the heavens and the earth, and one man and one woman, of whom you and we, and all the men of the world, were and are descendants, and all those who come after us. But on account of the multitude which has sprung from this man and woman in the five thousand years since the world was created, it was necessary that some men should go one way and some another, and that they should be divided into many kingdoms and provinces, for in one alone they could not be sustained.

Of all these nations God our Lord gave charge to one man, called Saint Peter, that he should be lord and superior of all the men in the world, that all should obey him, and that he should be the head of the whole human race, wherever men should live, and under whatever law, sect, or belief they should follow; and he gave him the world for his kingdom and jurisdiction.

And he commanded him to place his seat in Rome, as the most appropriate spot from which to rule the world; but he also permitted him to have his seat in any other part of the world, and to judge and govern all Christians, Moors, Jews, Gentiles, and all other sects. This man was called pope, as if to say, admirable great father and governor of men. The men who lived in that time obeyed that Saint Peter, and took him for lord, king, and superior of the universe; so also they have regarded the others who after him have been elected to the pontificate, and so has it been continued even till now, and will continue till the end of the world.

One of these pontiffs, who succeeded that Saint Peter as lord of the world, in the dignity and seat which I have before mentioned, made donation of these isles and Terra-firme [mainland] to the aforesaid king and queen and to their successors, our lords, along with all that there is in these territories, as is contained in certain writings issued on the subject, . . . which you can see if you wish.

So Their Highnesses are kings and lords of these islands and land of Terra-firme by virtue of this donation; and some islands, and indeed almost all those to whom this has been notified, have received and served Their Highnesses, as lords and kings, in the way that subjects ought to do, with good will, without any resistance, immediately, without delay, when they were informed of the aforesaid facts. And also they received and obeyed the priests whom Their Highnesses sent to preach to them and to teach them our holy faith; and all these, of their own free will, without any reward or condition, have become Christians, and are so, and Their Highnesses have joyfully and benignly received them, and also have commanded them to be treated as their subjects and vassals; and you too are held and obliged to do the same. Wherefore, as best we can, we ask and require you that you consider what we have said to you, and that you take the time that shall be necessary to understand and deliberate upon it, and that you acknowledge the Church as the ruler and superior of the whole world, and the high priest called pope, and in his name the king and queen, Lady Juana, our lords, in his place, as superiors and lords and kings of these islands and this Terra-firme by virtue of the said donation, and that you consent and allow these religious fathers to declare and preach the aforementioned to you.

If you do so, you will do well, and that which you are obliged to do to Their Highnesses, and we in their name shall receive you in all love and charity, and shall leave you your wives, and your children, and your lands, free without servitude, that you may do with them and with yourselves freely that which you like and think best, and they shall not compel you to turn Christians, unless you yourselves, when informed of the truth, should wish to be converted to our holy Catholic faith, as almost all the inhabitants of the rest of the islands have done. And, besides this, Their Highnesses award you many privileges and exemptions and will grant you many benefits.

But if you do not do this, and maliciously make delay in it, I certify to you that, with the help of God, we shall powerfully enter into your country, and shall make war against you in all ways and manners that we can, and shall subject you to the yoke and obedience of the Church and of Their Highnesses; we shall take you and your wives and your children, and shall make slaves of them, and as such shall sell and dispose of them as Their

Highnesses may command; and we shall take away your goods, and shall do you all the mischief and damage that we can, as to vassals who do not obey, and refuse to receive their lord, and resist and contradict him; and we protest that the deaths and losses which shall accrue from this are your fault, and not that of Their Highnesses, or ours, nor of these cavaliers who come with us. And that we have said this to you and made this Requirement, we request the notary here present to give us his testimony in writing, and we ask the rest who are present that they should be witnesses of this Requirement.

9. Bernal Díaz del Castillo, *The Conquest of Mexico* (1550s)
Translated from Spanish by Alfred Percival Maudslay

Among the many tales of the conquistadors in the New World, perhaps none has proved as enduringly compelling as that of a soldier in the army of Hernán Cortés, Bernal Díaz del Castillo (1492–1584). Díaz was from a low-ranking noble family in Medina del Campo, Castile, and like many young men, he went to the New World in search of adventure and riches, leaving in 1514.

He wrote his account many years later, in the 1550s, and although he certainly had more education than most of his countrymen, he felt some sense of inferiority as a writer. Yet after he read an account of Cortés's adventures by Francisco López de Gómara, he wanted to write his side of the story, for that more polished account glorified Cortés while downplaying the role of his soldiers, and its author had not even been to the New World. Díaz spent many years writing and revising his account, which was only published long after his death, in 1632.

The book constitutes a valuable source for recreating the events in question while also offering a rare look at the rich civilization that the Spaniards found in Mexico. In addition, accounts such as this one do much to explain why countless Spaniards were soon migrating to the New World. The following passages trace the travels of Cortés's men and their Indian guide and translator, Doña Marina, from the coast of Mexico to the Aztec capital.

SOURCE: *The True History of the Conquest of New Spain by Bernal Díaz del Castillo, One of Its Conquerors*, ed. and trans. Alfred Percival Maudslay, 4 vols. (London: Hakluyt Society, 1908–12), 1: 143–44, 185–88, 221–23, 237–40; 2: 37–44.

One morning, . . . more than one hundred laden Indians [arrived in the Spanish camp], accompanied by a great Mexican cacique [chief]. . . . When these people arrived and came before our captain [Cortés], they first of all kissed the earth and then fumigated him and all the soldiers who were standing around him with incense which they brought in braziers of pottery. Cortés received them affectionately. . . . After welcoming us to the country and after many courteous speeches had passed, he ordered the presents which he had brought to be displayed, and they were placed on mats over which were spread cotton cloths. The first article presented was a wheel like a sun, as big as a cartwheel, with many sorts of pictures on it, the whole of fine gold, and a wonderful thing to behold, which those who afterwards weighed it said was worth more than ten thousand [pesos]. Then another wheel was presented of greater size made of silver of great brilliancy in imitation of the moon with other figures shown on it, and this was of great value as it was very heavy—and the chief brought back the helmet full of fine grains of gold, just as they are got out of the mines, and this was worth three thousand [pesos]. This gold in the helmet was worth more to us than if it had contained twenty thousand [pesos], because it showed us that there were good mines there. Then were brought twenty golden ducks, beautifully worked and very natural looking, and some [ornaments] like dogs, and many articles of gold worked in the shape of tigers and lions and monkeys, and ten collars beautifully worked and other necklaces; and twelve arrows and a bow with its string, and two rods like staffs of justice, five palms long, all in beautiful hollow work of fine gold. Then there were presented crests of gold and plumes of rich green feathers, and others of silver, and fans of the same materials, and deer copied in hollow gold and many other things that I cannot remember for it all happened so many years ago. . . .

We slept the night in those huts, and all the caciques bore us company all the way to our quarters in their town. They were really anxious that we should not leave their country, as they were fearful that Montezuma would send his warriors against them, and they said to Cortés that as we were already their friends, they would like to have us for brothers, and that it would be well that we should take from their daughters, so as to have children by them; and to cement our friendship, they brought eight damsels, all of them daughters of caciques. . . . Cortés received them with a cheerful countenance, and thanked the caciques for the gifts, but he said that before we could accept them and become brothers, they must get rid of those idols which they believed in and worshipped, and which kept them in the darkness, and must no longer offer sacrifices to them, and that when he could see those cursed things thrown to the ground and an end put to sacrifices that then our bonds of brotherhood would be most firmly tied. He added that these damsels must become Christians before we could receive them, and the people must free themselves from sodomy, for there were boys dressed like women who went about for gain by that cursed practice, and every day we saw sacrificed before us three, four or five Indians whose hearts were offered to the idols and their blood plastered on the walls, and the feet, arms and legs of the victims were cut off and eaten, just as in our country we eat beef brought from the butchers. I even believe that they sell it by retail in the *tianguez* as they call their markets. Cortés told them that if they gave up these evil deeds and no longer practiced them, not only would we be their friends, but we would make them lords over other provinces. All the caciques, priests, and chiefs replied that it did not seem to them good to give up their idols and sacrifices and that these gods of theirs gave them health and good harvests and everything of which they had need; and that as for sodomy, measures would be taken to put a stop to it. . . .

When Cortés and all of us who had seen so many cruelties and infamies which I have mentioned heard that disrespectful answer, we could not stand it, and Cortés spoke to us about it and reminded us of certain good and holy doctrines and said: "How can we ever accomplish anything worth doing if for the honor of God we do not first abolish these sacrifices made to idols?" and he told us to be all ready to fight should the Indians try to prevent us; but even if it cost us our lives the idols must come to the ground that very day. We were all armed and ready for a fight as it was ever our custom to be so, and Cortés told the caciques that the idols must be overthrown. When they saw that we were in earnest, the fat cacique and his captains told all the warriors to get ready to defend their idols. . . . Cortés answered them in an angry tone . . . [and said] he was angry with them and would make them pay for it by taking their lives, . . . [and he] even threatened them with the power of Montezuma which might fall on them any day, [and] out of fear of all this they replied that they were not worthy to approach their gods, and that if we wished to overthrow them it was not with their consent, but that we could overthrow them and do what we chose.

The words were hardly out of their mouths before more than fifty of us soldiers had clambered up [to the temple] and had thrown down their idols which came rolling down the steps shattered to pieces. . . . When they saw their idols broken to pieces the caciques and priests who were with them wept and covered their eyes, and in the Totonac tongue they prayed to their gods to pardon them, saying that the matter was no longer in their hands and they were not to blame, but these [were] *Teules* [divine beings] who had overthrown them, and that they did not attack us on account of the fear of the Mexicans. . . .

The Spaniards, accompanied by Indian allies known as Cempoalans, then came to a "land belonging to the town of Xocotlan," where the cacique's name was Olintecle.

[The Indians here] asked [the Cempoalans who accompanied the Spaniards] what we did with the artillery we had brought with us, and the Cempoalans replied that with some stones which we put inside them we could kill anyone we wished to kill, and that the horses ran like deer and they would catch anyone we told them to run after. Then Olintecle said to the other chiefs: "Surely they must be *Teules*!" (I have already said that *Teule* is the name they give to their gods or idols and suchlike evil things.) Our Indian friends replied: "So at last you have found it out! Take care not to do anything to annoy them, for they will know it at once; they even know one's thoughts. These

Teules are those who captured the tax-gatherers of your great Montezuma and decreed that no more tribute should be paid. . . . They are the same who turned our *Teules* out of their temples and replaced them with their own gods and who have conquered the people of Tabasco and Champoton, and they are so good that they have made friendship between us and the people of Cingapacinga. In addition to this you have seen how the great Montezuma, notwithstanding all his power, has sent them gold and cloth, and now they have come to your town and we see that you have given them nothing—run at once and bring them a present!". . .

I remember that in the plaza where some of their oratories stood, there were piles of human skulls so regularly arranged that one could count them, and I estimated them at more than a hundred thousand. I repeat again that there were more than one hundred thousand of them. And in another part of the plaza there were so many piles of dead men's thigh bones that one could not count them; there was also a large number of skulls strung between beams of wood, and three priests who had charge of these bones and skulls were guarding them. We had occasion to see many things later on as we penetrated into the country for the same custom was observed in all the towns. . . .

This account of a battle in Tlaxcala on September 5, 1519 offers a look at how the Spaniards managed to overcome their numeric disadvantage.

There was not one of the wounded men who did not come forward to join the ranks and give as much help as he could. The crossbowmen were warned to use the store of darts very cautiously, some of them loading while the others were shooting, and the musketeers were to act in the same way, and the men with sword and shield were instructed to aim their cuts and thrusts at the bowels [of their enemies]. . . . We had not marched an eighth of a league before we began to see the fields crowded with warriors with great feather crests and distinguishing devices, and to hear the blare of horns and trumpets.

All the plain was swarming with warriors and we stood four hundred men in number, and of those many sick and wounded. And we knew for certain that this time our foe came with the determination to leave none of us alive excepting for those who would be sacrificed to their idols.

How they began to charge on us! What a hail of stones sped from their slings! As for their bowmen, the javelins lay like corn on the threshing floor; all of them barbed and fire-hardened, which would pierce any armor and would reach the vitals where there is no protection; the men with swords and shields and other arms larger than swords, such as broadswords and lances, how they pressed on us and with what valor and what mighty shouts and yells they charged upon us! The steady bearing of our artillery, musketeers and crossbowmen, was indeed a help to us, and we did the enemy much damage, and those of them who came close to us with their swords and broadswords met with such swordplay from us that they were forced back and they did not close in on us so often as in the last battle. The horsemen were so skillful and bore themselves so valiantly that, after God who protected us, they were our bulwark. However, I saw that our troops were in considerable confusion, so neither the shouts of Cortés nor [those of] the other captains availed to make them close up their ranks, and so many Indians charged down on us that it was only by a miracle of swordplay that we could make them give way so that our ranks could be reformed. One thing only saved our lives, and that was that the enemy were so numerous and so crowded one on another that the shots wrought havoc among them, and in addition to this they were not well commanded, for all the captains and their forces could not come into action and from what we knew, since the last battle had been fought, there had been disputes and quarrels between the captain Xicotenga and another captain. . . . Besides this, ever since the last battle they were afraid of the horses and the musketry, and the swords and crossbows, and our hard fighting; above all was the mercy of God which gave us strength to endure. . . .

In this engagement, one soldier was killed, and sixty were wounded, and all the horses were wounded as well. They gave me two wounds, one in the head with a stone, and one in the thigh with an arrow; but this did not keep me from fighting, and keeping watch, and helping our soldiers, and all the soldiers who were wounded did the same. . . .

Then we returned to our camp, well contented, and giving thanks to God. We buried the dead in one of those houses which the Indians had built underground, so that the enemy should not see that we were mortals, but should believe that, as they said, we were *Teules*. We threw much earth over the top of the house, so that they should not smell the bodies, then we doctored all the wounded with the fat of an Indian. It was cold comfort to be even without salt or oil with which to cure the wounded. There was another want from which we suffered, and it was a severe one—and that was clothes with which to cover ourselves, for such a cold wind came from the snow mountains that it made us shiver, for our lances and muskets and crossbows made a poor covering. . . .

Díaz then describes the arrival in the Aztec capital.

In the morning we arrived at a broad causeway and continued our march toward Iztapalapa, and when we saw so many cities and villages built in the

water and other great towns on dry land and that straight and level causeway
going toward Mexico, we were amazed and said that it was like the enchant-
ments they tell of in the legend of Amadís, on account of the great towers
and *cues* and buildings rising from the water, and all built of masonry. And
some of our soldiers even asked whether the things that we saw were not a
dream? It is not to be wondered at that I here write it down in this manner,
for there is so much to think over that I do not know how to describe it,
seeing things as we did that had never been heard of or seen before, not even
dreamed about.

Thus, we arrived near Iztapalapa, to behold the splendor of the other
caciques who came out to meet us, who were the lord[s] of the town named
Cuitlahuac, and the lord of Culuacan, both of them near relations of Montezuma. And then when we entered the city of Iztapalapa, the appearance
of the palaces in which they lodged us! How spacious and well built they
were, of beautiful stone work and cedar wood, and the wood of other sweet
scented trees, with great rooms and courts, wonderful to behold, covered
with awnings of cotton cloth.

When we had looked well at all of this, we went to the orchard and garden, which was such a wonderful thing to see and walk in, that I was never
tired of looking at the diversity of the trees, and noting the scent which each
one had, and the paths full of roses and flowers, and the many fruit trees
and native roses, and the pond of fresh water. There was another thing to
observe, that great canoes were able to pass into the garden from the lake
through an opening that had been made so that there was no need for their
occupants to land. And all was cemented and very splendid with many kinds
of stone [monuments] with pictures on them, which gave much to think
about. Then the birds of many kinds and breeds which came into the pond.
I say again that I stood looking at it and thought that never in the world
would there be discovered other lands such as these, for at that time there
was no Peru, nor any thought of it. [Of all these wonders that I then beheld]
today all is overthrown and lost, nothing left standing.

Let us go on, and I will relate that the caciques of that town and of Coyoacan brought us a present of gold, worth more than two thousand pesos,
and Cortés gave them hearty thanks for it, and showed them much affection,
and he told them through our interpreters things concerning our holy faith,
and explained to them the great power of our Lord, the Emperor. . . .

Early [the] next day we left Iztapalapa with a large escort of those great
caciques whom I have already mentioned. We proceeded along the causeway which is here eight paces in width and runs so straight to the City of

Mexico that it does not seem to me to turn either much or little, but, broad as it is, it was so crowded with people that there was hardly room for them all, some of them going to and others returning from Mexico, besides those who had come out to see us, so that we were hardly able to pass by the crowds of them that came; and the towers and *cues* were full of people as well as the canoes from all parts of the lake. It was not to be wondered at, for they had never before seen horses or men such as we are.

Gazing on such wonderful sights, we did not know what to say, or whether what appeared before us was real, for on one side, on the land, there were great cities, and in the lake ever so many more, and the lake itself was crowded with canoes, and in the causeway were many bridges at intervals, and in front of us stood the great City of Mexico, and we—we did not even number four hundred soldiers! And we well remembered the words and warnings given us by the people of Huexotzingo and Tlaxcala and Tlamanalco, and the many other warnings that had been given that we should beware of entering Mexico, where they would kill us, as soon as they had us inside.

Let the curious readers consider whether there is not much to ponder over in this that I am writing. What men have there been in the world who have shown such daring? But let us get on and march along the causeway. When we arrived where another small causeway branches off . . . where there were some buildings like towers, which are their oratories, many more chieftains and caciques approached clad in very rich mantles, the brilliant liveries of one chieftain differing from those of another, and the causeways were crowded with them. The Great Montezuma had sent these great caciques in advance to receive us, and when they came before Cortés they bade us welcome in their language, and as a sign of peace, they touched their hands against the ground, and kissed the ground with the hand.

Then we halted for a good while, and Cacamatzin, the lord of Texcoco, and the lord of Iztapalapa and the lord of Tacuba and the lord of Coyoacan went on in advance to meet the Great Montezuma, who was approaching in a rich litter accompanied by other great lords and caciques, who owned vassals. When we arrived near to Mexico, where there were some other small towers, the Great Montezuma got down from his litter, and those great caciques supported him with their arms beneath a marvelously rich canopy of green colored feathers with much gold and silver embroidery and with pearls and *chalchihuites* suspended from a sort of bordering, which was wonderful to look at. The Great Montezuma was richly attired according to his usage, and he was shod with sandals [*cotoras*], for so they call what they wear on their feet, the soles were of gold and the upper part adorned with precious stones. The four chieftains who supported his arms were also richly clothed according to their usage, in garments which were apparently held ready for them on the road to enable them to accompany their prince, for they did not appear in such attire when they came to receive us. Besides those four chieftains, there were four other great caciques who supported the canopy over their heads, and many other lords who walked before the Great Montezuma, sweeping the ground where he would tread and spreading cloths on it, so that he should not tread on the earth. Not one of these chieftains dared even to think of looking him in the face, but kept their eyes lowered with great reverence, except those four relations, his nephews, who supported him with their arms.

When Cortés was told that the Great Montezuma was approaching, and he saw him coming, he dismounted from his horse, and when he was near Montezuma, they simultaneously paid great reverence to one another. Montezuma bade him welcome and our Cortés replied, through Doña Marina, wishing him very good health. And it seems to me that Cortés, through Doña Marina, offered him his right hand, and Montezuma did not wish to take it, but he did give his hand to Cortés and then Cortés brought out a necklace which he had ready at hand, made of glass stones . . . which have within them many patterns of diverse colors, these were strung on a cord of gold and with musk so that it should have a sweet scent, and he placed it round the neck of the Great Montezuma and when he had so placed it he was going to embrace him, and those great princes who accompanied Montezuma held back Cortés by the arm so that he should not embrace him, for they considered it an indignity.

Then Cortés through the mouth of Doña Marina told him that now his heart rejoiced at having seen such a great prince and that he took it as a great honor that he had come in person to meet him and had frequently shown him such favor. . . .

Coming to think it over, it seems to be a great mercy that our Lord Jesus Christ was pleased to give us grace and courage to dare to enter into such a city; and for the many times He has saved me from danger of death, as will be seen later on, I give Him sincere thanks. . . .

They took us to lodge in some large houses, where there were apartments for all of us, for they had belonged to the father of the Great Montezuma . . . and at that time Montezuma kept there the great oratories for his idols and a secret chamber where he kept bars and jewels of gold, which was the treasure he had inherited from his father Axayaca, and he never disturbed it. They took us to lodge in that house, because they called us *Teules*, and took us for such, so that we should be with the idols or *Teules* which were kept there. However, for one reason or another, it was there they took us, where there were great halls and chambers canopied with the cloth of the country for our captain, and for every one of us beds of matting with canopies above, and no better bed is given, however great the chief may be, for they are not used. And all these palaces were [coated] with shining cement and swept and garlanded.

As soon as we arrived and entered into the great court, the Great Montezuma took our captain by the hand, for he was there awaiting him, and led him to the apartment and salon where he was to lodge, which was very richly adorned according to their usage, and he had at hand a very rich necklace made of golden crabs, a marvelous piece of work, and Montezuma himself placed it round the neck of our captain, Cortés, and greatly astonished his [own] captains by the great honor that he was bestowing on him. When the necklace had been fastened, Cortés thanked Montezuma through our interpreters, and Montezuma replied, "Malinche, you and your brethren are in your own house, rest awhile," and then he went to his palaces, which were not far away, and we divided our lodgings by companies, and placed the artillery pointing in a convenient direction, and the order which we had to keep was clearly explained to us, and that we were to be much on the alert, both the cavalry and all of us soldiers. A sumptuous dinner was provided for us according to their use and custom, and we ate it at once. So this was our lucky and daring entry into the great city of Tenochtitlán, Mexico, on the eighth day of November, the year of our Savior Jesus Christ, 1519.

10. Demands of the *Comuneros* (1520)

Ferdinand and Isabella had been remarkably successful in carrying out the union of the two Crowns, but their lack of a male heir threatened to undo that work. As a result of the premature death of their only son, as well as other deaths in the family, their youngest daughter Juana stood to inherit the throne, but Juana, known as "La Loca," was widely deemed incapable of ruling Spain. Because of Juana's mental state and her marriage to a member of the Habsburg family (rulers of the Holy Roman Empire), it fell to Ferdinand and Isabella's grandson (and Juana's son) Charles to inherit the Spanish throne in 1516.

Unfortunately, Charles was not Spanish, having been born in Flanders (now Belgium), and he spoke no Castilian. When Charles came to Spain in 1517, he brought with him a large entourage of Flemish advisers, and many Castilians suspected that these foreigners sought to enrich themselves at the expense of the Castilian treasury. Resentment also arose from changes in the balance of powers between the Crown and the Cortes, a kind of parliament whose ability to offset monarchs' powers had been eroding over the years. In 1520, discontent culminated in a rebellion that quickly spread throughout many parts of Spain.

The rebels, known as *Comuneros*, were primarily townspeople, but they included clergymen and nobles as well as commoners. Although this was never a well-coordinated national movement, the demands appearing in this reading reflect common themes that the various local groups articulated—especially the demand that the king respect and consult the Cortes and other local representative institutions. Before long the rebellion began turning into a general social upheaval, leading many nobles and rich commoners to abandon it, and by 1522 the last rebel bands surrendered to the royal forces.

SOURCE: Don Martín Fernández Navarrete, Don Miguel Salvá, and Don Pedro Sainz de Baranda, eds., *Colección de documentos inéditos para la historia de España*, vol. 1 (Madrid: Imprenta de la Viuda de Calero, 1842), 272–83.

Succession

After him [Charles] no woman can succeed to the throne in this kingdom; if there are no sons, then sons of daughters and granddaughters born and baptized in Castile shall inherit the throne; but this cannot happen unless they are born in Castile.

The Royal Council

In the council there must be as many members as there are bishoprics in this kingdom of Castile, chosen in this way: in each bishopric three men of letters over forty years of age will be nominated; the king or his governor will choose one of them, who will remain a member of the council for that bishopric for life; and when he dies, three more will be nominated in the same way; in this way each bishopric will choose one member of the council, and the king cannot add or remove anyone, nor can he impede or suspend the sentences and decrees that these members pronounce.

Officials

When a Cortes must be called, the royal domains of each bishopric and archbishopric shall choose two officials to go to the Cortes, one from the nobility and one from the commoners, and the king shall show them no favor; and each bishopric shall choose a cleric to go to the Cortes, and the knights shall choose two knights, and two members of the orders, one Franciscan and one Dominican; and without all of these there can be no Cortes. . . .

Governor

If a king be not yet of age or absent from the kingdom, the officials of the court and the council shall meet to form a Cortes and choose a governor from among the knights; the latter and the members of the council shall govern the kingdom and shall provide a tutor and regent for the lad or the simpleton [i.e., a mentally incompetent king], along with officials of his house, who shall be able to remove tutors, regents, and other officials when they deem it necessary, naming others.

Justice

The king shall not be able to name a *corregidor* [district magistrate] in any place; instead, each city and town shall on the first day of the year choose three nobles and three commoners, and the king or his governor shall choose one noble and one commoner; these two shall be civil and criminal judges for three years.

Royal Offices

Offices in the royal house must be given to persons born and baptized in Castile, and the king, while he is in Castile, cannot make use of persons who are not born in Castile.

Age

Those chosen to be mayors or officials in given places have to be at least thirty years of age, while members of the council must be at least forty, so that they shall have some experience.

Money

The king shall not be allowed to take any coins out of the kingdom (or allow them to be taken), nor gold or silver dust, and no coin can circulate or have value in Castile if it was not minted and stamped in the kingdom.

Removal of Bread and Meat

The king shall not allow anyone to take bread or meat out of the kingdom without the permission of the Cortes and its decree that it is not needed in the kingdom. . . .

Arms

Everyone shall be allowed to carry the offensive and defensive weapons that they wish to carry, and no law shall prohibit their carrying them; and all shall be obliged to bear arms in this manner; each member of the lower estate shall be obliged to have a sword, a dagger, a helmet, a lance, and a shield; those of the lower estate are those who do not have fifty thousand *maravedís* worth of property . . . ; those of the middle estate are those with between fifty thousand and two hundred thousand, while those of the highest estate are each obliged to have two swords and two daggers (one for oneself and one for a squire), as well as a pike, a halberd, and a shield . . . ; belonging to the highest estate are those who have more than two hundred thousand *maravedís* worth of property. . . .

War

Whenever the king wishes to make war he shall summon a Cortes and inform its members, and those of the council, explaining the reasons for the war, so that they can see whether it is just or willful. And if it is just, and against Moors, may people see that it is necessary and may they take account and know whether it is necessary to provide funds for it . . . ; without their consent the king cannot fight any war.

11. Charles V,
Statement on Luther (1521)

By 1517, Martin Luther, an obscure German monk and a Roman Catholic, was [Really] issuing challenges to the Church's current doctrine and practice. Luther was not [Reductionist] the first Catholic to protest against practices such as the Church's sale of letters of indulgence, which raised money for the Church on the pretext that the souls of the purchaser's deceased loved ones could escape purgatory and ascend to heaven. Because Luther expressed resentments that many other Germans felt— including many powerful nobles—he managed to escape the swift punishment that had met other such troublemakers.

Luther resided in the lands under the authority of the Holy Roman Empire, whose current emperor, Maximilian, died in 1519. Maximilian's grandson Charles had become king of Spain (known as Charles I in that capacity) when King Ferdinand died in 1516, but he now also became Holy Roman Emperor as well, being crowned in 1520 (and known as Charles V as Holy Roman Emperor). In 1521, he turned to the matter of this German monk's rebellion against the Church, calling a meeting of princes and clergymen, the Diet of Worms. At that meeting, Luther spoke, expressing his grievances against the Church with remarkable boldness, after which Charles issued the following reply.

SOURCE: Prudencio de Sandoval, *Historia de la vida y hechos del emperador Carlos V*, book 10, section 10 (Pamplona: Bartolomé Paris, 1614), 512–13; the text also appears in Alfonso García-Gallo, *Manual de historia del derecho español*, 3rd ed., vol. 2 (Madrid: A.G.E.S.A., 1967), 728–29.

You know that I am descended from the most Christian emperors of the noble German nation, the Catholic kings of Spain, the archdukes of Austria, and the dukes of Burgundy, who all were, until death, faithful sons of the Holy Roman Church, and they have always been defenders of the Catholic faith, the sacred ceremonies, decretals, ordinances, and laudable customs, for the honor of God, the propagation of the faith, and the salvation of souls. After their deaths they left, by natural law and heritage, these holy Catholic rites, for us to live and to die following their example. As a faithful imitator of my ancestors, I have by the grace of God maintained those rites until now. And so I am determined to maintain everything my ancestors and I have maintained so far, especially that which my predecessors ordered at the Council of Constance and at other councils. What is true and a great shame and offense to us is that a single monk, going against God, mistaken in his opinion, which is against what all of Christendom has held for over a thousand years to the present, wishes to pervert us and to proclaim, by his opinion, that all of said Christendom has always been in error. I am therefore determined to use all my kingdoms and possessions, my friends, my body, my blood, my life, and my soul. For it would be a great shame for you and me, the noble and greatly renowned German nation, appointed by special privilege and singular pre-eminence to be the defenders and protectors of the Catholic faith, as well as a perpetual dishonor for both of us and our posterity, if in our time not only heresy, but the suspicion of heresy and the degradation of the Christian religion were due to our negligence.

After the impertinent reply Luther gave yesterday in our presence, I declare that I now regret having delayed so long the proceedings against him and his false doctrines. I am resolved that I will never again hear him talk. He is to be taken back immediately according to the arrangements of the mandate with due regard for the stipulations of his safe-conduct. He is not to preach or seduce the people with his evil doctrine and is not to incite rebellion. As said above, I am resolved to act and proceed against him as against a notorious heretic, asking you to state your opinion as good Christians and to keep the vow given me.

12. The Inquisition (1536–1567)

Few aspects of Spain's history have received more attention than the Inquisition. The "Holy Office," as it was also known, had been created in various countries in medieval Europe, but it had ceased functioning in most parts of the continent when, in the early years of the reign of Ferdinand and Isabella, it was established in Spain. The Inquisition's primary objective in Spain was to defend the Catholic faith from any kind of deviation from orthodoxy, especially to deal with the problem of the *conversos*, former Jews whose conversion to Christianity was suspect. Soon, however, the Inquisition also targeted Erasmian humanists, Protestants, and those suspected of practices such as sorcery.

In recent decades, some historians have argued that the Spanish Inquisition has been portrayed in an overly negative light, as part of the "Black Legend" about Spain. These scholars point out, for example, that the Inquisition did not proceed recklessly, but rather sought carefully to know the truth and acquitted many people; that the methods of torture it used were simply common judicial practice throughout Europe at that time; that in practice it was often more lenient and flexible than some have suggested; and that the number of people it burned at the stake has often been exaggerated. Even keeping such points in mind, however, many of the charges made against the Inquisition are true, and the Inquisition was a powerful and feared institution whose importance in Spanish history should not be dismissed.

The first selection here, a report from 1536 on a case in Toledo, suggests the kind of practices that could bring one before the Inquisition, including those that were rooted in everyday aspects of popular culture.

The Trial of Francisca Díaz
Translated from Spanish by Benjamin Keen

SOURCE: Bartolomé Bennassar, *The Spanish Character: Attitudes and Mentalities from the Sixteenth to the Nineteenth Centuries*, trans. Benjamin Keen (Berkeley: University of California Press, 1979), 267–69. Copyright © 1979 The Regents of the University of California. Reprinted by permission of the University of California Press.

We the inquisitors against heretical perversity and apostasy in this very noble city and archbishopric of Toledo, commissioned and deputized by the apostolic authority, having jointly with the vicar and ordinary judge examined the criminal suit against Francisca Díaz, wife of Alonso de Arenas, hatter, inhabitant of this city, in which she is accused by the venerable *bachiller* Diego Ortiz de Angulo, prosecutor of the Holy Office, who declares the above-said Francisca Díaz heretical . . . because she has committed many acts of sorcery and invocations of demons to the great offense of God our Lord and His Holy Mother Church, to the scandal of the Catholic people and the

Christian religion; and in particular, because the said Francisca Díaz sought out a person whom she believed to be a sorceress and prayed her to work some sorcery in order that a man whom she greatly loved and by whom she had had a son should marry her. And the sorceress ordered her to go between ten and eleven o'clock at night to the threshold of her house, and say: "Devils of the oven, bring him around; devils of the marketplace, bring him to me dancing; devil of the butcher shop, bring him to me." . . .

And the above-said Francisca Díaz often invoked demons as instructed by the sorceress, believing and holding for certain, like a heretic and idolatrous infidel, that the devil would accomplish what she had asked, attributing to the devil works and power of God. . . . Moreover, the said Francisca Díaz, like a protector and defender of heretics, sought to hinder the work of the Holy Office of the Inquisition. When a certain person who had been advised to inform the Holy Office of the Inquisition of what she (Francisca Díaz) had done against the faith wished to do this, she (Francisca Díaz) advised him to do nothing of the kind, telling him to beware the devil and not go to the Inquisition; she also visited another person and told her that if she were summoned to the Inquisition in regard to this affair, she must not diverge in her testimony from what another person had said . . . for even if she perjured herself, it would suffice to place a *blanca* [copper coin] in the poor-box of a church and say an Ave Maria to be absolved; and she did many other things that merited severe punishment. That is why the said prosecutor asked us to proceed against the said Francisca Díaz as a heretic, an apostate from our holy Catholic faith who sought to hinder the work of the Holy Office, and a sorceress who invoked demons. . . .

Now, having confessed to us that she said and did all the things and acts of sorcery of which she is accused, but that she had no intention of believing in the devil or his works, as appears in detail in the said confession, and that she asked us to be merciful with her when we impose a penance for her offenses . . . , we determine that we could, if we wished, complying with the rigor of the law, punish her severely for having invoked demons, but since the said Francisca Díaz appeared before us of her own free will to confess her faults, when no testimony had yet been presented against her in this Holy Office, and she seems to have confessed her faults clearly and openly and has asked us for penance . . . , we condemn her to appear in the present *auto de fe* as a penitent, a wax candle between her hands, so that after the reading of our sentence she may abjure the crime of heresy of which she is accused; and we admonish her to shun these things henceforth and cease to commit these acts . . . and we order her to perform the other acts of penance that we impose on her.

The Trial of Elvira del Campo
Translated from Spanish by Henry Charles Lea

In the following case from 1567, as described in the Inquisitors' report, a woman has been accused of practicing Judaism secretly, something often found out by a person's adherence to Jewish law. The defendant, Elvira del Campo, had been denounced by two household employees, who noticed that she would not eat pork. She was pregnant when arrested, but what follows took place not long after her baby was born; the defendant was convicted but not executed.

SOURCE: Henry Charles Lea, *A History of the Inquisition of Spain*, vol. 3 (New York: Macmillan, 1922), 24–26.

She was carried to the torture chamber and told to tell the truth, when she said she had nothing to say. She was ordered to be stripped and again admonished, but was silent. When stripped, she said: "Señores, I have done all that is said of me and I bear false witness against myself, for I do not want to see myself in such trouble; please God, I have done nothing." She was told not to bring false testimony against herself but to tell the truth. The tying of arms was commenced; she said: "I have told the truth; what have I to tell?" She was told to tell the truth and replied: "I have told the truth and have nothing to tell." One cord was applied to the arms and twisted and she was admonished to tell the truth but said she had nothing to tell. Then she screamed and said: "I have done all they say."

Told to tell in detail what she had done she replied: "I have already told the truth." Then she screamed and said: "Tell me what you want for I don't know what to say." She was told to tell what she had done, for she was tortured because she had not done so, and another turn of the cord was ordered. She cried: "Loosen me, Señores, and tell me what I have to say: I do not know what I have done. O Lord have mercy on me, a sinner!" Another turn was given and she said: "Loosen me a little that I may remember what I have to tell; I don't know what I have done; I did not eat pork for it made me sick; I have done everything; loosen me and I will tell the truth." Another turn of the cord was ordered, when she said: "Loosen me and I will tell the truth; I don't know what I have to tell—loosen me for the sake of God—tell me what I have to say—I did it, I did it—they hurt me, Señor—loosen me, and I will tell it."

She was told to tell it and said: "I don't know what I have to tell—Señor, I did it—I have nothing to tell—Oh my arms! release me and I will tell it." She was asked to tell what she did and said: "I don't know; I did not eat because I did not wish to." She was asked why she did not wish to and replied: "Ay! loosen me, loosen me—take me from here and I will tell it when I am taken away—I say that I did not eat it." She was told to speak and said: "I did not eat it, I don't know why." Another turn was ordered and she said: "Señor, I did not eat it because I did not wish to—release me and I will tell it." She was told to tell what she had done contrary to our holy Catholic faith. She said: "Take me from here and tell me what I have to say—they hurt me—Oh my arms, my arms!" which she repeated many times, and went on: "I don't remember—tell me what I have to say—O wretched me!—I will tell all that is wanted, Señores—they are breaking my arms—loosen me a little—I did everything that is said of me."

She was told in detail truly what she did. She said: "What am I wanted to tell? I did everything—loosen me for I don't know what I have to tell—don't you see what a weak woman I am?—Oh! Oh! my arms are breaking." More turns were ordered and as they were given she cried: "Oh! Oh! loosen me for I don't know what I have to say—Oh! my arms!—I don't know what I have to say—if I did I would tell it." The cords were ordered to be tightened, when she said: "Señores, have you no pity on a sinful woman?" She was told, yes, if she would tell the truth. . . . Then the cords were separated and counted, and there were sixteen turns, and in giving the last turn the cord broke.

She was then ordered to be placed on the *potro* [a kind of ladder with sharp-edged rungs]. She said: "Señores, why will you not tell me what I have to say? Señor, put me on the ground—have I not said that I did it all?" She was told to tell it. She said: "I don't remember—take me away—I did what the witnesses say." She was told to tell in detail what the witnesses said. She said: "Señor, as I have told you, I do not know for certain. I have said that I did all that the witnesses say. Señores, release me, for I do not remember it." She was told to tell it. She said: "I do not know it. Oh! Oh! they are tearing me to pieces—I have said that I did it—let me go." She was told to tell it. She said: "Señores, it does not help me to say that I did it and I have admitted that what I have done has brought me to this suffering—Señor, you know the truth—Señores, for God's sake have mercy on me. Oh, Señor, take these things from my arms—Señor, release me, they are killing me."

She was tied on the *potro* with the cords, she was admonished to tell the truth, and the garrotes were ordered to be tightened. She said: "Señor, do you not see how these people are killing me? Señor, I did it—for God's sake let me go." . . . She said many times: "Señores, Señores, nothing helps me. You, Lord hear that I tell the truth and can say no more—they are tearing out my soul—order them to loosen me." Then she said: "I do not know that I did it—I said no more."

Then she said: "Señor, I did it to observe that law." She was asked what law. She said: "The law that the witnesses say—I declare it all Señor, and don't remember what law it was—O, wretched was the mother that bore me." She was asked what was the law she meant and what was the law that she said the witnesses say. This was asked repeatedly, but she was silent and at last said that she did not know. She was told to tell the truth or the garrotes would be tightened, but she did not answer. Another turn was ordered on the garrotes and she was admonished to say what law it was. She said: "If I knew what to say I would say it." . . . Then she said: "Lord bear witness that they are killing me without my being able to confess." She was told that if she wished to tell the truth before the water was poured [down her throat, while her nostrils were plugged] she should do so and discharge her conscience.

She said that she could not speak and that she was a sinner. Then the linen *toca* [a funnel stuck down the throat] was placed and she said: "Take it away, I am strangling and am sick in the stomach." A jar of water was then poured down, after which she was told to tell the truth. She clamored for confession, saying she was dying. She was told that the torture would be continued till she told the truth and was admonished to tell it, but though she was questioned repeatedly she remained silent. Then the inquisitor, seeing her exhausted by the torture, ordered it to be suspended.

An *Auto de Fe*
Translated from Spanish by Hans J. Hillerbrand

Those found guilty were punished in various ways, with the most serious offenders being subjected to an *auto de fe*, or "act of faith." An *auto de fe* was a public ceremony in which those convicted generally marched, wearing humiliating clothing and signs, through town to a public square. The most serious offenders were then executed publicly, with burning at the stake being the favored method of execution for the unrepentant. The following passage describes an *auto de fe* that took place in Seville in 1559.

SOURCE: Hans J. Hillerbrand, ed., *The Reformation: A Narrative History Related by Contemporary Observers and Participants* (Grand Rapids, Mich.: Baker Book House, 1972), 467–69. Copyright © 1972 Baker Book House Company. Reprinted by permission of Baker Book House Company.

On the square of San Fernando two large platforms were erected—one for the Inquisitors and the cathedral chapter, the supreme tribunal and the monks of San Francisco. The other platform was for the penitents, the clergy and monks of other orders. An altar was erected here for the degradation

of the licentiate Juan González. On one side of the square another large
platform was erected for the town chapter; alongside the platform of the
Inquisitors a platform for the duchess of Bejar, other marquises, and eminent
gentlemen. Many noble ladies were found here. Alongside the platform for
the penitents was another platform for other earls and lords and noble ladies.
All around the square were numerous scaffolds upon which stood a great
throng of people. It was said that some people who came to see the *auto* had
arrived three days early. The crowd of people was so huge that it was impossible to find lodging in the city. . . . Between two and three hundred men,
equipped with lances, well-dressed and decorated, were selected to accompany the penitents. They were a pleasure to behold. They marched orderly
with drums and flags to the castle, where they received the penitents with
whom they then walked to the square. About four o'clock in the morning
fifty priests arrived with the cross of Saint Ann and went to the castle, where
forty monks of all orders had gathered. Together they accompanied the penitents, . . . eighty penitents with habit and candles, twenty-one persons condemned to fire with a statue of Francisco de Cafra (who had escaped). Then
came the magistrates with their marshal, then the cathedral chapter with the
sextons in front. Finally came the Inquisitors with their banner. . . .

Don Juan Ponce de León was turned over to them so that his confession could be heard and he [could be] brought back to the Catholic faith. He
was a damned Lutheran who, despite two years in prison, had not given up
his Lutheran errors. The rector heard his confession, and led him back to the
faith. Don Juan swore that he would die as a true Christian. He had been
involved in great error and heresy; for example, that there was no purgatory,
that the Inquisitors were anti-Christian, that one should not believe or obey
the pope. Also that one should not accept any papal bulls or heed the pope's
word in any matter; that it was not necessary to make confession to monks
or priests, but only to God, everyone in his heart. Also the most holy sacrament should not be adored.

On one occasion he had stood in the yard of the cathedral when the
most holy sacrament was carried by. He had quickly hidden behind a pillar
and counseled the people he met to do the same. He persuaded them not
to adore the sacrament. He was the first to receive Lutheran books from
Germany. . . .

He pretended that he went to confession. When he wanted to take
communion he sent his servants away with orders so that they were of the
opinion, on their return, that he had received communion in the meantime. . . . This Don Juan was sentenced to die at the stake. . . . But our Lord,

in his immeasurable goodness, caused him to see his error, and led him back to the holy Catholic faith. He died with many tears of remorse over his sins. Indeed, still at the stake he endeavored to persuade the others to desist from their errors and to convert themselves to the holy Catholic faith and to the Roman Church.

13. Juan Ginés de Sepúlveda,
Just War in the Indies (ca. 1547)

For centuries, Christians in Spain had considered the legal and moral justification for waging war against "infidels" such as the Muslims, so when the completion of the Reconquest in 1492 gave way to a fresh set of military conflicts across the Atlantic, Spaniards already had considerable experience in debating such matters. Yet before long some Spaniards began to contend that the inhabitants of this New World were not like the Muslims at all and that their treatment required careful consideration. While some saw the Indians primarily as a labor supply, a few members of the Church protested the brutal exploitation of what they saw as such simple and innocent people, and it did not take long for a full-scale debate to arise over policies toward the Indians. Among the most famous of the Spanish scholars to take part in this debate was Juan Ginés de Sepúlveda, a scholar now best known for his debates with Bartolomé de Las Casas before the royal court at Valladolid in the 1550s.

Those debates had no clear winner; although official policy often seemed to adhere more closely to Las Casas's position, Sepúlveda's arguments enjoyed considerable support, and actual policies on the ground in America generally did not follow Las Casas's views. In addition to representing Spanish colonialist ideology, Sepúlveda's tract also illustrates methods of scholarly argumentation and reasoning in that era.

SOURCE: "Diálogo sobre las justas causas de la guerra," *Boletín de la Real Academia de la Historia* 21 (October 1892): 291, 293, 305, 307, 309, 313, 315, 331, 333.

You must remember that authority and power are not of one kind, but rather many, for a father rules over his children in one way, with one kind of law, and a husband rules over his wife in another way, and a master rules over his slaves in another, and the judge over the citizens in another, the king over the peoples and the mortals who are subject to his authority, and though all these powers are different, if they rest on proper reason, they have their foundations in natural law, which may perhaps seem diverse, but is actually reduced, as the scholars teach, to a single principle, namely, that the perfect must rule over and dominate the imperfect, the excellent over its opposite. . . .

And so we see that with inanimate objects the form, being more perfect, presides and dominates, and matter obeys its rule; and this is even clearer and more obvious with living creatures, where the soul rules and is like a head of the household, and the body is subjected to it and is like a servant. And in the same way, in the soul the rational part is the part that rules and presides, and the irrational part is that which obeys and is subjected to it. And all of this is by divine and natural decree and law, which commands that the most perfect and powerful should rule over the imperfect and unequal.

This must be understood as applying to those things whose nature remains uncorrupted, and to men who are healthy in soul and body, because in those who are full of vice and depraved, it is true that the body often dominates the soul and the appetites dominate the reason, but this is a wicked thing and is against nature. . . . So equality among these two parts, or the domination of the lower part cannot help being harmful for all. To this law, man and the other animals are subject. By this law, wild beasts are tamed and subjected to man's domination. By this law, the man rules over the woman, the adult over the child, the father over his children, that is to say, the most powerful and most perfect over the weakest and most imperfect.

The same thing is seen among men, with some being masters by nature, and others being slaves. Those who exceed others in prudence and intelligence, if not in physical strength, are by nature masters; those, on the other hand, who are mentally slow and lazy, though they may have the physical strength to fulfill all their necessary obligations, are by nature slaves, and it is just and useful that they be, and we even see this sanctioned by divine law itself. For it is written in the Book of Proverbs: "He who is foolish shall serve the wise man." Such are the uncivilized and barbaric peoples, strangers to civil life and peaceful customs. And it will always be just and in accordance with natural law that such peoples be subjected to the rule of more cultured and civilized princes and nations, so that thanks to their virtues and the prudence of their laws, the others may set aside their barbarism and be reduced to a more civilized life and the pursuit of virtue.

And if they reject this authority, one can impose it upon them by the use of weapons, and such a war will be just, as natural law declares. "It appears that in a certain way war originates in nature, since part of it consists of the art of hunting, which is not practiced only against beasts, but also against those men who, having been born to obey, refuse servitude: such a war is just by nature." Aristotle said this, and Saint Augustine agreed. . . .

Therefore consider it certain and proven, given that very learned authors affirm it, that it is just and natural for prudent, wise, and civilized men to rule over those who are not, and this gave the Romans grounds to establish their legitimate and just empire over many nations, as Saint Augustine says in various places in his work, *De Civitate Dei*, which Saint Thomas [Aquinas] cites in his book, *De Regimine Principum*. And given this, you can easily see . . . that if you know the customs and nature of one and the other people, then the Spaniards have a perfect right to rule over these barbarians of the New World and the adjacent islands, who are as inferior to the Spaniards in prudence, intelligence, virtue, and civilization as children are to adults and women are to men, there being as much difference between them as there is between wild and cruel people and highly merciful people, . . . and I would even say between monkeys and men.

You will not expect me to make a long argument for the prudence and intelligence of the Spaniards. . . . Who does not know the other virtues of our people, the strength, the humanity, the justice, the religiousness? I am only speaking of the princes and of those whose industry and force they use to administer the republic; I speak, in sum, of those who have received a proper education; for if some are wicked and unjust, their faults should not thus taint the reputation of their race, which should be judged by the cultured and noble men and by the customs and public institutions, not by men who are depraved and like slaves, whom this nation, more than any other, hates and detests, although there are certain virtues that are common to all the classes of our people, such as strength and martial force, which the Spanish legions have demonstrated in all times. . . . And what can I say of the temperance, both in regard to gluttony and to lust, when there is hardly any nation in Europe that can be compared with Spain in frugality and sobriety? And if it is true that in recent times I have seen that through trade with foreigners luxury has invaded the tables of the great, nonetheless good men condemn this, and one may hope that the pristine and innate parsimony of the customs of the fatherland will soon be reestablished. . . .

Although the philosophers teach that warriors are very given to the pleasures of Venus, ours . . . do not generally go against the laws of nature. How deeply rooted the Christian religion is in the souls of the Spaniards, even of those who live amid the tumult of arms, is something I have seen in many very clear examples, among which the greatest is that after the sack of Rome . . . [in 1527], there was hardly any Spaniard among those who died of the plague who did not order in his will that all the property stolen from the Roman citizens be returned; no one from any other nation, as far as I know, fulfilled this duty of the Christian religion. . . . And what can I say of the kindness and humanity of our people, who even in battles, after victory is won, show their greatest care and concern for saving the greatest possible number of the defeated, protecting them from the cruelty of their allies?

Now compare these gifts of prudence, intelligence, magnanimity, temperance, humanity, and religion with those of those little men in whom you will scarcely find vestiges of humanity, who not only possess no learning at all, but indeed they do not even know writing, nor do they retain any monument of their history, but only a certain obscure and vague reminiscence of some things portrayed in certain paintings. Nor do they have written laws, but only barbaric institutions and customs. And if we examine the virtues, what temperance and what kindness can you expect from men who have been given over to all kinds of intemperance and wicked lewdness, and who ate human flesh? And please do not believe that before the Christians' arrival they lived in that peaceful kingdom of Saturn that the poets imagined, but on the contrary, they made continuous and ferocious war on each other with such rage that they did not value their victory if they did not satiate their monstrous hunger with the flesh of their enemies. . . . Moreover these Indians are so cowardly and timid that they can scarcely resist the presence of our soldiers, and many times thousands and thousands of them have scattered, fleeing like women in the face of very few Spaniards, even less than a hundred.

And in order not to dwell too long on this, in order to know what kind of men these are, it is enough to know the sole example of the Mexicans [Aztecs], who were considered the most prudent, cultured, and powerful of all. Their king was Montezuma, whose empire extended far and wide throughout those regions, and who inhabited the city of Mexico. . . . He heard of the arrival of Hernán Cortés and of his victories, and of his intention to come to Mexico to meet with him, . . . and, full of terror, he received [Cortés] in his city along with a small number of Spaniards, not more than three hundred. Cortés, having occupied the city in this way, felt such disdain for the cowardice, inertia, and crudeness of these men that he not only terrorized and forced the king and the princes who were subject to him to accept the yoke and the lordship of the kings of Spain, but out of suspicions he had that in a certain province [Montezuma] had plotted the death of some Spaniards, he put him in jail, filling the citizens with terror and shock, but they did not dare to take up arms to free their king. . . . Can there be any greater or more convincing testimony of how much some men exceed others in intelligence, strength of spirit, and courage, and that some men are slaves by nature?

For although some of them show a certain talent for building, this is not an argument for human wisdom, since we see beasts and birds and spiders build things that no human industry can fully imitate. And as for the way of life of those who inhabit New Spain and the province of Mexico, I have already said that these are considered the most civilized of all, and they themselves boast of their public institutions, because they have rationally constructed cities and kings who are not hereditary but rather elected by popular suffrage, and they carry on commerce among themselves like cultured people. But look how mistaken they are and how strongly I dissent from such an opinion, instead seeing in these very institutions proof of the crudeness, barbarism, and innate servitude of these men. For having houses and a somewhat rational way of life and some kind of commerce are things that the necessities of nature lead to, serving only to prove that they are not bears or monkeys and do not completely lack reason. But on the other hand they have established their republic in such a way that no one possesses anything individually, not even a house or a field one can bequeath to one's heirs, because everything is in the power of their lords, who they improperly call kings and under whose arbitrary will they live more than under their own. . . . And in doing all this without being compelled by force of arms, but rather in a voluntary and spontaneous way, it is a very certain sign of the servile and downtrodden souls of these barbarians. . . .

And so if you wish to reduce them, I would not say to our domination, but rather to a somewhat softer servitude, it would not be hard simply to change lords, so that in place of those they had, who were barbaric, impious, and uncivilized, [they will] accept the Christians, who cultivate the human virtues and the true religion. . . . And we have not even mentioned their impious religion and the wicked sacrifices with which they worship the devil, to whom they could think of no greater tribute to offer than human hearts. And . . . they sacrificed human victims, and they tore the hearts out of human chests and offered them on their wicked altars, and in this way they believed they were placating their gods according to proper ritual, and they fed themselves on the flesh of their sacrificed victims. This evil so exceeds human perversity that Christians consider it among the wildest and most abominable of crimes. How can we doubt that such uncivilized, such barbaric people contaminated with such impieties and wickedness have been justly conquered by such an excellent, pious, and exceedingly just king as Ferdinand the Catholic, and now the Emperor Charles, and by a nation that is exceedingly civilized and excellent in all kinds of virtues? . . .

With great reason, then, and with excellent and natural right may these barbarians be compelled to submit to the rule of the Christians. . . . And with the infidels thus being brought under submission, they will have to desist from their wicked crimes, and under the care of the Christians, with their just, pious, and religious admonitions, they will return to the sanity of the spirit and the probity of customs, and will gladly receive the true religion to their immense benefit, bringing them to eternal salvation. It is thus not only infidelity that is the cause of this extremely just war against the barbarians, but also their wicked ways, their prodigious sacrifices of human victims, the extreme injury they have done to many innocent people, the horrible banquets of human bodies, the impious cult of idols. But just as the new evangelical law is more perfect and gentler than the ancient Mosaic law, because that was a law of fear and this of grace, softness, and charity, wars must also be waged with gentleness and mercy, not so much to punish as to correct evils. . . . What more appropriate or beneficial thing could happen to these barbarians than to be subjected to the rule of those whose prudence, virtue, and religion must transform them from barbarians—such that they scarcely deserve the name of human beings—into civilized men, at least as civilized as they can be; from stupid and lewd into upright and decent men; from impious servants of the demons into Christians and worshippers of the true God?

They are already beginning to receive the Christian religion, thanks to the providential diligence of the Emperor Charles, excellent and religious prince. They have already been given public teachers of human letters and knowledge and, even more importantly, teachers of religion and customs. . . . And if they refuse our rule, they can be compelled by arms to accept it, and this war will be, as we have declared with the authority of great philosophers and theologians, just by the law of nature. . . . And the justice of this war appears all the more obvious if one considers that the high pontiff, representing Christ, has authorized it.

14. Bartolomé de Las Casas, Thirty Propositions (1552)

One of the first people to protest Spain's treatment of the Indians was Bartolomé de Las Casas (1474–1566). Las Casas went to the New World as a soldier in 1502, and after participating in the conquest he received his own allotment of Indians under the *encomienda* system. (In that system, the Indians were divided up and "entrusted" to individual Spanish lords, ostensibly for their protection, but in fact to give the colonists a labor supply; around 1550 a labor draft known as the *repartimiento* replaced the *encomienda*, though the two terms were often used interchangeably, and actual distinctions between the two systems were often minimal or non-existent.) During those years Las Casas grew increasingly upset over Spanish treatment of the Indians, and after becoming a priest in 1512, he proceeded to wage a vigorous lifelong campaign for better treatment for the Indians. Eventually named bishop of Chiapas, Las Casas returned to Spain several times to lobby the Crown, and in 1550 and 1551 he engaged in a famous series of debates over Indian policy with Juan Ginés de Sepúlveda before the king at Valladolid. Las Casas was remarkably successful in influencing royal policy, but mistreatment of the Indians in the New World generally persisted despite the legal reforms he helped fashion.

SOURCE: Bartolomé de Las Casas, *Aquí se contienen treinta proposiciones muy jurídicas* (Seville: Sebastian Trujillo, 1552).

1. The Roman pontiff, canonically elected Vicar of Jesus Christ, successor of Saint Peter, has the authority and power of Jesus Christ himself, the Son of God, over all the men of the world, whether Christians or infidels. [He uses it] whenever he sees that it is necessary to guide and lead men to eternal life and remove the obstacles to it. . . . He uses and must use such powers with the infidels who never entered the holy Church through holy baptism, exercising one kind of authority over those who never heard the news of Christ or his faith and another kind over the faithful who are still faithful or who were at one time.

2. Saint Peter and his successors had and still have the obligation . . . to see to it with all diligence that the Gospels and the faith of Jesus Christ be preached throughout the world. . . . It is not likely that anyone would resist the preaching of the Gospels and Christian doctrine.

4. Among those chosen to spread and preserve the faith and the Christian religion, . . . Christian kings are very necessary for the Church, so that with their arms and royal forces and temporal riches they may aid, support, preserve, and defend the ecclesiastical and spiritual ministers. . . .

5. The high pontiff, given the authority he has been given over the earth by Jesus Christ, may impose obligations on Christian princes and kings . . .

if he sees that it is necessary or very desirable . . . to undertake expeditions for Christian purposes, for which he can also require contributions from all of Christendom. . . .

6. No Christian king or prince may undertake such an expedition (other than in cases of extreme necessity) without the express or tacit permission and authority of the high priest, the Vicar of Jesus Christ. And if the need should arise outside of his own kingdom, and the pope confers or entrusts the task to a single prince, the others cannot interfere in it in any way.

7. In order to avoid confusion, the Vicar of Christ has, by divine authority, most wisely, prudently, and justly divided the kingdoms and provinces of all the infidels of all kinds whatsoever among Christian princes, entrusting and committing to them the spread of the holy faith, the expansion of the universal Church and the Christian religion, and the conversion and health of the souls within them as ultimate ends.

8. The high pontiff did not and must not make that division, commission, or concession principally and finally in order to grant grace or expand the states of the Christian princes with honors or more titles and wealth, but rather principally and finally for the spread of the divine cult, the honor of God, and the conversion and salvation of the infidels, which is the intent and ultimate aim of the King of kings and the Lord of lords, Jesus Christ, but rather he imposes on them a very dangerous burden and task, for which they must give very strict account at the end of their days before divine judgment. Therefore that division and commission is more for the good and benefit of the infidels than for that of the Christian princes.

9. It is a just and worthy thing that although the primary reward of the Christian kings for the services they render to God and to their mother the universal Church with their royal persons does not consist . . . in worldly and physical things, for those are all of little substance and are transitory; but rather the ultimate and true reward is to reign with Christ, . . . but the high pontiff grants to them and makes a remunerative donation in those kingdoms for the same reason for which he granted them in the first place, as is just. . . .

10. Among the infidels who have distant kingdoms that have never heard Christ's gospel or received the faith, there are legitimate lords, kings, and princes, and their legitimate lordship, dignity, and preeminence derive from natural law and the law of nations, insofar as that lordship is exercised in the regulation and governance of kingdoms, confirmed by divine evangelical law. . . . Therefore with the advent of Jesus Christ, those lordships, honors, and royal preeminences and all the rest were not universally or specifically removed.

11. The opinion contrary to the preceding proposition is erroneous and very pernicious, and whoever stubbornly defends it is guilty of formal heresy. Similarly it is highly impious, evil, and productive of innumerable robberies and acts of violence and tyranny, ruin, and larceny, irreparable damage and the gravest of sins, infamy, stench, and hatred of the name of Christ and of the Christian religion and an effective obstacle to our Catholic faith. . . .

12. The said infidels, both lords and their subjects, are not deprived of their domains, dignities, or other goods because of any sin of idolatry or any other sin, no matter how grave and evil it may be. . . .

13. The infidels cannot be punished by any judge in the world for the precise reason of the sin of idolatry or of any other sin, no matter how enormous, great, and evil it may be, committed during the whole time of their infidelity before they received holy baptism of their own free will, especially those whose infidelity is purely a matter of negation, unless they are among those who directly block the preaching of the faith, and who, when sufficiently warned, do not desist, because of evil intent.

14. It was necessary, by divine order, for the high pontiff Alexander VI, under whose pontificate the great New World we call the West Indies was discovered, to choose a Christian king upon whom to impose the task of providing and having the solicitude, diligence, and care to proclaim the Gospels and the law of Christ and to found and spread divine worship and the universal Church throughout all its kingdoms, and to convert and save the native inhabitants living there, and everything else necessary and appropriate for that purpose. And as payment for that task he granted [that king] the dignity and the imperial Crown and sovereign authority over those domains.

15. The monarchs of Castile and León, Ferdinand and Isabella, . . . had singular qualities, more than those of any other Christian princes, and so the Vicar of Christ granted them said care and task. It was by nothing other than divine authority that they were instituted and invested with the highest dignity that kings have ever had on this earth. . . . Among other excellent qualities they had two, which are: one, that in addition to inheriting from their ancestors the recovery of all of these kingdoms of Spain from the hands of the Mohammedan tyrants who are enemies of our holy Catholic faith, at the cost of much spilling of royal blood, they themselves, with their own royal persons, and with incomparable efforts recovered the great kingdom of Granada and finally restored it to Christ and the universal Church. The other was that at their own expense and by their own favor, expedition, and command, they discovered those broad and extensive Indies, using the bold Christopher Columbus, whom they honored with the title of First Admiral of the Indies. . . .

19. All kings and natural lords, cities, communities, and peoples of those Indies are obligated to recognize the kings of Castile as universal and sovereign lords and emperors as stated, after having received our holy faith and sacred baptism by their own free will, and if before they receive it they do not wish to do so, they cannot be punished by any judge or official.

20. The kings of Castile are obligated, by formal precept of the Apostolic See, and also by divine law, to seek with all due diligence to send qualified ministers to preach the faith throughout that world, calling and summoning its peoples to come to the wedding and feast of Christ. . . .

22. The kings of Castile are obligated by divine law to seek to have the faith in Jesus Christ preached in the way that he, the Son of God, left orders specifying. . . . The universal Church has always had the custom, and in its decrees it has ordered, and the holy scholars have argued and explained in their books, that this be done peacefully and lovingly, and softly, with care, and as teachers, with gentleness and humility, and with good examples, inviting the infidels, and especially the Indians, who are so gentle, humble, and peaceful by nature with gifts and donations, taking nothing from them. And in this way they will consider the God of the Christians to be good and gentle and just, and in this way they will want to be his and to receive his Catholic faith and holy doctrine.

23. To conquer them first by war is a method that is contrary to the law and the gentle yoke and light and soft burden of Jesus Christ. It is the same one that Mohammed and the Romans used, with which they terrorized and plundered the world; it is the same one that the Turks and the Moors use today . . . and so it is very evil, tyrannical, and unworthy of the melodious name of Christ, causing infinite new blasphemies against the true God and against the Christian religion, as very long experience in the Indies has shown and is still showing. For they consider Christ to be the cruelest, most unjust, and pitiless God of all. And consequently it is harmful to the conversion of any infidels, and it has led to the impossibility of infinite numbers of people there ever being Christian, in addition to all of the irreparable and lamentable evil and damage mentioned in Proposition 11. . . .

26. Given that there was never just cause or authorization from princes to make war on the innocent Indians who were safe and peaceful on their lands and in their houses, we affirm that the conquests there were, are, and will always be (in the absence of some new cause) null and lacking legality, unjust, evil, tyrannical, and condemned by all the laws from the time the Indies were discovered until today. . . .

28. The devil could invent no greater pestilence to destroy that whole world, to consume and kill all the people in it, and to depopulate it, as he

has depopulated such great and populous kingdoms . . . than the *repar-timiento* and the *encomienda* of those people. They divided them up and entrusted them to the Spaniards as if they were entrusting them to devils, or as if they were cattle being turned over to hungry wolves.

By this *encomienda* or *repartimiento*, which was the cruelest kind of tyranny and the one most worthy of the fires of hell that one could imagine, all of those people are prevented from receiving the Christian faith and religion, given that the Spaniards keep them working day and night in the mines and in doing personal service, . . . and giving them burdens to carry a hundred and two hundred leagues, as if they were worse than beasts. And they chase from the Indian villages the religious preachers, who teach them the doctrine and give them knowledge of God, so that there will not be witnesses to their violence and their cruelty, and their continuous larceny and homicide. Because of these *encomiendas* and *repartimientos*, they suffer continuous torments, robberies, and injustices, and also to their children, wives, and property. Because of these *encomiendas* and *repartimientos*, I have witnessed the death of more than fifteen thousand souls in forty-six years, without their having received the faith and the sacraments, and they have depopulated more than three thousand leagues of territory; and I say I have witnessed this. . . .

29. These *encomiendas* and *repartimientos* of men that have been carried out as I have said, as if they were beasts, were never ordered by . . . the kings of Castile, nor did they ever have any such intention.

15. Letter from Five Franciscans (1552)

Although several different orders took part in the project of Christianizing the Indians of the New World, the Franciscan order was particularly active in many areas of Spain's colonies. In retrospect, it is easy to see that these missionaries' work would barely have been possible without the military might of Spanish troops helping to crush any resistance to the newcomers' ways. The soldiers, in short, contributed greatly to the spiritual conquest the missionaries were carrying out, just as the missionaries contributed greatly to the project the soldiers were carrying out. Yet these groups often failed to see how they were really working together, focusing instead on their rivalries and power struggles with each other. The following letter, written by five Franciscan missionaries in the Guadalajara region of Mexico and sent to King Charles I in 1552, illustrates those resentments, and many of the complaints and charges contained in this letter were sounded over and over again in messages sent to Spain.

SOURCE: *Cartas de Indias* (Madrid: Imprenta de Manuel G. Hernández, 1877), 103–17.

To His Holy Catholic Majesty and Emperor,

First of all, we know that the primary concern of Your Majesty in these parts, as in the other kingdoms and domains, is that your vassals and subjects be instructed and taught in the things relating to our holy Catholic faith—and the need is greater in these lands than anywhere else, both because of the lack of the required number of ministers and because it is the Lord's will that you continue to increase the number of your vassals here, converting them to the knowledge of our holy Catholic faith and making them obedient and subject to our Lord God and to Your Majesty. In this kingdom of New Galicia, it seems at present that three members of our order, . . . through the grace of God, without any other arms than the cross of Christ and the word of the Gospels, have attracted a great number of peaceful Indians, who previously had not been subjected to the yoke of your royal empire (although by means of warfare they had been subdued and conquered by Spaniards at the expense of your royal treasury). . . .

There is such a great shortage of friars that we could not fully explain it without going on at great length . . . [and] even if there were ten friars in each monastery, it would not be enough to carry out the task as Your Majesty's royal conscience requires; and because of this we have left several monasteries empty for lack of friars. We beg Your Majesty, for the love of our Lord, to see fit to issue an order that for the good of this kingdom of New Galicia at least one hundred friars should come here. For with that many helpers, Your Majesty could be sure and certain of reaping riches and treasures in the spiritual realm as great as those gathered in the temporal realm here. If Your Majesty should see fit to grant us this favor, we hope—through God's grace, and without any cost to Your Majesty's royal treasury, nor any deaths or cruelties inflicted on your subjects and the poor natives of this land—to increase the number of those attracted to the service of God and Your Majesty through the word of the gospels, far exceeding the number that your captains have been able to attract by means of war, and at great cost to your royal treasury. . . . From our experience we are certain that more would be attracted through peace and love, like those who have already been attracted and made subjects through the means of a spiritual conquest carried out by friars. We have presently seen how Your Majesty's captains have operated through means of war around here: the number of deaths and cruelties is so great, as they pursue their worldly private interest, that it seems to us that it would be better to leave the Indians alone than to try to conquer them. A small number won over by good and love is really worth many more than that won over by any other means . . . both through the example that is given to the rest and through the service that is rendered to our Lord God. . . .

2. We beg Your Majesty to send orders to your officials of this kingdom in charge of governing this land that they give us more sincere help and assistance than they have so far given us in matters concerning the teaching of the holy Catholic faith and the conversion of these natives. For not only do they prevent us indirectly from doing our work and gathering the fruits we desire, but they also impede and hamper us directly, by leading the Indian natives to believe that they do not need to obey us or to do what we order for their proper instruction, . . . and some of them even work to disrespect and dishonor the ministers who serve God, offending them with their words. They close the door to us, so that, assailed with worldly dishonor, we leave the pueblos and the teaching of Christian doctrine, and so that they can more freely destroy and ravage the land and its natives without there being any witnesses of their crimes and excesses and the evils that take place, or anyone who can inform those who govern the land for Your Majesty. And this has happened very often in the kingdom of [New] Galicia—for some of your local officials turn a blind eye in order to please and satisfy the Spaniards, and instead of punishing such offenses and outrages, they give them all kinds of assistance. We thus certify to Your Majesty that because of this there is scarcely a single friar who is willing to go live in the monasteries of the kingdom of New Galicia, doing so only by virtue of the holy obedience they have been ordered to maintain.

3. We beg that Your Majesty see fit to order that the favor and the alms that have been allotted to us in the form of wine for saying mass, oil for the sacraments, and other necessities actually be given and provided as Your Majesty has ordered. For before we receive the alms that Your Majesty has ordered in this kingdom of New Galicia, we must go through great struggles with your officials, and they do not always give them. And this is particularly common when a friar has interfered with some personal services [the officials have required] in their mines and farms, or has impeded some other injustices that they have sought to inflict on the Indians of this pueblo. . . .

4. By certain decrees of Your Majesty we take it that Your Majesty has been told that we have been excessively grandiose in the building of our monasteries. If those who made such reports had understood and had looked into and found out the truth, which is the contrary, Your Majesty would order the punishment of those who deserve it. . . . For the information that has been given Your Majesty concerns this monastery and church of Guadalajara, . . . [but] it is made of adobe and mud, with a dormitory containing ten cells, and a cloister thirty feet wide, and the church is of medium size and made of adobe, with a few stripes of rough stone and lime to strengthen and support it, and with thick beams made of unfinished wood. The father who delivers these dispatches will inform Your Majesty more fully about all this as an eyewitness. And the other monasteries that have been built in this kingdom are just as poor and humble, as our estate and habit require, and as the love and compassion for these poor natives, who help us build them, demand.

5. We believe Your Majesty is already aware of the death of the bishop of the kingdom of New Galicia. We beg, out of reverence for our Lord, that Your Majesty see fit to order that such positions in these parts be filled by persons who show a more Christian concern for this new church, and who carry out and fulfill all that the pastoral office requires of them. It seems to us that it would be very wise to choose persons who have some experience in this land and specific knowledge of the miseries and travails of these natives, and who have given some indication and sign of this through their desire and their works. . . .

6. The order that exists for most of the clergymen who serve in some of the pueblos in these parts . . . is so regulated by divine laws and those of Your Majesty that we do not understand how those who govern can permit and consent to it. . . . For when they place priests in the pueblos, they levy taxes and fees on the poor Indians to pay their salaries, and if they are authorized to charge two hundred pesos, they actually charge five hundred; and there

are very great excesses and disorder in this, and the same happens with the food and supplies they are given, which is in such excess that there is scarcely any priest here who does not enjoy a standard of living comparable to that of a middle-level prelate in Spain. And under the pretext that it is for salary and food for the priest, so many other robberies are inflicted on those same natives that it would be very difficult to learn what would be necessary to punish the excesses. And among these priests, there is almost no one who knows the language, or who preaches or hears confession, and thus they do not gather the necessary fruits of their labor.

7. Great would be the service that God our Lord would receive, and the fear and restraint that would be placed on the bad and undisciplined Christians, including Spaniards and Indians alike, if Your Majesty saw fit to institute the Inquisition in this land. For the offenses committed against our Lord and his temples and ministers are so numerous that it is impossible to speak or write to Your Majesty of each one, but with the fear of the Inquisition there would be a great remedy and improvement. This is something that Your Majesty must see fit to implement.

8. It has seemed necessary to us to beg Your Majesty that the government of this kingdom not be entrusted to four *oidores* [local judges], but rather to a single one, in light of the great disadvantages and problems that there have been and still are in carrying out matters of governance, all of which end up in the harm and destruction of the poor natives. If Your Majesty should see fit to entrust this power to a single person, it would be necessary to choose someone who had the necessary zeal for the service of God and Your Majesty and the necessary love and affection for these poor people, and someone who felt the pain of their travails and miseries; for otherwise, there might be even greater destruction and the end of the lives of these Indians. Among the great benefits of Your Majesty's naming such a person to govern this area would be that he would execute the new laws [proclaimed in 1542, with the intention of helping the Indians] of Your Majesty in these parts, laws which, at least for those concerning the use made of the Indians, not only are not followed and observed, but even seem to have resulted in the very opposite happening, as if Your Majesty had specifically decreed that the laws had been revoked and people should do the opposite of what they said. For concerning tributes, the Indians are now greatly oppressed, especially in the kingdom of New Galicia, not only in terms of the number and quantity of tributes assessed, but also, contrary to what Your Majesty has ordered, in that they are required to pay things that one must go forty or fifty leagues away to find, passing from temperate to hot regions, where they suffer great damage to their health and persons and lives; many

of them even flee to war-torn lands, where they abandon the [Christian] faith, being forced to do so by this bad treatment.

9. Concerning the personal services required of the pueblos and slaves . . . the situation is so disorderly and corrupt that if Your Majesty does not implement a thorough solution, ordering that the laws be executed, . . . then we consider it certain, based on our experience, that the remaining Indians will all be finished off, for in many valleys and provinces where there used to be many pueblos and people, everything is now completely destroyed— something that cannot help but cause one great pain and tears. And if there were one person in charge of governing this kingdom, feeling the pain the natives feel, and being ordered by Your Majesty to execute and carry out your laws, he would do so with greater efficiency and will if others did not get in his way, and this would bring the complete redemption of the lives of those who are presently [in danger]. Yet on the other hand, if such a governor had the opinions and animosities that some of your *oidores* have, he would be able to finish them off even more quickly. . . .

Guadalajara, May 8, 1552

Fray Angel de Valencia, Fray Jhoan de Armallones, Fray Alonso de Roças, Fray Iacobo de Dacia, Fray Antonio de Segovia

16. Viceroy Luis de Velasco, Letter to King Charles (1553)

Under Ferdinand and Isabella, the monarchy had attained an unprecedented level of power over the nobility and other rivals, and when King Charles inherited the throne, he continued that trend, defeating the *Comunero* revolt in 1521. This assertion of royal authority also had strong effects on the Crown's colonial policy from the outset in America. Unable to pay for the conquest and development of the New World directly out of its own funds, the Crown had little choice but to rely on a system of incentives for the conquistadors. Imbued with the noble spirit of Castile, of course, the conquistadors, once their conquest was done, wished to grow rich without working by enslaving the Indians. Yet an early policy of dividing up of the Indians as slaves quickly gave rise to protests from some clerics, and before long a new system was implemented. Under that new system, known as the *encomienda* system, Indians were "entrusted" to the oversight of the former conquerors, who were to see to their Christianization and good care, in return for which they could expect labor and the payment of tribute from the Indians. The *encomienda* system may have seemed satisfactory to the settlers and the Crown in some ways, but before long it threatened to give rise to the kind of hereditary aristocracy the Crown wished to avoid in the colonies. Advocates of better treatment for the Indians, including Bartolomé de Las Casas, also lobbied the king to alter royal policies in America.

In response to such concerns and pressures, the Crown promulgated the New Laws of the Indies in 1542 and 1543. Those laws explicitly banned the enslavement of Indians, even as punishment for crimes, and they also prohibited the creation of new *encomiendas* or the inheritance of existing ones. Although ostensibly promulgated to address the mistreatment of the Indians, the new laws certainly figured prominently in the Crown's plans to maintain political control in the New World.

Unfortunately, the New Laws, along with subsequent regulations such as a 1549 decree freeing the Indians from the obligation of forced labor (though not from the payment of tribute to the colonists), provoked outrage among the Spanish settlers, leading to a major revolt in Peru. In New Spain (now Mexico), there was no full-scale military rebellion, but as the following letter from the viceroy shows, the policies crafted in Castile met considerable resistance from the colonists. Luis de Velasco, Mexico's second viceroy, also offers a valuable look at political, social, and economic conditions in the colonies at that time.

SOURCE: *Cartas de Indias* (Madrid: Imprenta de Manuel G. Hernández, 1877), 263–69.

In all the ships that have left from this land of New Spain, I have written to Your Majesty, giving long and detailed accounts of the situation in this land and what has been done since my arrival, following your orders and instructions, and I have received neither any response from Your Majesty nor any word that my letters have been described to you. And now, two and a half years since the first ones were written, I suspect that the great concerns and wars that have arisen are the reason why Your Majesty has not ordered that I be sent replies. May it please our Lord God that everything come out as well as we servants of Your Majesty desire.

The execution of the New Laws and provisions that were sent to me has caused great turmoil and need in this land, and those problems keep growing worse as a result of their implementation. Among the Spaniards there is great discontent and much poverty, and among the Indians more license and leisure than their undisciplined nature can afford. It is my suspicion that very grave problems must arise from one nation or the other, for this land is so full of Negroes and mestizos that their numbers far exceed those of the Spaniards, and they all wish to gain their liberty at the cost of their masters' lives, and this wicked nation may well join together with whomever rebels, be it Spaniards or Indians. To assure that this land remains devoted to our Lord and obedient to Your Majesty, there are certain measures that seem necessary to me, and almost inevitable if the land is not to end in ruin, and I will describe them. . . .

The main thing Your Majesty must order to be implemented is the system of distribution [of Indians] the conquerors and settlers propose, with the conditions that the favor Your Majesty sees fit to grant does not include giving anyone jurisdiction and that the tributes be very moderate, and that the *encomenderos* must pay a sixth or seventh of their income to support the churches and monasteries and the friars and priests who must oversee the administering of the sacraments and the indoctrination of the natives, thus entrusting the prelates with that task and taking it away from the *encomenderos*. In this way, it seems to me, Your Majesty will fulfill your royal conscience and duty to those who have served you, keeping the Spaniards on the land and assuring its safety. Those [friars] who inform Your Majesty that the land can be sustained without it being defended by [armed] Spaniards who have the necessary means and something to lose do you a great disservice, arguing that friars alone can maintain the land; in my view they are mistaken and do not know the natives well, for they are not sufficiently devoted to our holy faith, nor have they forgotten the evil ways they had in the time of their infidelity, and so we cannot entrust such a weighty matter to their virtue.

The next point is that Your Majesty should send away part of the Spanish population and the mestizos and Negroes, of whom there is such an excessive number here, on some conquest somewhere. If this is not done, Your Majesty should close the door to any kind of Spaniards, keeping them from coming to this land of New Spain, while also putting as many mestizos as possible on the ships heading for Spain, for they have a very bad influence on the Indians. Those who remain will learn the lesson of this example, seeing the others removed from the land.

Your Majesty should order that fewer licenses be given to import Negroes, for there are more than twenty thousand in this land of New Spain, and their number is growing very rapidly, and there are so many that they could cause great problems in the land.

The next point is that Your Majesty should grant the favor of giving membership in the Order of Santiago to some noblemen and hidalgos who have estates here in New Spain and who are deserving, which is not a large group; for this would oblige them once again to be faithful vassals and to live a Christian and virtuous life and to be firm in the service of Your Majesty. If the leading men here do so, it will do much to keep the lower sort in order. . . .

Your Majesty should order that all those who were given *encomiendas* must live and reside in the bishopric where their Indians are and maintain their homes in the principal cities and towns where the main churches are and where the prelates reside, so that all can be accounted for, avoiding the confusion that currently exists. For Mexico City and its surrounding areas are so full of people that supplies are in constant shortage. . . . [Some towns] inhabited by Spaniards are becoming depopulated because they are in hot climates, because they have few Indians, and because the Spaniards have not been allowed to use them and the tributes are set too low. . . .

As for matters of good government and the execution of justice, if the brevity of my experience does not mislead me . . . there should be three or four well-educated and trustworthy criminal judges in this royal *audiencia* [a district appellate court], earning as much as the civil judges and having the same powers as those in Valladolid and Granada, with jurisdiction over Spaniards and Indians alike. This would bring great benefits because justice would be carried out swiftly and strictly, which is so very necessary to settle things down in this land. The civil judges have so much work that they cannot get to the criminal matters quickly, and in this way crimes go unpunished, or prisoners die in jail before their case comes to trial; this has happened several times.

In addition, the civil judges appointed should not serve in that position for more than five or six years, so that they do not become rooted here or form secret commercial connections, which are more damaging to the republic than public ones; I cannot say for sure that the current ones have such secret connections, but they could well have them without it being known, for they work through third parties.

The next point is that the next viceroy here should have much more power than Your Majesty ordered that I should have. For whatever is ordered here in matters of good government is appealed to the *audiencia*, and most times the order is not implemented. This is very damaging, giving rise to audacities that create serious problems. The greatest sacrifice I have made in this post has been to put up with some of the civil judges . . . acting as if they were my superior. . . . I beg Your Majesty to order that this be remedied, sending someone to come investigate this *audiencia* and to find out how we serve and how we live, appointing more upright, experienced, and conscientious men than some of those who have been named so far. Your Majesty would do me a great favor by allowing me . . . to go die in Spain, where I have left behind a wife and children, who are in dire poverty, in order to come serve as Your Majesty commanded me to. And this need keeps growing stronger, for I have no farm or lands to exploit, and my salary really does not suffice for the high cost of living here. . . . And so my small estate here is mortgaged, and I have debts, and I hope not to leave them unpaid when I die. I beg Your Majesty to see fit to order either that I be given an appropriate salary or that I be allowed to quit, as I have requested, before I am completely finished off, for Your Majesty always grants mercies to those who serve you well, and I think that I am among those who are deserving, in light of the fidelity and care with which I have served for over thirty years. I find myself old and poor and a thousand leagues from my home and my debts and my friends, in a place where I have only Your Majesty's mercy to turn to. . . .

The mines and estates in New Spain are losing much of their value because of the loss of the [Indians'] personal services, for without those services, [the mines and estates] cannot be worked or provided with supplies. That which can be done with horses and other beasts of burden is very little, and little can be earned with what labor Spaniards, Negroes, and mestizos can supply, for they do not know how to work or smelt ore. Without Indians, Your Majesty should not believe that the mines can prosper, for they will be ruined if the Indians do not work there and Spaniards do not do the work, which I doubt they would do even if they were dying of hunger. And even if they wanted to do it, they are too few in number. . . . Your Majesty should see to it that the mining does not collapse with the freeing of the slaves, which will soon cause great harm to the royal treasury and to private individuals, for there is no mine rich enough to be worked with wage earners without the costs being twice as much as the revenues. . . .

Your Highness, in accord with the Council of the Indies, sent orders to me to execute all that the new laws and other provisions declare, and so it is being done. Yet there is great concern among the Spaniards, who are all affected. Among other things, the council has declared that it is personal service for the Indians to have to come to this city to bring tribute for the royal treasury and for private individuals. And since most of this tribute consists of supplies, and the duty of bringing these has been removed, there is great want in this city, and I can see no way to solve this problem, for if the Indians do not bring these things, there is no industry or diligence either on my part or that of the Spaniards that can supply the city even with bread, water, firewood, and feed for the horses, which is the force that there is in this city. Counting the number of people who normally live in this city, I find that including Spaniards, Indians, mestizos, Negroes, and foreigners here on business, there are some two hundred thousand mouths to feed. Your Majesty must think about how they will be fed, for there are not a thousand laborers among them. . . . I am doing my best about this, but it will not be enough, if the law has to be observed, to prevent this republic of Spaniards from being at great risk. Your Majesty should consider whether it is desirable for Spaniards to remain here. . . . [If not] Your Majesty should order those who can to return to Spain and should prevent others from coming here. While awaiting Your Majesty's reply, I will try to manage things as well as I can, but I beg Your Majesty to send orders as quickly as possible. May our Lord guard Your Majesty and grant you the increase of your kingdoms and domains.

Mexico City, May 4, 1553

17. Saint Ignatius Loyola, Autobiography (1555)
Translated from Latin by J. F. X. O'Conor, SJ

Don Iñigo de Oñea y Loyola, founder of the Society of Jesus, was born into a noble family in 1491 in the Basque province of Guipúzcoa. As a young man, he was not strongly religious, and he became a soldier. During a war against the French in 1521, Loyola was badly wounded, as this excerpt from his autobiography explains, and the experience changed his life dramatically.

This opening passage from the account of his life that he dictated (in the third person) when he was in his sixties not only relates his discovery of faith, but also offers a glimpse of the life of soldiers at that time, among other matters. Loyola, known to Catholics as Saint Ignatius Loyola, founded the Jesuits in 1540 as an order devoted to serving the pope, and this order proved especially valuable in the Church's campaign against the Protestant Reformation. Loyola led the order until his death in 1556.

SOURCE: *The Autobiography of St. Ignatius*, ed. and trans. J. F. X. O'Conor, SJ (New York: Benziger Brothers, 1900), 19–29.

Up to his twenty-sixth year the heart of Ignatius was enthralled by the vanities of the world. His special delight was in the military life, and he seemed led by a strong and empty desire of gaining for himself a great name. The citadel of Pamplona was held in siege by the French. All the other soldiers were unanimous in wishing to surrender on condition of freedom to leave, since it was impossible to hold out any longer; but Ignatius so persuaded the commander that, against the views of all the other nobles, he decided to hold the citadel against the enemy.

When the day of assault came, Ignatius made his confession to one of the nobles, his companion in arms. The soldier also made his to Ignatius. After the walls were destroyed, Ignatius stood fighting bravely until a cannon ball of the enemy broke one of his legs and seriously injured the other.

When he fell, the citadel was surrendered. When the French took possession of the town, they showed great admiration for Ignatius. After twelve or fifteen days at Pamplona, where he received the best care from the physicians of the French army, he was borne on a litter to Loyola. His recovery was very slow, and doctors and surgeons were summoned from all parts for a consultation. They decided that the leg should be broken again, that the bones, which had knit badly, might be properly reset; for they had not been properly set in the beginning, or else had been jostled on the journey [so] that a cure was impossible. He submitted to have his flesh cut again. During the operation, as in all he suffered before and after, he uttered no word and gave no sign of suffering save that of tightly clenching his fists.

In the meantime his strength was failing. He could take no food and showed other symptoms of approaching death. On the feast of Saint John the doctors gave up hope of his recovery, and he was advised to make his confession. Having received the sacraments on the eve of the feasts of Saints Peter and Paul, toward evening the doctors said that if by the middle of the night there were no change for the better, he would surely die. He had great devotion to Saint Peter, and it so happened by the goodness of God that in the middle of the night he began to grow better.

His recovery was so rapid that in a few days he was out of danger. As the bones of his leg settled and pressed upon each other, one bone protruded below the knee. The result was that one leg was shorter than the other, and the bone causing a lump there made the leg seem quite deformed. As he could not bear this, since he intended to live a life at court, he asked the doctors whether the bone could be cut away. They replied that it could, but it would cause him more suffering than all that had preceded, as everything was healed, and they would need space in order to cut it. He determined, however, to undergo this torture.

His elder brother looked on with astonishment and admiration. He said he could never have had the fortitude to suffer the pain which the sick man bore with his usual patience. When the flesh and the bone that protruded were cut away, means were taken to prevent the leg from becoming shorter than the other. For this purpose, in spite of sharp and constant pain, the leg was kept stretched for many days. Finally the Lord gave him health. He came out of the danger safe and strong with the exception that he could not easily stand on his leg, but was forced to lie in bed.

As Ignatius had a love for fiction, when he found himself out of danger he asked for some romances to pass away the time. In that house there was no book of the kind. They gave him, instead, *The Life of Christ*, by Rudolph, the Carthusian, and another book called the *Flowers of the Saints*, both in Spanish. By frequent reading of these books he began to get some love for spiritual things. This reading led his mind to meditate on holy things, yet sometimes it wandered to thoughts he had become accustomed to dwell upon before.

Among these there was one, though, which, above all the others, so filled his heart that he became, as it were, immersed and absorbed in it. Unconsciously, it engaged his attention for three and four hours at a time. He pictured to himself what he should do in honor of an illustrious lady, how he should journey to the city where she was, in what words he would address her, and what bright and pleasant sayings he would make use of, what manner of warlike exploits he should perform to please her. He was so carried away by this thought that he did not even perceive how far beyond his power it was to do what he proposed, for she was a lady exceedingly illustrious and of the highest nobility.

In the meantime the divine mercy was at work substituting for these thoughts others suggested by his recent readings. While perusing the life of our Lord and the saints, he began to reflect, saying to himself: "What if I should do what Saint Francis did?" "What if I should act like Saint Dominic did?" He pondered over these things in his mind, and kept continually proposing to himself serious and difficult things. He seemed to feel a certain readiness for doing them, with no other reason except this thought: "Saint Dominic did this; I, too, will do it." "Saint Francis did this; therefore I will do it." These heroic resolutions remained for a time, and then other vain and worldly thoughts followed. This succession of thoughts occupied him for a long while, those about God alternating with those about the world. But in these thoughts there was this difference. When he thought of worldly things it gave him great pleasure, but afterward he found himself dry and sad. But when he thought of journeying to Jerusalem, and of living only on herbs, and practicing austerities, he found pleasure not only while thinking of them, but also when he had ceased.

This difference he did not notice or value, until one day the eyes of his soul were opened and he began to inquire the reason of the difference. He learned by experience that one train of thought left him sad, the other joyful. This was his first reasoning on spiritual matters. Afterward, when he began the Spiritual Exercises, he was enlightened, and understood what he afterward taught his children about the discernment of spirits. When gradually he recognized the different spirits by which he was moved, one, the spirit of God, the other, the devil, and when he had gained no little spiritual light from the reading of pious books, he began to think more seriously of his past life, and how much penance he should do to expiate his sins.

Amid these thoughts the holy wish to imitate saintly men came to his mind; his resolve was not more definite than to promise with the help of divine grace that what they had done he also would do. After his recovery his one wish was to make a pilgrimage to Jerusalem. He fasted frequently and scourged himself to satisfy the desire of penance that ruled in a soul filled with the spirit of God.

The vain thoughts were gradually lessened by means of these desires — desires that were not a little strengthened by the following vision. While watching one night he plainly saw the image of the Blessed Mother of God with the Infant Jesus, at the sight of which, for a considerable time, he received abundant consolation and felt such contrition for his past life that he thought of nothing else. From that time until August 1555, when this was written, he never felt the least urge of lust. This privilege we may suppose from this fact to have been a divine gift, although we dare not state it, nor say anything except what has already been said. His brother and all in the house recognized from what appeared externally how great a change had taken place in his soul.

He continued his reading meanwhile and kept the holy resolution he had made. At home his conversation was wholly devoted to divine things, and helped much to the spiritual advancement of others.

18. Ysabel de Guevara,
Hardships in the Río de la Plata Region (1556)

The most familiar images of the Spanish conquistadors in the New World concern the exploits of men such as Hernán Cortés and Francisco Pizarro, who conquered magnificent and wealthy cities. Yet many of the first Spaniards to explore the New World had very different kinds of experiences. One of the most inhospitable areas was the Río de la Plata region (now Argentina, Uruguay, and Paraguay), where the Spaniards found no cities or gold; the first Spanish settlement at Buenos Aires in 1535–36, for example, was a complete failure and was abandoned. Years later, a Spanish noblewoman wrote the following letter to Princess Juana, wife of a Spanish governor, offering a glimpse of the difficulties many of the first Spaniards faced in such expeditions in the New World, while also showing that women's role in the conquest and settlement of the New World was greater than many familiar historical accounts suggest.

SOURCE: *Cartas de Indias* (Madrid: Imprenta de Manuel G. Hernández, 1877), 619–21.

Most High and Powerful Lady,

To this province of the Río de la Plata, a certain group of women came along with its first governor, Don Pedro de Mendoza, and fate would have it that I was among these women. And when the fleet arrived in the port of Buenos Aires, with one thousand five hundred men, and food was soon lacking, the hunger was so great that within three months one thousand died. This hunger was so great that not even that of Jerusalem could equal it, nor can any other be compared to it. The men were so weak that the poor women had to do all the work, including washing the clothing, tending to the sick, preparing what little food they had, cleaning them, standing guard, tending to the fires, arming the crossbows when the Indians sometimes came to attack, even lighting the fuses for the small artillery, rallying the soldiers who were capable of fighting, . . . giving them directions and keeping them in order. For at this time, although we women were sustaining ourselves on little food we had not become as weak as the men. Your Highness must believe that the women did so much to take care of everyone that if it were not for them, all would have perished. And were it not for the honor of the men, many other things could truly be written, attested to by witnesses. I believe that others will write to you at greater length, and so I will stop here.

Having gone through such a dangerous ordeal, they decided to head upriver, despite being so weak and despite winter approaching, with the few still alive leaving in two small sailboats, and the exhausted women took care of them and watched over them and prepared their food, hauling firewood on their backs from outside the boat, and encouraging them with manly words not to let themselves die, saying that they would soon come to lands where there was food, carrying them on their backs and placing them in the boats, doing so with as much love as if they were their own children. We then came upon a group of Indians . . . who had a great deal of fish, and we once again served [the men], looking for various ways of cooking the fish, . . . for they had to eat it without bread, and they were very weak.

Then they all decided to head up the Paraná River in search of provisions, a voyage in which the unfortunate women expended such effort that it was only by a miracle of God that they survived. For the women carried out all of the work with great concern, each one not wishing to suffer the shame of doing less than any other, and they worked the sails, did the navigation, sounded the depths of the waters, took over the oars from the soldiers who could not row, bailed water from the boat, and tried to keep the soldiers from losing heart at seeing the women do their work. The truth is that the women were not pressured into doing these things, nor did they do them out of any obligation, doing so only out of a sense of charity.

And so they arrived in the city of Asunción [in Paraguay], which, though now very fertile in provisions, was at that time so lacking in them that the women had to resume their labors, working with their own hands, watering the fields, weeding, and sowing and harvesting the crops without anyone's help until the soldiers recovered from their weakened state and began to take control over the land, getting Indian men and women to serve them, until finally they got the land into the state it is now in.

I have wanted to write about this and bring this to Your Highness's attention to let you know of the ingratitude I have faced in this land, for the distribution of Indians has now been carried out among those who are here, among both those who have been here for a long time and those who have not, without anyone thinking of me or my service, and I have been left out, having been given no Indians or any other kind of servant. I very much wish I were free to present myself before Your Highness, [to describe] the services I have rendered for His Majesty and the offenses that are now being done to me. But this is out of my hands, for I am married to a nobleman from Seville, named Pedro de Esquivel. . . . What I ask now is that you order that my fair share [of Indians] be given to me in perpetuity, and that in recompense for my services you order that my husband be given some position suitable to a person of his status; for he, for his part, has earned this through his services.

May our Lord grant your royal life many long years. From this city of Asunción, July 2, 1556. This humble servant of Your Highness kisses your royal hands.

Doña Ysabel de Guevara

19. Baltasar Porreño,
A Portrait of King Philip II (1628)

Philip II (reigned 1556–1598) has not generally fared well in retrospect, as his enemies both in Europe and in Spain itself have penned many a scathing portrait of the ruler of the greatest empire of his day. But if Protestant authors, for example, long vilified him as the epitome of the cruel and intolerant Spanish ruler, at least some Spaniards in his own era saw things very differently. One such Spaniard was Baltasar Porreño (ca.1565–1639), a clergyman and prolific writer from the Castilian town of Cuenca, whose favorite genre was biography. Although modern readers may see this as hagiography rather than biography, Porreño's description of Philip conveys the substance of what his Spanish admirers liked about him, and this portrait in some ways presents a catalog of Spanish images of virtue in the early modern era. Porreño never met Philip, though he did know his successor, Philip III, so he used a variety of written and oral sources as the basis of this work, which was first published in 1628, but which went through many more editions in subsequent years.

SOURCE: Baltasar Porreño, *Los dichos y hechos del Rey Phelipe II, llamado con justo razón, el Prudente* (Brussels: Francisco Foppens, 1666), 37–40, 46–47, 51, 76, 81–82, 86, 101–2.

He was so serious that everyone trembled in his presence, even the bravest, and even the most learned men grew unsettled, finding themselves at a loss for words when they went to give him their studied reasonings. . . . Rare were those who managed to speak without losing their concentration in seeing his incomparable seriousness. . . . And so on their first meeting with him, courageous men, tested by a thousand dangers, trembled in his presence, and no one looked at him without flinching. Archbishops, bishops, dignified scholars, eminent preachers, and orators grew unsettled in his chamber, so much that if not for his gentleness, they would not have said a word. He encouraged those who were unsettled and taken aback, telling them to calm themselves. . . .

Once finished with the war against France, he began transferring his men to Africa, sending a very large army of some 14,000 to Gelbes; he helped the Catholics in France and Germany; he subdued the rebellious Moors of Granada; he pacified the Indies; he calmed the kingdom of Portugal; he restrained the English and other heretics. . . . With great courage he confronted the Turk, an enemy common to all Christendom, breaking his pride at Lepanto [site of a Spanish victory in 1571].

Upon his being informed of the miserable disaster for Spain of the Armada sent against England, everyone expected that he would experience emotions as grave as those of Augustus Caesar, but without this sad news causing him to seem the least bit upset, he said, with more integrity than

Plato or Seneca could have had, "I did not send the Armada against the winds and fortune of the seas, but rather against men," saying this because he lost the Armada to bad luck in the [English] Channel. . . .

He witnessed the deaths of all of his loved ones: parents, children, wives, close advisers, ministers, and high-ranking servants; [he experienced] great losses to the treasury, bearing all these blows and setbacks with such evenness of spirit that he amazed the world. . . .

With great humility and devotion did he receive the letters that the Holy Mother Teresa of Jesus wrote to him, in which she advised His Majesty of various things and asked him for things for her order, and he granted those things generously; moved by the letters and by the opinion he had of her, he acted as her great protector and a father of her religion. . . . His devoutness and humility were so great that, in Valladolid one day, a holy friar from the Dominican Order, Friar Gerónimo Vallejo, entered the palace with a crowd of poor people, and, going up the staircases with this group, he encountered a physician of His Majesty, who scolded him, saying that poor people did not just walk into kings' palaces, because of the importance to the public good of the king's health, and because of the damage that the bad odors could do to it. Friar Gerónimo replied, "I was not aware that there were laws contrary to the laws of God in the house of a Christian prince, and that the doors to this path were closed to the needs of the poor." The physician complained to the king about Friar Gerónimo's words and actions, but His Majesty, being such a humble and devout prince, responded that the friar was right in everything he was saying and trying to do, and he ordered that a poor child from the crowd accompanying him be allowed in, and he gave the child alms . . . with his own hand. . . .

His religiousness was so great that, being in Zaragoza one day, on the first day of Lent, he did not want to take the ashes until all of the clergymen (even those who were not yet priests) had done so, and he then took them with such singular humility, ascending to the innermost step to the altar . . . without letting anyone put down a cushion or anything else upon which he might kneel. . . .

His religion and faith were so great that he made perpetual war on the heretic in England, Flanders, and France, and upon the idolater and pagan in the Indies, and upon the barbarian and infidel in Turkey, and upon all the enemies of the holy Catholic faith everywhere in the world. . . . And he spent excessive amounts supporting the Catholics, using up his patrimony with such generosity that, like another Josiah, he had to ask his vassals for contributions and to be perpetually in debt, despite being the most powerful of all the world's kings.

20. Philip II,
What to Learn Concerning Indian Tribute (1559)

The acquisition of enormous new territories in the New World presented many challenges for the Crown, and simply as a problem of administration, the colonies threatened to strain Spanish resources. The Crown, of course, was hoping that the colonies would benefit rather than deplete the royal treasury, so Spanish officials sought to come up with revenue in all possible ways, including those traditionally used in Spain. Unfortunately, before they could tax the Indians effectively, there was much they had to learn. The following royal instructions sent to Spanish officials in Peru in 1559 suggest that as they took on this problem, the Spaniards could not avoid viewing Indian societies through the lens of their own culture.

SOURCE: Francisco de Zabálburu and Don José Sancho Rayon, eds., *Nueva colección de documentos inéditos para la historia de España y de sus indias*, vol. 6 (Madrid: Imprenta de Manuel G. Hernández, 1896), 28–31.

Given the need to create order in what concerns the distribution of the Indians of the provinces of Peru, in perpetuity or otherwise, it is necessary to appraise and declare justly the tributes, rents, and other fees that the Indians have to pay, so that this can be done with greater justice and a more sound basis. You, the count of Nieva, my viceroy and captain general of those provinces . . . [and] the other officials should inform yourselves and find out the following, in keeping with the advice and consideration contained in one of the chapters of the instructions you were given.

First, we must find out what tributes the Indians were paying to their sovereign lord and to their governors and to the lords whose vassals they were, and what they were accustomed to paying.

Similarly, you shall find out what those Indians are currently paying, and whether this represents a greater or lighter burden than what they had been paying, and whether they have stopped paying their chiefs and lords what they had been paying, and what those tributes were worth in total, expressed in gold pesos, per year. In order to find this out, you shall have brought before you pictures or tablets, or other accounts from that time, through which you will be able to learn these things, and from all this you will find out who are honest and impartial persons who have no vested interest and who is knowledgeable about these things.

You shall also find out what kind of persons paid such tributes, and if it was only the workers they call maceguales, or if merchants and other kinds of people also paid them, and whether their hidalgos or other such persons were exempt. You shall also find out what time of the year they paid these tributes and what procedures there were in the collection and distribution of these payments.

Similarly, you shall find out whether the tributes were based on the lands they worked and cultivated, or on the property they owned, or on persons and thus by head.

You shall also find out what land and other property the Indians owned, and whether those who paid tributes were attached to manors, and how their tributes were paid to the lords of those lands, and whether the tributes were paid based on a general or individual lordship.

Similarly, you shall find out whether, when the Christian Spaniards came and conquered those provinces, they levied any new tributes on the Indians, in addition to the old tributes that they paid during their time of infidelity, and if so what [the Spaniards] did with those payments, and whether they considered this and refrained from requiring any other tributes and services, . . . or if there were new charges assessed upon the Indians for the purpose of supplying food for the Spaniards to whom the pueblos were entrusted.

You shall also find out the order then enacted by those who assessed the tributes owed to the encomenderos, and how this was done, and whether it was done in consideration of what they had been paying to their primary lord, . . . or whether it was something new, exceeding what they had been paying their lords.

You shall also find out how these assessments were done, and whether the pueblos were summoned to do this, and what consideration they were given in these assessments, and whether the pueblos consented to them, and how the pueblos gathered and what procedures were used in seeking their consent, and whether it was done by force or by free will, or contrary to it. . . .

And you must also find out if there were formerly personal services and what kinds, so that if there were we may understand what they could and should pay in lieu of them.

You should learn whether it would be good if the tributes were paid in the form of the products of the land and the things that exist in that province and not in others. . . .

Similarly, you must find out what the Indians have to give and pay in tribute in place of the tithe for the divine religion, clergymen, monks, and parish priests, for sacred vestments and for the building of churches and monasteries, taking into consideration the tithes that the Spaniards now pay, as well as the rents and tributes that the Indians formerly, in their time of infidelity, were accustomed to paying for the manor houses and sanctuaries, and any other properties and rents that were devoted to the temples of the

Indians, and to the sun, all of which can be found out from the old Indians and from old pictures. . . .

The part indicated for this does not have to be collected as a tithe, as it is here in Castile, but rather may be assessed based on a locality, for if the method of the tithe is used, the natives may be annoyed by the pressure from the ministers, scandalizing the natives, who, being ignorant, may say that the law of Jesus Christ was introduced to them in order to exact new tributes from them, . . . so once you find out what the natives must pay for the service of God, you should have them pay that to their temporal lords.

All of this you will do with the proper care and diligence we expect of you. . . .

Ghent, July 23, 1559.

21. The Struggle Against Protestantism (1559, 1566)

Translated from Spanish by Hans J. Hillerbrand

For Spanish officials, who lived in dread of the spread of Protestantism from northern Europe into Spain, the task of defending the country from heresy focused on keeping Protestant pamphlets and books from crossing the borders into Spain. Unfortunately for those officials, however, there were many Protestants in southern France, in areas not far from the Spanish border, making the prevention of the smuggling of printed and handwritten material difficult. In this first text from 1559, the Inquisition in Toledo reports on its efforts.

SOURCE: Hans J. Hillerbrand, ed., *The Reformation: A Narrative History Related by Contemporary Observers and Participants* (Grand Rapids, Mich.: Baker Book House, 1972), 466–67. Copyright © 1972 Baker Book House Company. Reprinted by permission of Baker Book House Company.

Even without special order I shall never fail to submit a report whenever developments warrant it. Such is now the case. Last Saturday, the fourteenth of this month, five pamphlets were found in five chapels of our church here. I am herewith transmitting one of these pamphlets to you. There was no trace of the culprit. All were in the same handwriting and had the same content. It rained very heavily that night and more than thirty additional pamphlets were found at many doors, virtually throughout the entire town. They were all written by the same hand and again identical in content. Despite great efforts no trace has been found thus far.

We are carefully and secretly applying ourselves to this task. The following has been done: All teachers were called in, one after the other, and were asked under oath if they knew the handwriting. They were given the first three lines, without the title, to have the pupils identify the writing without knowing the reason for the inquiry. All inns and hostels in Toledo have been reached to learn who has stayed there during the past two months, from whence they came, and what papers they had in their possession. This search was also undertaken in the hospitals. All writers were sought out and messengers were sent into outlying villages to learn if perchance someone lives there and writes. Notaries were called to identify the handwriting. These and other methods are used, according to the situation in all secrecy, for it seems that it is the intent of these manifestos to cause public commotion. No trace has been found, however. In light of the content of the pamphlets, it appears that an apostate monk is the author.

An agent of the Inquisition filed the following report in 1566.

By order of Don Francis d'Alua I associated in Montpellier, a French town, with several Lutherans who have close contacts with Spain in order to learn if they ship books to Spain or know of heretics there. In order to gather this information conveniently and without gaining undue attention, I pretended to be a heretic myself and indicated my intention to take some books, such as the works of John Calvin and Theodore Beza, to Spain. [I told them that] since I was afraid of the Inquisition, I did not dare to purchase any there. If they, as believers, desired to help me in this regard, I would take books pertaining to their religion along. These I would send to several ladies and other friends who had eagerly requested them. A bookseller and a merchant volunteered to bring the books secretly to Barcelona to the home of one of their friends who were, as they said, of their faith.

A thousand deceptions were necessary to gather this information. Eventually Don Francis gave me permission to buy several books and the merchant took them. In order to save expenses he will send them around the middle of Lent to the house of one of their friends. He gave me a letter which introduces me. Don Francis presumably informed you already of further details. He allowed me to proceed to Barcelona to uncover this deception. I learned the names of all his friends from him, for he told me that they were of his religion. I am staying here and expect the books in order to further the transaction for the service of God and Your Majesty.

22. Saint Teresa of Avila, Autobiography (1561–1565)

Teresa de Cepeda y Ahumada, commonly known as Saint Teresa of Avila (or Teresa of Jesus) was born into a relatively wealthy family—one with Jewish ancestry on Teresa's father's side—in 1515. As she explains here, she suffered serious illnesses as a young woman, and though she spent several years in a convent, she did so reluctantly for some time. Among her most notable accomplishments was her founding of a new religious order known as the Discalced (or barefoot) Carmelites, which was known for its staunch discipline and austerity. Clashing repeatedly with Church authorities, who were suspicious of her family origins, her internally directed spirituality, her visions, and her gender, Teresa pursued her aims, even turning to King Philip II for assistance in 1579. She died in 1582, was canonized in 1622, and was declared a Doctor of the Church in 1970.

A remarkable woman who wrote several books, she can hardly be considered typical of Spanish women of the sixteenth century, but some aspects of her life cast light on the situation and outlook of women at that time, and her tale is also helpful for understanding certain attitudes and mentalities during Spain's Counter-Reformation.

SOURCE: *La vida de la madre Teresa de Jesús escrita por su misma mano, con una aprobación del Padre M. Fr. Domingo Bañes su confesor y cathedrático de prima en Salamanca* (Strasbourg: J.H.E. Heitz, 1924).

With all that the Lord did for me, having virtuous and God-fearing parents would have been enough for me to be good if I were not so wicked. My father liked to read good books, and he had books in Spanish so he could read them to his children. These, along with the care my mother showed in making us pray and in teaching us devotion to our Lord and some saints, led me to begin to open my eyes to things when I was about six or seven. . . .

I had a brother who was about my age, and we often got together to read lives of the saints, which I liked best. . . . When I saw the martyrdom that the saints endured for God, it seemed to me that they paid very little for being able to go and be with God, and I wanted very badly to die that way, not because of any love I had for Him, but because I was impatient to enjoy the great benefits I had read that there were in heaven, and my brother and I talked about how we might do this. We agreed that we would go to the land of the Moors, begging . . . that they cut our heads off, . . . but having parents proved the greatest obstacle to our plan. . . .

I have often thought about how much damage parents do when they do not see to it that their children see only virtuous things. . . . My mother liked books of chivalry, and that pastime did less harm to her than to me. . . . I started to pick up the habit of reading them . . . and it did not seem wrong to me to spend many hours, day and night, in such a vain pursuit, even though hidden from my father. . . . I started to dress up, and to worry about my appearance, paying great attention to my hands and hair and to scents and to all the vanities one can have in this area. . . . I did not have bad intentions, for I did not want anyone to offend God because of me. This excessive concern for my appearance lasted for some time, and things that did not seem any great sin to me for many years I can now see were very bad. . . .

Were I to give advice, I would tell parents that when their children are that age they should be very careful about the persons who have contact with them; for this is the source of much evil, given that our nature is much more inclined toward evil than good. And so it happened to me that . . . I was exposed to great damage by a cousin who was often in our house. She was so frivolous that my mother tried very hard to keep her out of the house (it seems that she could foresee the evil that would come to me because of her), but she had so many occasions to come to the house that there was nothing she could do. I enjoyed spending time with this girl. With her I chatted and gossiped, for she encouraged me in all the things I liked to do, and even showed me new ones, and she let me in on her conversations and vanities. Until I got to know her, which was when I was about fourteen, or maybe older, . . . I do not think I had gotten away from God through mortal sin, nor lost the fear of God, even if I cared more about honor. . . .

I do not think I spent more than three months in these vanities when my parents took me to a monastery . . . where they brought up such persons, although not ones with ways as wicked as mine. . . . For the first eight days I was very unhappy . . . but soon I was happier than I had been in my father's house . . . and although I was still deeply opposed to being a nun, it pleased me to see such good nuns, who were plentiful in that house, women of great honesty and piety and prudence. Yet still the devil did not cease to tempt me. . . .

I began to understand the truth I had known as a child, that the vanity of the world meant nothing, and soon I began to fear that if I died I would go to hell. Although my will was still not inclined toward being a nun, I saw that it was the best and safest state, and so little by little I became determined to force myself to become one. For three months I remained in this struggle, forcing myself with the reasoning that the travails could not be worse than those of purgatory, and I had indeed deserved to go to hell. . . .

When I took the habit, the Lord soon helped me to understand how he favors those who make an effort to serve him. . . . Being in that state then gave me great happiness, which has never disappeared ever since, and God turned the dryness in my soul into great tenderness; everything about religion made me happy, and it is true that I sometimes spent hours sweeping the floor, filling hours that I had spent on my amusements and appearance; realizing that I was free from that gave me such new enjoyment that it alarmed me. . . .

The changes in my life and my eating habits soon damaged my health . . . and I soon began fainting more and more often, and my heart began ailing, frightening anyone who saw me. . . . And the illnesses were so bad that . . . my father took me to a place well known for curing illnesses. . . . I spent almost a year there, and I suffered such severe tortures there in the cures they attempted that I do not know how I was able to bear them. . . . I tried as hard as I could to see Jesus Christ, our Savior and Lord, before me. . . .

I remained in that place for three months amid very great suffering, for the cure was more arduous than my constitution could bear; after two months the medicine had almost finished me off, and the difficulties of my heart ailment, which I had gone there to have cured, were even more arduous, so that sometimes that ailment seemed to have me in the grips of very sharp teeth, so horrible was it. Lacking strength (for I could eat nothing, but only drink . . .) I had deteriorated so badly that my nerves began to shrink, creating pains so unbearable that I could not sleep by either day or night, and I experienced a profound depression.

I could not have been in such straits for more than three months, for it seemed impossible to be able to suffer so greatly. Now I am amazed, and I consider the forbearance that His Majesty gave me to be a great mercy of the Lord, for one could see that it came from him. It did me much good that I had read the story of Job in the *Morals* by Saint Gregory, by which the Lord seems to have prepared me. . . . All my conversations were with God. I constantly had these words of Job in my thoughts, and I repeated them to myself: "As we have received good things from the hands of the Lord, why would we not also bear the bad things?" It seems that this gave me strength. . . .

One night I had a fit, which left me unconscious for four days; they administered the sacrament of the last rites, and at every hour and moment they thought I was dying, and they did nothing but read me the Credo, as if I could understand anything. They were so sure I was dead that I later found wax on my eyelids. . . . For a day and a half, there was a grave open in my monastery, awaiting my body. . . . But the Lord wished for me to revive, and soon I wished to go to confession; I confessed with great tears, but it seems to me that they did not flow because of a sense of regret for having offended God, which would have sufficed to save me. I had been deceived by those who had told me that certain things were not mortal sins, but I have certainly seen now that they were. . . . It seems to me that my salvation would have been in danger had I died then, partly because my confessors were so poorly educated, but also because I was so wicked. . . .

I was in such a state after those four days that only the Lord knows the unbearable tortures I felt. My tongue was bitten to pieces; my throat, through which nothing had passed, . . . was so weak that even water could not pass through it. Everything seemed out of place, and my head was in a daze; I was all shriveled up, . . . and I could move neither my arms, nor my feet, nor my hands, nor my head, as if I were dead, and others had to move me. I could only move one finger on my right hand. . . . This went on until Easter. . . .

I was so anxious to return to my monastery that I had myself taken there. They received the one whom they thought was dead, but with my body appearing worse than dead, it was frightening to look at me. It is indescribable how extremely thin I was, nothing but bones, and, as I said, I spent more than eight months like this. I remained paralyzed, though slowly improving, for almost three years. When I began to be able to crawl, I gave praise to God. . . .

[My monastery] gave me great liberty, more than even the very old women had. . . . I think it did me great damage to be in a monastery that did not lock the women in. For liberty, which women who were good could have, . . . would certainly have led me, being so wicked, to hell if the Lord had not rescued me. . . . So it seems very dangerous to me for a monastery to give women liberty. . . .

Oh, what terrible evil! What terrible evil for monks and nuns (here I am not referring more to women than men) where the rules of religion are not strictly observed! . . . Because of our sins, the way of imperfection is more often traveled, and because that path is broader, it is more often chosen. . . . I do not see why one should be surprised that there are so many evils in the Church today, for those who should be the model from whom others learn virtue have erased the work that the spirit of the saints of the past has left for religion. . . .

One day . . . while praying I saw—or I sensed, to be more accurate, for I saw nothing with the eyes of the body or soul—that Christ was standing next to me, and it appeared to me that he was speaking to me. And because I was completely unaware that such a vision could exist, it scared me greatly at first, and I could only cry; but he spoke a word of reassurance to me, I regained my usual calm and had no fear. Jesus Christ seemed to be right by my side, and because it was not an imaginary vision, I could not see the form distinctly, but I could sense that it remained very clearly by my side, and that it witnessed everything I was doing. . . .

I went straight to my confessor very anxious to tell him about it. He asked me in what form I saw it. I told him that I did not see it. He asked me how I knew it was Christ. I told him I did not know how I knew, but I could not fail to understand that he was next to me, and I saw, or sensed, clearly, and that the effects on my soul were much greater than anything I had ever felt while praying. . . . We women, who know so little, have no way to express this, and educated men can do a better job of explaining such things. For if I say that I did not see with the eyes of either my body or soul, how can I explain that it was clearer to me than it would have been had I seen with my eyes? . . .

I spent several days with this vision near me, and it was so helpful to me that I did not stop praying. . . . One day, while I was praying, the Lord saw fit to show me only his hands, which were so exceedingly beautiful that I cannot describe them. . . . A few days later I also saw that divine face, and I was completely entranced. I could not understand why the Lord was showing himself to me little by little, for later he had the mercy of letting me see his entire person, but later I figured out that His Majesty was proceeding according to my natural weakness. May he always be blessed, for such a lowly and wicked subject could not bear such glory, and as he knew this, the pious Lord went about it carefully. . . .

Soon he removed all doubt about whether this was an illusion, and soon I saw my foolishness. I could spend many years trying to think of how to invent something so beautiful and I would still fail, for it exceeds anything that can be imagined in this world, even its whiteness and brilliance. It is not a brilliance that can be seen, but rather a soft whiteness, and the brilliance is such that it brings extreme delight to see it, and one cannot tire of seeing such divine beauty. It is such a different kind of light from that of this world that even the light of the sun seems dull next to it. . . . It is like seeing very clear water that runs over crystal, with the sunshine shimmering in it, compared with very dark waters on a cloudy day. . . . In sum, it is such that no matter how great a person's understanding, one could never, in all the days of one's life, imagine how it is. . . .

As my visions grew more and more frequent, one who had previously helped me . . . began to say that this was obviously the work of the devil. Seeing that I could not resist, he ordered me to cross myself whenever I saw a vision and to point my finger accusingly at it, and to be certain that it was the devil, and this way it would not return. And he told me not to fear, that God would protect me and would take it away from me. This was very disturbing to me, for as I could not believe it was not God, his instructions were frightening to me. And as I have said, it was so hard for me to want it to go away, but in the end I agreed to do as he said. I begged God to deliver me from deception . . . and I prayed to Saint Peter and Saint Paul, whom the Lord had told me . . . would protect me from being deceived. And so I often saw them very clearly at my left side, and not in an imaginary way. . . .

Having to point like that when I saw this vision of the Lord gave great sorrow, . . . and it reminded me of the injuries that the Jews had done to the Lord, and I begged him to forgive me, for I was doing it out of obedience to one who stood in his place. . . . He told me not to worry, and told me I was doing well to obey. . . .

Sometimes the Lord wished for me to see a vision of this kind: I saw an angel at my left side, in corporeal form, which I do not usually see. . . . He was not large, but rather small and very beautiful, with his face burning, so that he seemed like one of the highest angels, who are always aflame. I could see that he had in his hands a broad arrow of gold, at the tip of which there seemed to be a small flame. It seemed to me that he was stabbing me in the heart with it, and it reached even to my entrails, and when he pulled it out it seemed as if it was dragging my entrails out, and it left me burning with great love for God. The pain was so great that it made me moan, and the sweetness of this extreme pain was so excessive that I did not want him to stop, and my soul would be content with nothing less than God. It was not a bodily pain but a spiritual one. . . .

I was once in an oratory when the devil appeared on my left side in an abominable form. I focused on his mouth, because it looked terrifying when he spoke. It seemed as if a great flame was coming out of his body, which was brightly illuminated without any shadow. He frightened me in saying that although I had slipped out of his hands, he would return to get me. I was very scared and I crossed myself as well as I could, and he disappeared, but then soon returned. This happened to me twice. I did not know what to do; I had some holy water there, and I threw it toward him, and he did not return.

Another time I was tortured for five hours with such terrible pains and internal and external anxiety that I could not believe it was possible to suffer so greatly. Those who were with me were terrified and did not know what to do or how to help me. . . . The Lord allowed me to understand that it was the devil, for I saw a horrible little Negro boy growling desperately over losing what he had thought he had. And when I saw him I laughed, and I was not afraid. . . . I have often learned from experience that there is nothing that chases devils away for good like holy water. The powers of holy water must be very great. . . . Well, as the torture was not stopping, I asked those with me if they would not laugh if I asked them for some holy water. They brought it to me, sprinkled it on me, . . . and I threw some toward where the little Negro was, and he fled right away, and all of the pain went away as if taken away by God's hand. . . .

After much time, . . . I was praying one day when all of sudden, without knowing how, I seemed to find myself in hell. I understood that the Lord wanted me to see the place the devils had ready for me, and which I deserved for my sins. This only took an instant, but I believe I could never forget it even if I were to live for many years. The entry seemed very long and narrow to me, like a very low, dark, and narrow oven. The floor seemed to be of very dirty mud, with a pestilential odor, with many evil reptiles there. At the end was a little nook in a wall, like a cupboard, where I saw myself confined. This was all pleasant to look at compared with what I was feeling. . . .

I felt a fire in my soul, and I could not describe how it felt, with physical pains so unbearable that, although I have experienced extremely severe pains in my life, . . . those were nothing in comparison with what I felt there, and to think that they would never end. But that is nothing in comparison with the agony of the soul, a feeling of constriction, a stifling feeling, such a palpable affliction and one with such desperate and severe anxiety that I do not know how to describe it. . . . I do not know how it was, but I understood that it was a great mercy, and that the Lord wanted me to see with my own eyes what he had freed me from with his mercy. . . .

Since then, everything seems easy to me in comparison with that memory of having to suffer what I did there. . . . How many times, Lord, have you freed me from such a frightful prison? . . . It was from that place that I came to feel so sorry for the many souls who are condemned, especially the Protestants (for they had been members of the Church, having been baptized), and it also made me want very badly to save souls, for it seems right to me that I should gladly accept death many times in order to save one single soul from such extreme torture.

23. Margaret of Parma,
The Situation in the Low Countries (1566)

When Philip II became king in 1556, he inherited not only Spain and its American colonies, but also the many European lands that his father, Charles, had possessed as part of the Habsburg patrimony. The wealthiest of those European lands were the Low Countries, including the present-day Netherlands and Belgium, and it would be hard to overstate their economic importance to Spain both as markets for Spanish exports—primarily Castilian wool—and as suppliers of capital and manufactures. Unfortunately for Philip, the Protestant Reformation had made considerable headway in those lands by the 1560s, even though a majority of the inhabitants remained loyal Catholics. Protestantism took several different forms in the Low Countries, with Lutherans, Anabaptists, and Calvinists being the most significant denominations; the Calvinists were particularly adamant in their hatred for the Catholic churches' religious imagery and displays of wealth, which struck them as corrupt and contrary to the true message of the New Testament. Protestantism in the Low Countries, in short, was one of the most alarming and difficult problems Philip faced.

For some time, Philip had sought to stop the growth of Protestantism in Spain's possessions in the Netherlands and Flanders through the usual means, including the Inquisition and the publishing of "placards" decreeing royal instructions on matters of religion. Yet Philip, inclined toward absolutist methods of government, was also engaged in a power struggle with the local nobility, who asserted their traditional rights to govern through the Estates General (a set of political institutions somewhat like the Iberian Cortes). So although the local nobility had little desire for a general social upheaval or violence by the classes below them, Philip could not count on the local ruling class's cooperation in his campaign against Protestantism.

In the summer of 1566, matters took a turn for the worse when a serious food crisis struck the Low Countries, creating an even more volatile atmosphere. In August of that year, Philip's half-sister, Margaret of Parma, who was acting as his regent in the Low Countries, sent him a series of letters reporting on the unfolding crisis.

SOURCE: Baron de Reiffenberg, ed., *Correspondance de Marguerite d'Autriche, duchesse de Parme, avec Philippe II* (Brussels: Delevingne et Callewaert, 1842), 182–85.

My lord, in the wake of my other letters, I cannot fail to warn Your Majesty of the continuation of the sacking of the churches, cloisters, and monasteries here, where these sectarians and their followers are toppling and smashing all the images, altars, epitaphs, organs, sepulchers, books, church ornaments, chalices, sacramental objects, and, in general, everything devoted to the worship of God; I am assured that in Flanders alone they have already sacked more than four hundred churches and will not stop until they have finished; they have even set fire to the interior of the church and cloister of the Dunes, where they burned the library. They did the same in the Abbey of Clermaretz . . . , and also Watton Abbey, and they are still threatening to go even further in doing the same in all the churches in Artois. Your Majesty is warned that in all these monasteries and cloisters, they are smashing all the sepulchers of the counts and countesses of Flanders, among others. Today I have received word that they have pillaged and sacked the great church of Notre Dame of Antwerp, and all other cloisters and parish churches, while the people watched, without saying anything in objection; and they were about one hundred in number, all from among the rabble.

And I understand that they, not being content with all this, have left the city to do the same at Saint Bernard Abbey, two other places in Antwerp, where they are still at present, and they say that they will not stop until they have finished off everything in the area. . . . They have also sacked the cloisters at Ghent, and, as I understand it, they are currently finishing off the cathedral and parish churches [there]. In the area of l'Alleud, they have chased away all the priests, and in various places they have begun to inflict punishments on those who do not wish to come to hear [their] preaching, thus forcing good people to become their followers.

I am threatened and warned that they will do the same thing this very day, or else tomorrow, in this city [Brussels], and I am deliberating on the means of preventing this, though with little hope of finding a way to do so, for if they wish to do evil, they will not stop until everything is sacked and destroyed. I see no alternative to their pillaging everything, for I find no help or solution to these evils, as those in the Estates General tell me that I have no choice but to grant freedom of conscience, authorizing the [Protestant] preaching, and can only seek a cease-fire and an end to the sacking and pillaging of churches. . . .

May it please Your Majesty to tell me what should be done. . . .

Brussels, August 22, 1566

24. Letter from Four Indian Governors (1567)

As Spanish missionaries carried out their task of spreading Christianity in the New World, one of the problems they faced was that of incomplete or deceptive conversions (something familiar to the Spaniards from their previous efforts to convert Jews and Muslims in Spain). Many of the Indians certainly embraced Christianity in full sincerity, but it was not uncommon for Indians to accept the new religion while still adhering to their prior beliefs and rituals—a practice that fit comfortably within the Indians' polytheistic outlook, but one the missionaries found unacceptable. In this 1567 letter to King Philip II, four Indian chiefs from the Yucatán region of Mexico wrote to complain of their treatment at the hands of Franciscan missionaries.

SOURCE: *Cartas de Indias* (Madrid: Imprenta de Manuel G. Hernández, 1877), 407–10.

After we had the fortune of coming to know our Lord God as the only true God, leaving behind our blindness and idolatry, and Your Majesty as temporal lord, and after we opened our eyes properly to the knowledge of the one and the other, a persecution came upon us, the greatest that can be imagined. In the year 1562, the monks of Saint Francis, whom we had had brought here to indoctrinate us, instead began to torture us, hanging us by our hands, whipping us cruelly, hanging stone weights from our feet, torturing many of us on racks, and pouring a great deal of water into our bodies; and from these tortures many of us have died and been crippled.

Amid this tribulation and travail, and while we were trusting in the justice of Your Majesty to hear us and protect us, the Honorable Diego Quixada came to help the torturers, saying that we were idolaters and sacrificers of humans, and other things that are completely untrue, and that even in the time of our infidelity we did not commit. And finding ourselves crippled by the cruel torments, with many having died from them, and having been robbed of our lands and more, when we saw the disinterment of the bones of our departed ones, who had been baptized and who died as Christians, we reached a point of desperation. And, not being content with all that, the monks and authorities of Your Majesty carried out a solemn act of the Inquisition in Mani, one of your pueblos, in which they took out many statues and disinterred many of the dead and burned them there publicly and also condemned many to serve the Spaniards as slaves for eight and ten years, and they also made them wear penitents' hats. And all these things greatly alarmed and frightened us because we did not know what it was all about, having been recently baptized and preached to. And when we returned to our vassals, in order to tell them to listen and to follow the regulations, they arrested us and imprisoned us and took us in chains, like slaves, to the monastery in Mérida, where many of our people died, and there they told us that they would have to burn us, without our even knowing why.

At that time the bishop, whom Your Majesty had sent to us, arrived, and he, despite releasing us from jail and freeing us from the death sentence and allowing us to remove the penitents' hats, did not clear us from the false accusations and testimony made against us, saying that we were idolaters and sacrificers of humans, and that we had killed many Indians. He is, after all, from the order of the Franciscans, and he works for them, but he sought to console us, saying that Your Majesty will see that justice is done.

An official from Mexico came to look into all this, and we thought that he would take care of this, but he did nothing.

Then Governor Luis de Cespedes came, but instead of clearing us, he added to our tribulations, taking away our children and wives so that they would serve the Spaniards, against their will and ours, causing us such great sorrow that the simple people now say that we were not so oppressed during our time of infidelity, because at least our ancestors never took anyone's children away from them, nor did they take wives away from husbands to use them as Your Majesty's authorities now do, even having them serve Negroes and mulattos.

And even given all our afflictions and travails, we love our fathers and we give them all the necessities, and we have built them many monasteries and provided ornaments and bells, all at our own expense, done by our people; in payment for all these services they treat us like vassals, even taking away from us the positions of authority we inherited from our ancestors, a thing we had never suffered before. And we obey Your Majesty's justice, hoping that you will send some remedy for all this. . . .

If Your Majesty wishes to investigate this, you may send anyone to look into it and learn of our innocence and the great cruelty of the fathers. And if the bishop had not come, we would all have been finished. And although we wish Fray Diego de Landa well, in addition to the other fathers who tortured us, merely hearing their names makes our innards churn. And so, may Your Majesty please send us other priests to indoctrinate us and preach the law of God, because we wish for our salvation very much.

The monks of Lord Saint Francis, in this province, have written various letters to Your Majesty and to the leader of their order, on the instructions of Fray Diego de Landa and his brethren, who were the ones who tortured, killed, and scandalized us, and they also gave certain letters written in the language of Castile to certain Indians they knew so that they would sign them, and so they did sign them and send them to Your Majesty. May Your

Majesty understand that these are not our letters. Those of us who are lords of this land do not have to write lies or falsehoods or contradictions. May Fray Diego de Landa and his brethren do penitence for the evil they did to us, and may our descendants remember to the fourth generation the great persecution they brought to us. . . .

May our Lord God guard Your Majesty for a long time. . . .

Humble vassals of Your Majesty, whose royal hands and feet we kiss.

Don Francisco de Montejoxio   Jorge Xin
Governor of the Province of Mani   Governor of Panaboren

Juan Pacab   Francisco Pacab
Governor of Mona   Governor of Texul

25. Francisco Núñez Muley,
A Morisco Plea (1567)

The liberal terms Ferdinand and Isabella granted the Moors upon their surrender in Granada in 1492 were not honored for long, for in 1499 the zealous archbishop Francisco Jiménez de Cisneros lobbied for a policy of intolerance toward Islam in Granada. Under that new policy, Muslims were forced either to convert or to emigrate, leading to a major uprising known as the first Alpujarras revolt. Although the rebels were defeated, and although all who remained had to accept Christianity, local officials stopped short of trying to eradicate every trace of Muslim culture and religion. Those who stayed, known as Moriscos, were thus Christian (at least outwardly), but they continued to speak Arabic, and they retained many aspects of their traditional culture.

In 1508, Spanish officials issued regulations targeting those remaining aspects of Moorish culture, but local officials made little attempt to enforce the rules, and an unofficial compromise prevailed for many years. In 1567, however, with the military threat from the Turks rising, those bent on eradicating all traces of Moorish culture obtained the proclamation of new regulations, which required the Moriscos to give up their language, clothing, and other customs. In response to these new rules, a Morisco nobleman sent this statement to the local authorities in Granada.

Such protests were in vain, but the enactment of the regulations helped provoke another rebellion, known as the second Alpujarras revolt (1568–1570). Once again, the Moriscos put up staunch resistance but eventually lost. This time, the Spanish government chose to disperse the Moriscos throughout Castile, bringing in Christians to settle in Andalusia.

The term *zambras* refers to a kind of festival the Muslims of southern Spain enjoyed, featuring exuberant dancing and singing.

SOURCE: Luis del Mármol Carvajal, *Historia del [sic] rebelión y castigo de los moriscos del reyno de Granada* (Madrid: Imprenta de Sancha, 1797), 152–62.

When the natives of this kingdom converted to the faith of Jesus Christ, there was no condition that obliged them to give up their way of dressing or their language, nor the other customs they had concerning their festivals, *zambras*, and recreations. And to speak truthfully, the conversion was done by force, contrary to the provisions of the treaty signed by the Catholic monarchs [Ferdinand and Isabella] when King Abdilehi [Boabdil] turned over this city. While Their Majesties remained alive, I do not, with all my years, recall any attempt to go back on that agreement. Then, during the reign of Doña Juana, their daughter, it came to seem appropriate (to whom I do not know exactly) to order that we give up our Morisco clothing, but when certain drawbacks to this plan were pointed out, it was suspended, remaining that way when the most Christian emperor Don Carlos [Charles V, I of Spain] came to the throne.

It then happened that a low-ranking man from our nation, trusting in the protection of . . . a local official for whom he worked in this district, dared to write certain passages against the priests and clergymen, without consulting with the leading men of the community. . . . On behalf of the clergymen, the Honorable Pardo, abbot of San Salvador del Albaicín [in Granada] responded, . . . using his authority to inform his superior that the newly converted were still Moors, and that they lived as Moors, and that an order should be given that they abandon their ancient customs, which prevented them from being Christians. The emperor, as a most Christian prince, ordered investigators to go throughout this kingdom to find out how its natives were living. The very same clergymen carried out this investigation, and they were the ones who made the deposition against them. . . . Many things were decreed against our privileges . . . and they were suspended. . . .

Now the same clergymen have taken up the issue again, to harass us in many ways all at once. Anyone who looks at the new rules from a distance will think they would be easy to follow, but the difficulties they imply are very great, as I will explain in detail, so that, in coming to share the pain of this miserable people, one will take pity on them with love and charity. . . .

The clothing our women wear is not even Moorish clothing; it is simply the local clothing, like the clothing in Castile, and as in other places the headdresses, clothing, and shoes serve to distinguish people. Who can deny that the clothing of the Moors and Turks is very different from these people's clothing? And even among themselves there are many differences; for the clothing in Fez [now Morocco] is not like the clothing in Tlemcen [now Algeria], nor is that of Tunis like that of Morocco, and the same can be said of Turkey and the other kingdoms. If the sect of Mohammed had its own clothing, it would have to be the same everywhere, but the habit does not make the monk. We see Christian clergymen and laymen from Syria and Egypt dressed in the Turkish style, with headdresses and full-length caftans; they speak Arabic and Turkish and do not know Latin or Spanish, and yet they are Christians. . . .

This being as it is, what good can it do anyone to take away our clothing, keeping in mind that we have spent a great deal of money on it, money earned in the service of the previous kings? Why would they want to make us lose the more than three million gold pieces we have tied up in this clothing, wiping out the merchants, traders, jewelers, and others who make their living by making clothing, shoes, and jewelry in the Morisco style? If the more than two hundred thousand women there are in this kingdom have to buy all new clothing, from head to toe, where will the money come from? . . . Think of the poor woman who cannot afford to buy a Castilian skirt, a mantilla, a hat, and clogs. . . . What will she do? What will she wear? Where will she get the money for this? . . .

I have often heard the ministers and prelates say that favors would be done for those who dressed in the Castilian style, but so far, of the many who have done so, I can see none who have been either bothered or favored; we are all treated the same. If they find a knife on any one of them, they throw him in jail, and he loses his property in fines and penalties. We are persecuted both by ecclesiastical and secular authorities, and despite all this, we remain loyal vassals, obeying His Majesty, ready to serve him with our properties, and it can never be said that we have committed any treason from the day when we surrendered.

When the Albaicín rebelled [in 1499, over forced conversions and other measures], it was not a rebellion against the king, but rather in favor of things he had signed his name to, which we consider sacred. Before the ink was even dry, they broke the terms, seizing women who had Christian ancestors in order to force them to be what they had once been. Let us see, lord: in the Comunero revolt [in 1520], did the people of this kingdom rise up? For sure, in favor of His Majesty, as the marquis of Mondéjar and Don Antonio and Don Bernardino de Mendoza, his brothers, sided with him against the Comuneros . . . with more than four hundred soldiers from our nation, and they were the first people in all of Spain to take up arms against the Comuneros. And Don Juan de Granada, brother of [Muslim] King Abdilehi, was also a general in Castile in the royal army, and he worked to pacify things as much as he could, and he acted as a good vassal of His Majesty should. It is thus only fair that those who have maintained such loyalty be favored and honored and protected in their properties, and that Your Lordship should favor, honor, and protect them, as the previous authorities in this place did.

Our weddings and festivals and the pastimes to which we are accustomed do not in any way prevent us from being Christian. I do not even see how these things can be considered Moorish ceremonies; good Muslims were never found doing these things, and the holy men left as soon as the *zambras* and the singing and music began. . . . These *zambras* do not exist in Africa or Turkey; it is a local custom, and if it were a religious ceremony, it would have to exist in the same form everywhere. . . .

What good does it do to make us keep our doors open? That would allow thieves to rob us, rapists to force themselves on our women, and policemen and scribes the opportunity to destroy poor people. If someone

wanted to be a Moor and take up Moorish ways, couldn't they do so at
night? Yes, for sure, for the sect of Mohammed requires solitude and seclu-
sion. For those with bad intentions, it matters little whether they open or
close the door, and there is still punishment for those who are doing what
they should not, since nothing is hidden from God.

Can it really be true that the baths serve a ceremonial purpose? No, certainly not. Many people gather at the baths, and most of the bathers are
Christians. The baths are not clean, while the rites and ceremonies of the
Moor require cleanliness and solitude. How could one undertake suspicious
activities there? Baths were created for the cleaning of the body, and to say
that men and women get together there is beyond belief, for where so many
people go there cannot be any secret. There would be other ways for them
to get together if they wanted, and men do not enter the baths when women
are there. There have always been baths in all provinces, and if they were
abandoned in Castile, it was because they weakened men and undermined
their warrior spirit. Yet the natives of this kingdom do not have any wars to
fight, nor do women need such strength, but only need to be clean. If they
cannot wash there, nor in the creeks, fountains, and rivers, nor even in their
houses, as they are prevented from doing, then where should they bathe? . . .

What does it mean to require that women go about with their faces
uncovered, if not to give men the occasion to sin, as they see the beauty
they tend to find so attractive? And consequently, unattractive women will
not find anyone to marry them. They cover themselves so they will not be
recognized, as Christian women do; it is a decency designed to avoid problems, and for this reason the Catholic king [Ferdinand] ordered that no
Christian should uncover the face of a Morisca woman, under severe penalty.
This being so, and there being no offense to matters of religion, why must the
natives be harassed about the covering or uncovering of their women's faces?

The old surnames we have serve for people to know each other, and
without them knowledge of persons and lineages will be lost. What good
does it do to have such memories be lost? . . .

Then let us speak of the Arabic language, which is the greatest issue
of all. How can one take away people's native tongue, with which they
were born and raised? The Egyptians, Syrians, Maltese, and other Christian
peoples speak, read, and write Arabic, and they are just as Christian as we
are; and you will not find that any writing, contract, or testimony has been
written in Arabic since the conversion took place. To learn the Castilian language is something we all wish to do, but it is out of people's hands. How
many people can there be in the villages and places outside this city, or even
within it, who only manage to speak Arabic in very diverse ways, using very

different accents, so that one has only to hear someone from Alpujarras speak to know what clan they are from. . . . It would be very difficult, almost impossible, for the old people to learn Spanish in the days they still have left, much less in the brief period of three years, even if they did nothing but go to school the whole time. This is clearly a rule that was created to harm us, for . . . they want us to learn it by force and abandon the one we know so well, creating the opportunity for penalties and accusations, and those who cannot accomplish such a difficult task may leave this land and flee to other places out of fear of those penalties.

26. The Council of State,
Events in Antwerp (1576)

The rebellion that broke out in the Low Countries in the 1560s turned into a long war, creating a prolonged strain on the Spanish Crown's already beleaguered finances. In 1575, Philip's government declared bankruptcy, impeding the Crown's access to loans from international bankers. At that point, Philip found himself unable to pay his troops in the Army of Flanders. The following report drawn up by the local Council of State describes what ensued in Antwerp.

SOURCE: *Correspondance de Philippe II sur les affaires des Pays Bas*, ed. M. Gachard, vol. 5 (Brussels, Ghent, and Leipzig: C. Muquardt, 1879), 8–10.

Brussels, November 6, 1576

Sire, since we last wrote to Your Majesty, things have grown worse and worse, as Spanish soldiers here, after having taken over, sacked, and burned part of the city of Maastricht, killing a large number of bourgeois and other inhabitants of that place, have now violently invaded, occupied, burned, sacked, . . . and pillaged the town of Antwerp and the bourgeois and other inhabitants here, including priests as well as laymen, women as well as men, carrying out all sorts of hostile actions with as much cruelty as possible, to our great and unspeakable regret. Because we are sure that [mutineer] Gerónimo de Roda and his followers will have given Your Majesty an account of this from their point of view, in order to justify their actions, we have felt it necessary to advise Your Majesty about the truth of the case.

That is in effect that said Roda and his followers, not content with holding the citadel in Antwerp, have endeavored to take over the whole city. . . . [The town's authorities] worked out a reciprocal promise not to attack each other. Yet notwithstanding this agreement, the soldiers in the citadel had all of the cavalry that was in Maastricht come join them, along with all of the other mutinous soldiers who had been in Alost. . . . [Given] the fear of the inhabitants of Antwerp that the aforementioned accord might not be kept by those who had already given such great indication of their bad intentions by the fact of their threats to massacre and to destroy everything, they once again had reason to seek greater assurance of their security. . . . [A detachment of civil guards then came to protect the city], but at the very same moment when they arrived, the aforementioned [mutinous] soldiers from Alost arrived at the citadel. . . . [At this point] the said Spaniards, especially the soldiers from Alost, along with some officers from Germany who had come from Maastricht, Tirlemont, and elsewhere, joined together, and with great fury began breaking the agreement, and, with the help of the artillery, began firing down from the citadel into the city. . . . What then ensued was a massacre not only of the civil guard but also of the good bourgeois and other inhabitants, regardless of nation, who were on the streets and in their houses. And the Spanish soldiers then set fire to several townhouses and other places in that city, destroying, according to reports we have received, very large blocks and neighborhoods of the city, described in detail in a document we have enclosed. They even destroyed the city hall, built only a few years ago, as you know, at great cost, a rare and very magnificent building, a drawing of which we understand Your Majesty was recently sent. We assure Your Majesty that the damage done by the burning of this building alone is inestimable, considering the great and unspeakable interest that over a million persons have in it, and not only subjects of Your Majesty but also of other countries; for what was burned included all of the property records and contracts among private persons and other very old documents, together with the charters, accords, and treaties made with the foreign nations who have over time come to live and to negotiate in this city, so that the damage done exceeds any possible estimate.

The death toll in this massacre, according to reports, is more than eight thousand persons, [including] . . . the officers of Count Everstein and the count himself along with . . . Lord de Bièvre, who had been in charge of the estates of the six hundred light horsemen; taken prisoner was the son of the count of Egmont, who was in charge of a regiment of Walloons [among others]. . . .

This, sire, is a summary of what happened in Antwerp, to our very great regret. . . . As a result of all this, the most beautiful city in Europe has been ruined. . . . May God will that similar evils not recur, allowing Spanish soldiers to threaten at any moment that they will go on like this until they have done even worse things, turning everything upside down. What is still causing so much worry among the Estates [General] and everyone else is the fear that [Philip's military envoy] Don Juan will not make it here in time to resolve all of this, and that, out of desperation, and in order to protect themselves from such violence, [the locals] may turn to foreign princes—an eventuality whose negative consequences Your Majesty, in your great wisdom, can easily see.

27. Philip II,
The Portuguese Succession (1579)

In 1578, King Sebastian of Portugal died fighting the Moors in North Africa, leaving no sons to inherit his throne. Succeeding Sebastian was an elderly relative, Cardinal Henry, who also had no sons, and in the final two years of Henry's life, several candidates put forward their claims to succeed him as king of Portugal. The three most likely candidates were Don Antonio, prior of Crato (an illegitimate son of the Portuguese royal family), the duchess of Braganza, and Spain's King Philip II. Philip's candidacy enjoyed some support among the Portuguese nobility and upper classes, given the commercial advantages of access to Spain's empire, but many lower-ranking clergymen and other Portuguese subjects, who did not stand to benefit so directly, resented the idea of a Castilian king ruling over them. Philip thus had to use extensive diplomatic and financial resources to secure the Portuguese throne, but when Cardinal Henry died in 1580, Philip indeed became king of Portugal. In this letter from August 1579, Philip gives his ambassador in Lisbon instructions and presents the arguments for his candidacy.

SOURCE: "Carta de Felipe II al Duque de Osuna San Lorenzo, 24 agosto 1579," in *Colección de documentos inéditos para la historia de España*, vol. 6 (Madrid: Imprenta de la Viuda de Calero, 1845), 649–61.

Having been informed by your last letters of the recollections that the Most Serene King [Henry], my uncle, retains, and the hope that there is for his full recovery, I have found much greater happiness and contentment than I can tell you. . . . Now you will visit him and offer him my congratulations on his recovery, telling him what I am telling you here. . . .

You must tell [the king] . . . how important it is for the service of our Lord God and for the universal benefit of Christianity that the matter of the succession of the kingdoms of this crown, which he has in his power, be resolved properly and promptly. And I have no doubt that with his unique prudence and deeply Christian zeal he must have foreseen the great usefulness and advantage that will be secured not only for all of Spain but also for the rest of Christendom if I should be declared and sworn to be his legitimate successor, . . . and I hope and trust in his great goodness and rectitude, since with the information that persons of good faith have given him, he must have understood the well-known justice of my case. And still, in light of my desire to see this matter resolved and brought to conclusion simply and peacefully, . . . I ask and entreat him once again very affectionately that he see fit to resolve this by declaring me his successor. . . .

Considering this, . . . may he see fit to exchange his role of judge for that of a father of his kinsmen, among which I have the place of first-born son, and as a common father may he try to reconcile and resolve these disputes for the universal good of the vassals of that crown and the particular good of his nephews; I will look after all of them very gladly because of my great desire to see to it that it is never necessary to come to hard measures with my own blood relatives, with my own nation, with my own children, whom I have in this place. . . . Aside from the obligation common to all Christian princes, he has the very particular obligation as an ecclesiastical prince of great virtue and piety to make the propagation of the gospel and the benefit and growth of the universal Church and our holy Roman Catholic faith the basis of all his actions; he will do our Lord God a great service by not obstructing, but rather implementing, such an important and appropriate measure as this, which is being offered with the union of these two crowns, to introduce and exalt the name of our Lord Jesus Christ and his divine law and holy religion in the regions of the East, where it cannot be spread as it must be by the forces of a single kingdom.

May he command that people see that with the formation of this union, one of the greatest benefits and comforts that can ever be offered is being created for the Church and for all Christianity in general, for it will be an extremely effective means of restraining and defeating the forces, insolence, and tyranny of the Turk, the perpetual enemy of Christianity, with the diversion we will be able to make in the Orient and in Asia, which will force [the Turk] always to be so much on guard that it will restrain him and prevent him from freely invading our coasts as he has done up to this point.

The same security will be had regarding Africa, along with a great chance of invading it, with the conquest not being divided, and with my frontiers and those of those kingdoms having a single owner. . . .

In joining my kingdoms with those, both will be defended very easily from pirates, from the Ocean Sea as well as the Mediterranean, and it will be possible to be so completely rid of them that those living on the coast will be able to live like those in the interior.

In joining with the forces of my states those of a nation as courageous as the Portuguese, and one so respected in the world for its arms and its conquest of the sea and land, Spain's reputation in the field of navigation will grow so much that all the other nations will recognize and respect it as the most powerful and praiseworthy province of Christendom.

If any damage should result to Portugal because of this union, it will be so limited as to be given little consideration compared to the universal and common advantages for the Church and all of Spain to which we have referred; indeed . . . not only will those kingdoms not be damaged, but in fact they will receive specific benefits in being added to mine. . . . This is so obvious that no dispassionate judge will fail to admit that all the benefits of

Castile will be communicated to these kingdoms, with the only things leaving them being those which are not needed. . . .

In turning to specifics, one can see clearly that the three estates will each extend its reach throughout these kingdoms, the clergy with offices and ecclesiastical benefits, the nobility and gentry with positions and posts throughout all of them, and the people with their endeavors and the navigation of the West Indies, which will be of great interest to them.

Lisbon, a city so famous and esteemed for its greatness and loyalty, will be even more so as the capacity and convenience of its port will make commerce grow to the point that it has no equal in Europe. . . .

So that it can be seen that I am doing everything possible to achieve this objective and to avoid all kinds of problems, you will offer on my behalf that if he declares and swears that I am his prince and the legitimate successor of that Crown, I will willingly concede these favors and privileges. . . .

That because those of the ecclesiastical estate . . . should enjoy the privileges of that estate, we will look kindly upon the bestowing of honors and benefits in these kingdoms in accordance with their merits. . . .

That we will favor the religious orders of these kingdoms impartially and very willingly with gracious acts and alms as we believe they deserve based on how observantly they serve Our Lord and his Church.

That for the good of the state, of the nobles, and the gentry of those kingdoms we promise to preserve the royal house and family with all its functions, maintaining its privileges and customs in its establishments and its dwellings without altering anything the kings of Portugal have done. . . .

That we will always allot offices in government and the justice system in all of the kingdoms and tribunals of this Crown to natives of Portugal. . . .

That when I am absent from Portugal I will bring with me all the ministers and officials necessary for the proper expediting of matters of government.

That I will admit Portuguese to the offices of my household in accordance with the customs of Burgundy, [treating them] no differently from the Castilians and the other vassals of my nations. . . .

That for the good of the people and the whole of these kingdoms, and so that commerce and good communications should increase with those of Castile, I will see to it that internal customs ports are opened on both sides so that merchandise may pass freely as it did before the customs duties that are now charged were implemented.

That we will order a reduction in half of the twenty percent duties that are now paid on merchandise entering Lisbon and other ports.

That for the entry of bread from Castile for the provisioning of that kingdom we will order that all appropriate privileges be granted.

That in the same way we will order that there be a proper agreement with those of that kingdom regarding that which will allow them to travel to my Indies, granting them all the privileges that are called for.

That when they declare and swear that I am the successor in that kingdom I will grant them . . . three hundred thousand *ducados* for the ransom of captives, two hundred thousand for ransoming hidalgos . . . and one hundred thousand for poor captives, this at the disposal of Lisbon.

That although the claims of the most illustrious Lady Catherine, duchess of Braganza, my cousin, to the royal succession of that kingdom have as little foundation and justice as is known, I will look kindly upon treating her as liberally as the love and family relations that exist between us require, increasing her household and wealth and authority in that kingdom as well as these. . . .

That given the love that the natives of this kingdom have for their monarchs we would like to promise that we will normally reside in it, but because of the government of the other kingdoms and states that God has entrusted to me [I cannot]. . . . But we will try to be in this kingdom as much as we can, and whenever there is no other duty that prevents this, we will leave our son, His Most Serene Prince, there so that he may be raised among the Portuguese, and so that he may get to know them, love them, and respect them as they deserve, and as I do. And in the times when neither I nor he can reside there the best possible accord will be reached with those of that kingdom to create the situation that is most agreeable and appropriate for its good government. . . .

There must not be any room for my opponents' misconception that I am a foreign prince, since I have so much Portuguese blood in me, much more than of any other place; moreover, as is known, it is the nature of princes that they are not restricted to one place or kingdom as private citizens are, but rather are part of the entire breadth of their states. . . .

You may also tell him that he knows full well that this difference between Portuguese and Castilians has no more substance than a vain and false man does, for the one and the other are equally Spanish, and they differ so little in language, in manners, and in customs, and many of the great and middling families of Castile descend from Portugal through the masculine line, and all of the nobility of both kingdoms is linked through affinities and family relationships, and among us there are so many that they cannot be recounted, so that one can easily see that this vain opinion is only based on popular ignorance. . . .

In the same way you will tell him that because my rights to succession in that kingdom are so certain and well known, as everyone understands, I do not need to reply to the slander of those who, with evil intentions, seek to convert this grace into poison, saying that out of doubts over the justice of my case I turn to liberal means. . . .

To complete your discussion with him, you must on my behalf beg and ask the Most Serene King, my uncle, to consider the miseries and public calamities that one may truly fear if my great rights and the well-known justice of my claim to succession of that kingdom are not honored, and I ask him as a kind of father not to deny me the right of the first-born son, which God and the laws have given me, nor to oblige me to take any other path than that of the gentleness, love, and generosity that I propose; and [ask] that he prevent . . . the disputes that have existed and may exist, for he can and must act justly for the benefit of Christendom and all the kingdoms of Spain, and especially those of that crown that God had entrusted to him. . . . That which among private citizens is a mere dispute tends, among princes, to be war, the spilling of blood, the misery and ruin of kingdoms, which could never be blamed on me, for I offer the possible means of avoiding it with great confidence that the Most Serene King, my uncle, must embrace it and accept it all in accordance with his great prudence, rectitude, and Christianity. And you will advise me when you have a response . . . for I will be on guard until I hear the answer in detail.

28. Luis de León,
The Perfect Wife (1583)

Born in 1527 in Castile, Luis de León was educated at the University of Salamanca and later taught there as well. As an Augustinian friar, he became caught
up in a conflict with the Dominicans, and he was arrested by the Inquisition,
spending several years in prison in the 1570s. After he was cleared, he continued to write, becoming famous in his own times. In this piece, written to advise
a female friend who had just married, the friar uses a famous text from the Old
Testament, Proverbs 31, as the basis of his comments on women's proper behavior and place in society. The book proved quite popular, and some Spaniards
continued to use it as a wedding present for women as late as the twentieth century, during the regime of Francisco Franco. Luis de León died in 1591.

SOURCE: Luis de León, *La perfecta casada, por el maestro F. Luys de Leon,
texto del siglo XVI*, ed. Elizabeth Wallace, reprint of 3rd ed., prologue by Elizabeth
Wallace (Chicago: University of Chicago Press, 1903).

To Lady Maria Varela Osorio.

This new state in which God has placed Your Grace, subjecting you to
the laws of holy matrimony, is a royal path, more open and less tiresome
than others, but it does not lack its difficulties and pitfalls, and it is a path
on which one also may stumble, err, and encounter danger, so it calls for
a guide, just as the others do. For serving one's husband, governing one's
family, and raising one's children, and the responsibility toward God that
goes along with all of this, . . . are tasks that each call for great caution, and
without heaven's assistance these tasks as a whole could not be carried out.
On this point many women are mistaken, thinking that getting married consists of nothing more than leaving one's father's house and passing over to
that of one's husband, leaving servitude behind for liberty and pleasure. And
they think that in having a child from time to time and then handing it
over to the arms of a governess they are complete and perfect women. And
although Your Grace's good judgment and inclination toward virtue, which
God gave you, assure me that I should not fear that you will be like those
women I describe, my compelling love for you and the concern for your
well-being that burns within me nonetheless spur me to provide you with
some advice. . . .

So I will teach you about this journey that Your Grace has begun, not
from what my experience has taught me, for it is foreign to my profession,
but rather from what I have learned from the Sacred Scriptures. . . . In truth,
the state of matrimony is at a lower grade of perfection than that of celibacy
and virginity, but out of the necessity that exists in this world that the human

race be preserved, and so that children of God will be born to honor the earth and please the heavens with glory, marriage was always very honored and privileged by the Holy Spirit in the Sacred Scriptures.

From those Scriptures we know that this state of being is the first and most ancient of all, and we know that it was not invented after our nature was corrupted by sin and condemned to death, but rather ordered from the beginning, when men were complete and perfect in paradise. They also teach us that God Himself arranged the first marriage, and that He joined the hands of the first couple and blessed them, as if He were the first priest to perform a marriage ceremony. . . .

Among many other passages in the divine books that deal with this subject, the most fitting place where it is discussed . . . is in the final chapter of Proverbs, where God, through the mouth of Solomon . . . paints a full picture of a virtuous wife. . . . For those who aspire to be that (and all who marry should), they may look at her as they would look in a crystal-clear mirror and learn what to do. . . . Two things are thus necessary: to know what you are and what conditions you face . . . and to embrace those conditions sincerely. . . . The essence of what God asks each person is to follow the obligations of his or her position, fulfilling the fate that has fallen to them. . . .

The cross that each one must bear in order to join Christ is precisely the obligation and the burden that each one has as a result of the place they have been given. . . . So may you engrave it in your heart with all firmness that to be a friend of God is to be a good wife, and that the good of your soul lies in being perfect in your place. . . . For it is well known that when a woman carries out the tasks that go with her position, her husband loves her, her family is in harmony, her children learn virtue, peace reigns, and her household's property grows. . . .

Take a look at your neighbors and others, and recall what you have heard of other households. How many women have you known of who, because they have not minded their place but rather pursued their whims, were constantly fighting with their husbands and disgracing them? How many have you seen who were saddened and shamed by disagreements with their sons and daughters, who did not want to obey? How many have struggled in extreme poverty because they did not watch carefully over their household's fortune, or, more precisely, because they were the cause of its ruin? So it is that there is nothing richer or happier than a good woman, nor worse nor more miserable than a wife who is not good. . . .

And it happens that . . . women, being so concerned with matters of honor, craving to be prized and honored (as all weak souls are), and competing in very childish and petty things, . . . become careless and forget the basis of their own virtue and praiseworthiness. A woman likes to appear more beautiful than another, and even if her neighbor has a better skirt, or perhaps gets a better hairdo, she does not accept it patiently. . . . [But] the praise one gets in this way is petty, vain, and fleeting, and does not even merit being called praise; the praise, on the other hand, that is solid and real, and which flourishes in the mouths of wise people . . . does not wither with age or time, but rather grows over the years. . . . The good woman's family reveres her, and her children love her, and her husband adores her, and her neighbors bless her, and those today and those to come laud and extol her. In truth, if there is anything under the sun that deserves to be respected and prized, it is the good woman. Compared to her, even the sun is not brilliant, and the stars are but dark, and I know of no precious jewel that stands out and shines with such clarity and splendor in men's eyes like that treasure of immortal qualities of honesty, sweetness, faith, truth, love, kindness, softness, joy, and peace. . . .

"She seeks wool and flax and works with willing hands" (Proverbs 31: 13).

It does not say that the husband buys flax for her to work on, but rather that she seeks it. . . . The first part of being industrious is to make good use of things [including] excess things and those that seem ruined, and she values things that her husband ignores, providing herself with wool and flax and other things like this, which are like the weapons and the battlefield where the good woman discovers her virtue. For joining her skills with her industriousness and that of her maids, . . . she will find her house overflowing with abundance and full of wealth.

But perhaps some delicate ladies will now say that this portrait is crude, and that this woman is the wife of a working man, and thus a woman from a different estate than their own, and thus that we are not speaking of them. To this we respond that this wife is the perfect model for all wives, and the measure by which those of higher and lower estates must be judged. . . .

And it is proper and necessary for all . . . not to be wasteful and dissolute, and to be industrious and to increase one's property. And if leisure and wasting time have led some to believe that carelessness and idleness are part of nobility and grandeur, and if those who call themselves ladies make a point of doing nothing and of taking care of nothing, and if they believe that earning a living and farming are lowly endeavors contrary to nobility, then they should quit fooling themselves and see the truth. For if we look back at the past, we will find that whenever virtue has reigned, farming and

work have gone along with it. . . . Abraham, a very rich man and the father
of all true nobility, broke the earth, and David, invincible and glorious king,
not only tended flocks before he became king, but even after he became king
he continued to live off his lands and his flocks. And as for the Romans, lords
of the whole world, we know that they went from the plow to the consulate, that is, to commanding and governing all the earth, and that they then
returned from the consulate to the plow. . . .

Almost in the time of our grandparents, we find clear examples of this
virtue, as in the case of the Catholic queen, Lady Isabella. . . . And if those
ladies who see themselves this way, and who call themselves duchesses and
queens, are not persuaded by reason, let them try this for a brief time; let
them take up the distaff, the needle, and the thimble, surrounded by their
ladies-in-waiting, and let them make rich products, working into the night,
fighting off sleep, . . . and let the young thoughts of their ladies-in-waiting
be occupied in this way, so that, inspired by the example of their lady, they
may compete among themselves, seeking to be the most industrious. And if
because of the wealth of their own persons or their households this labor is
not necessary for them (though there is no household so great or royal that
it would not bring honor and plenty upon itself by doing so), then let them
do it not for themselves but for the good and the welfare of a hundred poor
people and a thousand needs of others. . . .

"She rises while it is still night and provides food for her household, and
tasks for her maidens" (31: 15).

This wife we are portraying as an example for good wives is the wife of a
man who lives, as we have said, from farming. . . . For in such households
the family must get up very early in the morning and does not return to the
home until nightfall, and that family must also take with them the food for
their lunch. . . . And as Solomon said, the good wife does not give this job
to one of her servants while sleeping late in her bed; instead, she rises first,
rising even earlier than the sun, and with her own hands she provides for her
people and her family. . . . For if the lady of the house, who is and must be
the example and the teacher of her family, from whom each one of her maids
must learn what goes with her position, forgets her duties, then the others
will forget theirs and remain asleep. . . . So the wife must get up early so that
her family will too. For she must understand that her household is a body,
and she is its soul.

"She makes herself coverings; her clothing is fine linen and purple" (31: 22).

By this statement, God wishes to tell good women that they should only put on what they could wear in church, that is, that all their clothing and adornments should be holy . . . and that their outfits should not be cut following the despicable and worldly whims of fashion, but rather according to the demands of decency and modesty. So here God indicates holy clothing, condemning the profane. He says purple and linen, but he does not call for the embroidery that is worn these days, nor the decorations, nor the gold worn in fine chains. He says clothing, but he does not say diamonds and rubies. She puts on what can be sewn and made at home, but not the pearls that are hidden in the depths of the sea. He accepts simple clothing but does not permit frills, ruffles, or cosmetics. . . .

Especially regarding facial cosmetics, there is great excess even among women who are otherwise decent. . . . Yet I fear to discuss this, for who would not be afraid to oppose something so common? And who will dare to persuade women to want to appear as they are? . . . . This is not only a difficult task, but also a dangerous one, for they will soon hate the one who takes these things away from them. . . .

But what does it matter if I condemn them, when there are so many to absolve them? And if they listen to those who indulge their taste for these things that leave them disgusting and ugly, then they should not hate me, but simply listen with equanimity and attention; for all I wish to do is to teach them that they are beautiful, which is the main thing they want. Because I do not want them to indulge in the sin that some do in putting on makeup, but only to get them to realize that it is a deceptive thing, which gives them the opposite effect of that which is promised. . . .

Those who consider makeup beautiful do not realize that it is dirty . . . and that most of the materials from which it is made are disgusting. . . . And if they are not dirty, why do women remove them at night and wash their faces so thoroughly, and why, after they have practiced to deceive during the day do they wish to spend the night clean? . . . How can they persuade themselves that [cosmetics] make them beautiful? Isn't cleanliness the basis of beauty? . . .

But they say that the colorings are very important. "To whom?" I ask. For women with pretty faces are beautiful even if they are dark-skinned, and I do not know if they would be any prettier if they were white-skinned; those who are ugly remain ugly even if they make themselves as white as snow. Because before putting on the varnish, if they were ugly, at least they were clean, but after putting it on they become ugly and dirty, which is the most despicable kind of ugliness.

Good color is worth a great deal if it is really good color, but this is not good color, nor is it even close, but simply a deception that all can spot. . . . Who is so stupid to want to be fooled, or so dumb that they do not recognize this ruse? . . . It is also very important to consider . . . the damage to the conscience and the offense to God. . . . [Women] persuade themselves either that it is not a sin or that it is a very minor one, but the opposite is true. . . . For they do a grave insult to their own bodies, which are not theirs, but rather God's, consecrated to Him upon baptism, and so must be treated as a holy temple with honor and respect. . . .

So once again we must ask, "Why does she put on makeup?" Because, to tell the truth, the answer is, out of excessive self-love, insatiable appetite and vanity, ugly envy, dishonesty rooted in the heart, adultery, prostitution, a crime that never ceases. What do you women who use makeup think it means to do so? It is to wear the ugliness of your desire on your faces.

Yet all of you who wear makeup do not have evil desires; it is only courteous to believe so. But if you do not awaken your own desires with makeup, you nonetheless awaken others' desires, so with these dirty pretensions, you either publicize your own dirty desires or you corrupt those of the men who look at you. And it is all an offense to God.

"She opens her mouth with wisdom, and the law of kindness is on her tongue" (31: 26).

Two things make up this good of which we are speaking, discreet reason and sweetness of speech. The first is called wisdom and the second kindness, or better yet, gentleness. . . . For a stupid and talkative woman . . . is something intolerable. And one cannot bear to see those who are forward and of hard and bitter speech. . . . What really constitutes stupidity is not to know oneself and to consider oneself wise. . . . The best advice we can give such women is to beg them to be quiet, and being poor in wisdom, they should try to speak rarely. As Solomon said, "If a fool is silent, he will often be considered wise." . . . It would be best if all women sought to be quiet, both those who have good reason to conceal their small amount of knowledge and those who could without shame reveal what they know; for in every woman, silence and speaking rarely are not only a pleasing condition but also a necessary virtue. . . .

For just as nature . . . made women to be closed in inside the home, it also obliges them to keep their mouths closed; and just as nature barred them from trade and commerce outside the home, so it also freed them from what goes with trade and commerce, which is a great deal of discussion and words. Because speech is born from understanding, and words are but images or signals of what the soul harbors within it; so it is that nature did not make the good and decent woman for the study of the sciences or for working out difficult matters, but rather for a single simple domestic task; and so it is that nature limited her understanding, and consequently gave her a limited amount of words and reason. . . .

The beauty of life lies in nothing other than everyone conforming to what their nature and their place demands of them. The woman's place, in contrast to her husband's, is a humble place, and moderation and shame are like natural gifts for a woman, and there is nothing less appropriate or more incompatible with humility and modesty than being talkative and loquacious. . . . For knowing how to be quiet is truly her own form of wisdom. . . .

So much for the first matter. But the second problem, harshness and lack of grace, arises more from a wicked will than from a wayward nature, and so is a more curable disease. This is something that good women should duly note, for I do not know if there is anything more monstrous . . . than a harsh and aggressive woman. Harshness comes from nature among lions and tigers, and even among men, and given the needs of the endeavors in which these creatures must ordinarily engage, they have good reason to be somewhat harsh. Frowning and scowling and acting disdainfully is proper at times; but if a woman acts like a lion, what is there left that is feminine about her?

If you look at her whole composition you will see that she was born for kindness. And just as with wildcats, the claws, the fangs, the fierce mouth, and the bloodthirsty eyes invite them to cruelty, so with the woman the peaceful appearance of her entire disposition obliges her spirit not to be any less restrained than her body is soft. And do not think that God created women and gave them to men only for them to take care of the house, but also to console men and make them happy; and so that in her, the tired and annoyed husband shall find relief, and the children love, and the family kindness, and all, generally, an agreeable reception. . . .

"She moves throughout all the corners of her house, and does not eat the bread of idleness" (31: 27).

This means that in awaking, the woman has to provide all the things for her house and to put them in order, and does not have to do what many these days do, which is to eat breakfast as soon as they put their feet on the floor— or even before getting out of bed—as if they had spent the entire night digging a ditch. Others sit down to their mirror for the job of painting their faces and are riveted there for three or four hours, until it is afternoon and the husband comes to eat and there is nothing ready for him.

Solomon refers to this diligence in this verse not because he had not said it already, but rather to implant it further in the memory by repeating it, and he thus shows how well he understood women and how careless they can be and how inclined they are toward relaxation. And he also says it because, by telling the woman to move throughout her house, he wishes her to be familiar with the space where she should tread . . . and with the location of her career, which is her own house and not the streets and plazas, nor the orchards and the houses of others. . . . And so she never needs to go out of the house, for her feet are for walking throughout the corners of her house, and not for walking through the fields and streets. . . . For if it is her natural place to take care of the house, how can it be permitted that she be out in the streets visiting and wandering? . . .

God did not make women with the cleverness that business requires, nor with the strength that war and farming demand, so they should reconcile themselves to what they are and content themselves with what their fate is, staying in their houses, for God made them only for that. The Chinese bind their daughters' feet so that when they grow up they cannot go out, though their feet are sufficient for walking inside the house. Just as men are made for public life, so women are made for indoor life, and . . . it is for women to stay inside and remain covered. Even in the church, where the necessities of religion and the service of God take them, Saint Paul wanted them to remain covered so that men would scarcely be able to see them. Would you accept that out of their caprices they move through the plazas and streets, making a spectacle of themselves? . . .

"Give her of the fruit of her hands, and let her works be praised in the public places" (31: 31).

No good strikes human eyes more strongly, nor causes greater satisfaction in men's hearts, than a perfect woman, nor is there anything that opens men's mouths with greater happiness or kinder words. . . . Some praise her for staying home, while others laud her discretion, and others extol her modesty, her purity, her kindness, her honest and sweet softness. They speak of her clean face, of her spotless clothing, of her work, and her watchful eye over the family. . . . They praise her raising of the children, the proper treatment of her maids. . . . They say that she is holy toward God and pleasant toward her husband. . . .

Her neighbors say this to others, and parents make a model of her in teaching their children and their grandchildren, so her fame keeps growing everywhere and memories of her remain clear from generation to generation. And the years do no damage to memories of her, which do not age with time, but rather flourish more and more with each passing day, because they have their roots in fertile ground, and they cannot decay any more than the structures built in the heavens can crumble. Nor is it possible in any way that this praise can die out for one who, while she lived, was a perpetual source of praise for the goodness and grandeur of God, to whom alone exaltation and glory are owed. Amen.

29. Pedro de Ribadeneyra, Exhortation for the Soldiers (1588)

In the sixteenth century, the vast Spanish empire was being challenged on a number of fronts. The advent of the Protestant Reformation had joined religion with economic and geopolitical considerations, confronting Spain with a major rebellion by the Dutch (then under Spanish rule) as well as threats from England, a rising maritime power. As part of Spain's strategy to subdue the Dutch rebels, Philip II decided to mount a major naval assault on England, sending the mighty "Invincible Armada" north in 1588. Amid the preparations for the attack, clergymen such as the Jesuit Pedro de Ribadeneyra (1527–1611) gave sermons and speeches designed to inspire the Spaniards to victory.

SOURCE: *Obras escogidas del padre Pedro de Rivadeneira* (Madrid: M. Ribadeneyra, 1868); the text also appears in Pedro de Ribadeneyra, *Historias de la contrarreforma* (Madrid: Biblioteca de Autores Cristianos, 1945), 1333–49.

Invincible captains and mighty soldiers, if you did not know the zeal, piety, spirit, and valor with which Your Mercies have desired that this journey to England, blessed by God, should end happily, I would need many words and have to bring to bear many arguments to persuade you how important it is. But because these mighty hearts and brave spirits do not need words . . . I wish to be brief, describing to you some of the arguments that come to mind to confirm the happiness and the joy of this occasion, in order to thank our Lord God, who offers Himself for your glory and for the honor and growth of Spain.

This journey, gentlemen, has in its favor all of the reasons of a just and holy war that there can possibly be in the world. And though it may at first seem an offensive rather than a defensive war, in that we are attacking another kingdom instead of defending our own, if we look more closely we will see that it is indeed a defensive war in that we are defending our sacred religion and our most holy Roman Catholic faith; we are also defending the extremely important reputation of our king and lord, and that of our nation; we are also defending all of the property and wealth of all the kingdoms of Spain, and along with that, our peace, calm, and quiet.

No one could possibly know without having seen or read of them the injuries that are done to God and his saints each day in England, for they are so many that they cannot be counted, and so bizarre that they cannot be believed. I am not speaking of the evil acts that were committed in that kingdom in the time of Henry VIII, father of this Elizabeth who now reigns in England . . . or of the thousand monasteries of great servants of God laid waste, and ten thousand churches profaned and destroyed, the temples robbed, the sanctuaries sacked; the ancient memorials of the saints toppled to the ground, their bodies burned and their sacred ashes scattered to the wind; the nuns violently thrown out of their convents; the sisters devoted to God raped and virgins deflowered; countless servants of Christ torn limb from limb with atrocious and extreme tortures, with such fierce cruelty and impiety that in no kingdom of heathens, Moors, and barbarians has the Catholic Church suffered greater persecution. I do not wish to go back over the things of the past, nor recall calamities that happened to the Catholics of the kingdom after Henry VIII ceased to obey the Church, because once I started I could never finish.

I only wish to describe the current miserable state of affairs now existing under this Elizabeth, daughter of Anne Boleyn, whom Henry married after tiring of the holy Queen Catherine [of Aragon], legitimate daughter of the Catholic monarchs, with whom he had lived peacefully for twenty years and had children. This Anne was the sister of one mistress of the king and the daughter of another, so that, as some have rightly said, she was the daughter of this very same king, who married his own daughter so that there would be born (oh abominable, unjust, and unheard of thing!) such a horrible and frightening monster, who is the daughter and sister of her mother and the granddaughter of her father, and who imitates her father-grandfather in her cruelty and her disobedience of the pope and imitates her mother-sister in her heresy and dishonesty, for which, by the order of the same King Henry, her head was publicly cut off.

So this Elizabeth, daughter of such parents, has made herself head of the Church of England, and being a woman, and thus naturally subject to the male, as Saint Paul says, and not being able, following God's commands, to speak in church, she wishes to be recognized as the spiritual head of the clergy and of the monks, bishops, and prelates of the Church, whom she fires, appoints, interviews, disciplines, and punishes. . . . And because they have not wished to obey her, she has persecuted, mistreated, deposed, jailed, imprisoned, and finally murdered all the Catholic bishops in England.

She is the one who has ordered the Catholic preachers to be silent and has ordered the heretics to speak. She is the one who has gathered, sheltered, supported, and favored all of the most pestilential ministers of Satan and the diabolical teachers of all the errors and the madness that have been invented against our sacred religion in our own time, summoning them to her kingdom, and they have come to her from France, Scotland, Germany, and the other provinces infected with heresy. And they have come to England as if coming to the main university of their doctrine, or to a cave full of snakes, or to a haven for thieves and pirates. . . . She is the one who has removed the images of the saints, persecuted their relics, and perverted the use of the Holy Sacraments, forbidding that mass be said in her kingdom and ordering that the Roman pontiff, the Vicar of Christ, and the supreme head of the Church of the faithful on earth, be neither recognized nor obeyed. . . .

She is the one who each day promulgates new and extremely rigorous laws against the Catholic faith, executes them with extreme force, and continually spills the innocent blood of those who profess it, even if they be noble knights, powerful lords, venerable priests, or holy monks, . . . who die through wretched tortures, being hanged half-alive with their entrails and hearts being ripped out, chopping them into pieces and displaying their body parts on the towers, bridges, and roads of the cities. She is the one who has so greatly afflicted and oppressed all of the Catholics of her kingdom, who are the largest and best part of it, with unjust laws, with new and severe orders, and with the most atrocious punishments, carried out by the most inhuman men, with slander and false accusations, sentenced by wicked and soulless judges. People cannot even speak a word, nor move a muscle, nor even breathe as Catholic Christians without losing their goods, without being exiled or confronted, or held in some horrible dark dungeon. . . .

She is the one who, inspired by the heretics whom we have said she has in her kingdom (having embraced the infernal desire to propagate, promote, and spread throughout the world the fire of her false religion), has sought with all her skill and shrewdness to make this destructive and consuming fire spread throughout the entire world, beginning with the nearest kingdoms and states. She is the one who has destroyed the kingdom of Scotland and subjected its king to the miseries we see. She is the one who by deception arrested . . . Queen Mary, his mother, who was both queen of Scotland and France and heir to the kingdom of England, and after twenty years of hard and bitter imprisonment, she ordered her to be killed because she was a Catholic, having her head cut off by the executioner of London. . . .

She is the one who is supporting the long, costly, and bloody war of the states of Flanders [modern-day Belgium, then part of Spain's empire] against our lord the king. . . . She is the one who has taken over Holland, occupying its cities, forts, and ports, infested our seas, robbed the estates of their merchandise, and with her money, soldiers, arms, supplies, advice, and her tricks, has stirred those states up against old friends and new allies . . . and against our king, our holy religion, and God.

She is the one who, with new spirit and zeal, testing our patience, has dared to attack the states of the West Indies, burning our islands, robbing our people, seizing and sinking our ships, entering our cities by force and sacking them, putting our justice and our royal governors in a difficult position and all the kingdoms of Spain in a state of alarm and confusion.

And . . . she has had the audacity . . . to assault and rob our ports in Spain, first in Galicia and then in Cádiz, attacking, robbing, burning, and sinking part of our Armada when it was in port. And she would have burned, sacked, and destroyed that city itself if God, in His mercy, had not stopped them, and if the duke of Medina had not personally come to the rescue. This Elizabeth has done before our very eyes, in view of the whole world. . . .

This very same Elizabeth is the one who, . . . hoping to uproot our holy and Catholic religion from all of our kingdoms, has made alliances with heretical princes, has sent her ambassadors to Moscow and her fleets even to Constantinople to solicit the help of the Turk and to summon him against us, and to bring him to our lands to terrorize us and afflict us in our own houses, taking away from us, if possible, our properties and our lives, and what is most important, the law of God and the Catholic faith, the eternal salvation of our souls.

The saints in the heavens will accompany us, and particularly the patron saints of Spain and the holy protectors of this very England, who are persecuted by the English heretics, and who wish for and ask God for their vengeance, and they will come out and greet us and help us. . . . The cries of an infinite number of imprisoned Catholics are waiting for us, along with the tears of many widows, who lost their husbands because they kept their faith; also the sobs of countless maidens who will either have to give their lives or abandon their properties and their souls; also the children and infants, who, if not rescued, will be lost by having been raised with the milk of heresy. Finally, innumerable farmers, city dwellers, nobles, knights, lords, priests, and Catholics from all walks of life, who are afflicted, oppressed, and tyrannized by the heretics, are waiting for us for their liberty.

Along with us go faith, justice, truth, and the blessing of the pope, who holds God's place on earth, as well as the desires of the good and the prayers and pleas of the whole Catholic Church. God is more powerful than the devil, truth more powerful than lies, the Catholic faith more powerful than heresy, the saints and angels in the heavens more powerful than all the power of hell, the invincible spirit and robust Spanish arms more powerful than the decadent spirits and frozen and weak bodies of the heretics. The pure and good conscience, the clean heart, burning with love and zeal for the glory of God, will not be absent, but will go with us, as will the fine intention to fight principally for the Catholic faith and for our law and our king and our kingdom. Let us live a Christian life without scandals and public offenses to God; may there be piety in us toward Him, union and brotherhood among the soldiers, obedience to the commanders, Spanish spirit, force, and courage, and with this we have nothing to fear, for victory is ours.

30. Pedro de Ribadeneyra,
On the Causes of the Armada's Defeat (1588)

In May 1588, an "Invincible Armada" of 130 Spanish ships set out for England, but the recent death of Spain's best commander left the fleet under the less able command of the duke of Medina-Sidonia. Although many in Spain were highly confident of victory, the English fleet had many experienced commanders and sailors, and its ships were more mobile; those advantages, combined with some adverse winds at a crucial moment, resulted in a Spanish defeat. Only 76 of the 130 ships returned to Spain, while the English lost no ships at all. The defeat in an endeavor that had been so costly and in which so many hopes had been invested provoked a great deal of soul-searching in Spain, particularly given predictions of a divinely guided victory.

SOURCE: *Obras escogidas del padre Pedro de Rivadeneira* (Madrid: M. Ribadeneyra, 1868); the text also appears in Pedro de Ribadeneyra, *Historias de la contrarreforma* (Madrid: Biblioteca de Autores Cristianos, 1945), 1351–55.

I beg Your Lordship to pardon me if it should seem a new or improper thing for me to write what I will say here, for it is only my love and zeal to serve the Crown that leads me to write this. . . .

The judgments of our Lord God are highly secret, so we cannot know for sure what His Divine Majesty intended in such an extraordinary event as that which happened to Your Majesty's powerful Armada. Yet despite this being a cause that was so much His, and that was undertaken with such holy intentions, and that was so highly praised throughout these kingdoms and so desired and solicited by the whole Catholic Church, the pious prayers and tears of so many and such illustrious servants of His were not answered, making us fear that there are great reasons why our Lord God has sent us this task. . . . For given that He does not do things by chance, nor does a single leaf fall from a tree without His will, . . . it is a most reasonable thing to wonder . . . why God did not grant us success.

Personally, I consider it certain that He has not wished to deny it to us, but rather just to delay it for a while, and in the meantime render us many other and greater mercies that we need more. . . . Our Lord has wanted to test our faith, awaken our hope, enliven our prayers even more, reform our ways, purify our intentions and cleanse them of the dust of our own temporal interest and contentment. . . .

Yet setting aside these things that we might gain from the events that happened to this Armada, I wish to point out the things that, after some prayer and much consideration, have occurred to me, and which may be causes of this calamity and universal punishment, so that, if Your Lordship should believe it proper, Your Majesty may judge the appropriate path to take. . . . It seems to me that this is a matter whose necessity goes beyond the specific need to pursue the war and seek out the enemy, if we do not want the enemy to come to us and make war on us in our own homes.

The first is that Your Majesty should grant relief to many persons in this kingdom, and particularly in Andalusia, who have been wronged and . . . despoiled of their means of sustenance and support for their children, without being compensated or even heard, but rather imprisoned and afflicted for having wished to defend their possessions. I have heard that this has happened with such excess and violence, that serious and God-fearing people said before the Armada left that it was impossible for it to be victorious, for it went loaded down with the sweat and the curses of so many miserable people. . . . And this is especially the case because much of what has been taken, though it was taken in the name of Your Majesty and the Armada, was not taken for your royal service, but rather to enrich those who took it.

The second point is that Your Majesty, with your very great prudence, should examine . . . what reasons there might be why such a sizable economy as Your Majesty's shines so dimly and is sinking. . . . If poor management of the economy or the corruption of those in charge [is the cause], it is necessary to take care of this problem, punishing the thieves severely as destroyers of the republic, and showing mercy toward those who administer as they should. Because if this is not done, evil men will be encouraged and good men discouraged. So it is necessary to deal very carefully with this matter, for the economy is the foundation of the army, and even in peacetime it is essential to the kingdom to make people obey and to know that the king is powerful. And this matter is all the more deserving of attention in that Your Majesty's economy is not only yours, but that of all of your kingdoms, or more precisely, that of all Christendom, being for its benefit, making it necessary to look carefully at this problem.

The third point is that Your Majesty should look closely at whether, in affairs having to do with England, . . . more concern has been given to the security of the state than to the glory of God and the growth of the Catholic faith, and whether, in order not to offend the queen of England, Your Majesty has failed to protect those who have been persecuted and oppressed by her for being Catholic and loyal to God. For just as our Lord God is so jealous of His honor and wants all Christians, and especially kings, to strive to further it, . . . any carelessness in this matter offends Him very much. . . .

The fourth point is that more care must be given to removing public sins and scandals, especially when it comes to great persons who have the obligation to set a good example. For with the evil they spread, they infect or corrupt the republic. Since Your Majesty is the head and lord of it, and can so easily resolve and correct the excesses with a single demonstration of your will, it seems that the Lord may call you to account for what is not done. . . .

The last point, but not the least in importance, is that Your Majesty should consider that the greatest wealth of the kingdom is not an abundance of gold and silver, nor of goods, nor of other things concerning the necessity, or the adornment and luxury of human life, but rather the proliferation and abundance of courageous and magnanimous men who can be pillars of the republic in war and in peace. And although Your Majesty is so powerful and is the greatest monarch that there has been among Christians, you are sorely lacking in such men, as the outcome of this expedition has demonstrated. Such men are not born fully made, but must be made through the experience of time, and they will only be made by putting them to the test and then honoring and rewarding those who serve you well. For although the Spaniards are arrogant and are enemies of learning, ordinarily wishing to begin where others end up, they are nonetheless very loyal and obedient to their king. . . . And if Your Majesty should favor them, rewarding those who serve you well, I believe that there will be men to fill your kingdom and carry out all the tasks of peace and war. . . . And this is all the more important in that our lord the king is already old and tired, needing persons who can allow him to rest, looking after his life and health, which is so important to the whole Catholic Church, especially since our lord the prince is still so young and does not yet have the force needed to govern so many kingdoms.

31. Martín González de Cellorigo, The Restoration of the Republic (1600)

Spain, despite retaining a vast empire in the late sixteenth century, had been experiencing severe difficulties, including military defeats in Europe and a series of financial crises that led the Crown to declare bankruptcy three times in the late 1500s. Consequently, more and more Spanish writers began offering their diagnoses and prescriptions; these analysts, known as *arbitristas*, continued to appear throughout the seventeenth century, as such writings became almost a national pastime for the educated classes.

This text by a government official sounded many themes others would later echo, including the problem of population decline, the passion for gold and silver, disregard for farming, industry, and manual labor, and the neglect of the domestic economy in favor of the colonies. The author also makes a number of moral critiques, as did other reformers of that era.

SOURCE: Martín González de Cellorigo, *Memorial de la política necesaria y util restauración a la república de España y estados de ella, y del desempeño universal de estos Reynos* (Valladolid: Iuan de Bostillo, 1600). The work has been reprinted; see José L. Pérez de Ayala, ed., *Memorial de la política necesaria y util restauración a la república de España* (Madrid: Instituto de Cooperación Iberoamericana, 1991).

Spain has always been considered a fertile and abundant land, and it is, for all who seek to enjoy its fertility while recognizing that human effort must do its part. If it seems infertile it is because it has not been given a tribute appropriate to God's gift to men, for were it cultivated as the law of nature dictates and teaches us, it would suffice to support an infinite number of people. . . . Its reputation is such that all who write of it consider it the richest and most fertile land in Europe, even saying that its horses are faster than the wind. . . .

What is most certain is that our republic has declined so greatly from its former state because we have disregarded natural laws, which teach us to work, and because we have put wealth, which is acquired through natural and human industry, into gold and silver, and because we have ceased to follow the true and right path. It is Spain's subjects who are seriously guilty of this, all the more in these days in which they are fortunate to have a prince and a lord who . . . is so solicitous of his subjects' welfare. . . .

However well governed a republic may be, if the subjects do not follow their king, they will not avoid being afflicted with poverty and abandoned by their friends, surrounded by enemies, and full of miseries; indeed a kingdom can be fertile in lands, abundant in wealth, replete with arms, powerful in vassals, triumphant in battles, and justly governed and yet still decline from its grandeur much more than any other republic. Prosperity, which is one of the strongest enemies virtue has, tends to prevent the vassals from taking all the proper actions necessary to keep them in the state in which their king seeks to sustain them if they do not temper their wealth and the happiness of their good fortune with moral policies and good customs, if they do not avoid as much as possible the laziness that has destroyed so many kingdoms, and if they do not embrace work and seek the artificial sustenance of their good industry, which has preserved so many peoples.

There is no lack of astrologers who . . . seek to warn of and predict the decline of republics, particularly ours. . . . They say that the birth, growth, stability, decline, and fall of republics depend on the movement of the stars and the operation of the signs and planets. . . . Others say that a republic, having slowly grown in power until it reaches the peak of its perfection and grandeur, cannot last, given the variability and the uncertainty of human affairs, and that even the highest republics are brought down. . . . Others attribute [the decline of republics] to human nature, believing it certain that they slowly grow old, meeting their end through their internal illnesses. . . .

One cannot fail to respond to those who see such force in natural causes, who see such dependence on the stars, inferring from them the future order of things and what God has in store for you. . . . It would be wrong not to admit the marvelous effects of the celestial bodies on all the things of nature on land and in the air, through which the immense power of God manifests itself. . . . Having admitted this, one cannot fail to deny the falsehood that proponents of this science pronounce, so contrarily to our Catholic truth. [A long denunciation of astrology and numerology follows.]

The decline in population, which has been perceived for many years in this realm, did not arise so much from wars as from the shortcomings in all things caused by the laziness of our people. . . . With people having put their wealth into gold and silver and into making loans that pay interest, it is as if a general epidemic had thrown this kingdom into misery by persuading all, or most, to live off this money. . . . This is what has so obviously destroyed this republic . . . because in relying on these payments they have abandoned the virtuous occupations of farming and raising animals and all those things that naturally sustain men. . . . So one can indeed say that the wealth that was supposed to have enriched has instead impoverished, because it has been so poorly used that it has led the merchant not to trade and the farmer not to farm. . . .

Spain has turned its eyes so completely toward the Indies, from which gold and silver is coming, that the kingdom's communications with its neighbors have stopped, and if all the gold and silver that its natives have found and are finding in the New World were to enter here, it would not make Spain as rich and powerful as it would have been without it. . . . A lot of money in a kingdom perverts relations among men. . . .

There is nothing worse than the excessive wealth of some and the extreme poverty of others, which has done so much to disorient our republic, just as have the many *mayorazgos* [entailed estates] that take place each day, and as has the use of loans, which enrich some and ruin others. And though it would not be good to say that everyone must be equal, it would not be unreasonable to say that the two extreme situations are equally bad. . . . Spaniards . . . have begun to imitate others and have started competing among themselves for honor, authority, and the display of wealth, always trying to keep up with all others, perverting the natural order of things . . . [in which] some were born to serve and obey while others were born to command and govern, as Aristotle . . . and others who have followed him, have maintained. . . .

What seems the most striking reason for the decline of our republic and the deepening of its problems is the shrinking of the population, which formerly made the country rich and powerful. . . . For this kingdom to be restored now with the number of citizens it needs, there is no alternative to bringing people from abroad or else giving orders that those here now not be allowed to leave. And of these two options, it is better to retain the natives than to seek foreigners. This can be accomplished by putting things right in the state, so that the kingdom no longer needs to send its people abroad. . . .

As for the origins of this depopulation, we can see that a major reason has been the small amount of concern paid to remedying many fallen men and women . . . so that they could pursue this goal and obtain the virtuous fruits of marriage, thus fertilizing our republic with good people, born of legitimate and honorable parents. And as for the other reasons why Spain is considered a sterile country . . . , it is not a defect of the land but rather a failure of the people. Because the land is quite capable of producing as many people as needed for civil life and for sustaining more than it does. Here it is not insignificant that Spain's women have such a poor reputation among men, and that in avoiding matrimony they abandon procreation and turn to extreme vices. And this derives from not punishing public sins when it is necessary to restrain the bad ways of the many who, finding an easy path to the indecency of their appetites, do not wish to submit to the yoke of matrimony. . . .

The problem also derives from women being very expensive under the present ways. . . . Many, sinking themselves into indecent vices, abandon matrimony, and even very virtuous young ladies, because they lack dowries, end up losing their virtue because of the excesses of others, who pursue their appetites by spending without limit, and in other shameful things, causing men to abhor matrimony because they do not see in their homes what they see in others'.

Many honorable young ladies find no solution because there is no one in the republic to deal with this; so it is one of the most important things, if we wish to avoid sins, to increase the number of clergymen. And it has become so common to dismiss good things and respect evil ones that people look down on those who seek to solve this problem, which is one of the most virtuous things anyone can do. The failure to punish the wrongdoing and the excesses of women who break the laws of marriage, punishing them with all the severity that such a grave sin merits, comes at a cost to procreation; too much liberty for women leads men to abhor marriage—some enjoying illicit affairs, which they have with such women, and others wishing to avoid altogether a situation that causes such pain. . . .

There is no republic, no matter how barbarous, that does not punish this sin severely. The Romans, by the Julian Law, inflicted grave penalties upon them. The Hebrews . . . in less rigorous times, stoned them. . . . The Egyptians cut off their noses, which is the most effective punishment for women, considering the ugliness resulting from such a penalty. . . . For although cruelty is reprehensible, it keeps the subjects observing the law, and being too liberal makes them disregard the law. . . .

Many virtuous women who could bear fruit for our republic are left alone because men are so concerned about dowries, wanting women to support them. . . It is necessary . . . to lead women to more measured and moderate ways. . . . And we must be firmer, regulating their clothing and their excessive dress by restoring the Oppian Law defended by Cato in Rome, which prohibited women from wearing richly colored clothing or wearing more than an ounce of gold. . . . And just as, according to Euripides, there is nothing greater or more necessary for a republic's preservation than a wife's obedience to her husband, in the same way a husband worthy of the name has no right to mistreat his wife. . . . God's written law . . . calls the husband lord and master, showing that it is his place to command. . . .

It is fate that gold and silver be taken out of Spain, and that this kingdom only holds temporarily the wealth that it soon returns to other kingdoms, who are like lords over it. . . . Because as money is not true wealth, and that which is more truly valuable attracts money to it, that which is less valuable gets taken to that which is more valuable. . . . It is a very false opinion held by those who claim that the poverty of this kingdom has arisen because of money leaving it through the wars in Flanders and other states belonging to the Crown of Castile. . . . Hence our own people should be able to learn from what they see practiced to their advantage and their disadvantage: to their advantage in trade with the Indies, in which the natural and manufactured products that are lacking over there attract to Spain the gold and silver found over there; and to their disadvantage through the things that could be enjoyed in this kingdom by their manufacture, but which are not made here, so that the gold, silver, and minted coins go to foreigners. . . .

It is also a mistake not to understand that the relative quantity of money does not raise or lower the wealth of a kingdom, because given the fact that money is nothing more than an instrument for purchases and sales, a small amount of money has the same effect as a large amount. . . . With the large amount of money that has been minted, leases, rents, and taxes have gone up, reaching levels that could not be paid if there were not in the kingdom such a large quantity [of money]. . . . And the same is true for foreign products, which have become more expensive because of the large supply of money. . . . That which was bought with one *real* now cannot be bought with fifty. The Romans saw this, . . . as their history tells us; when Paulus Emilius brought back gold and silver from the kingdom of Macedonia, . . . prices of things went up . . . by a third. And when Julius Caesar had the spoils of Egypt brought back to Rome, interest rates and exchange rates fell and the prices of things went up sharply. The same happened to our people in Peru, where with the abundance of money and the lack of everything else (if the histories are correct), a piece of clothing cost a thousand *ducados* and a horse six thousand and a cask of wine three hundred. And . . . a pound of grapes was sold for a pound of silver. . . . This is the result of having a lot of money, silver, and gold when the necessities of life are lacking. . . .

It is very important to the king to see to it that his subjects not let themselves keep making the error they are currently making, and that all the vassals and those who have recently inherited land understand that it is a clear mistake to base their wealth on what they have based it on so far and to live off of *censos* [a common kind of loan often made to farmers] . . . because their use has up until now been the plague and the ruin of Spain. The merchant, for the sweetness of the fixed gain of *censos*, sets aside his commerce, the official disdains his office, the farmer abandons his farming, the shepherd his flock, the noble sells his lands, exchanging the hundred they were worth for the five hundred he hopes to make in interest, without considering that when they turn to this deal the firm revenue of their lands dries up and money goes up in smoke. For each man who works the land has to support not only himself, but also his landlord and his lender and the collector of the tithe and the agent who collects his interest payments and others who seek his money; and soon one can see that for each person who works there are thirty who do not. Then come the creditors' lawsuits, the enormous costs of the credit transactions, and, with so many relying on these payments, their fortune collapses when loans are not repaid. With the *censos*, very illustrious families have been ruined, and other, lower people have exchanged their careers, jobs, and farming for idleness, and the kingdom has become a lazy and vice-ridden republic. . . .

The practice of crafts is very necessary in all republics, because just as the fruits of the earth sustain us, so do all the other things produced by crafts and acquired skills. Their use . . . [brings] all that is necessary to civil life . . . without having to spend money and rely on the industry of other countries. One should seek to make one's own crafts so eminent that foreign kingdoms need them. . . . As a result, the subjects will see an increase in their fortunes, their honor, and the blessings that are obtained with labor and virtuous occupation, as well as in the procreation of their children, for in good republics the hardest-working people are the most abundant. And the king, having hard-working subjects, will have in abundance all the consequent fruits, and with the growth of the population, kings' revenues will also grow, and because of that, so will their grandeur and authority. . . .

It would be going against the will of God . . . to want to enjoy the fruits of the earth without working, for they must be earned through the sweat of our brow. And so we must solve the abuses of the land through all possible means, including giving orders to the wayward and idle people of the republic. Those whom a republic gives assistance should be compelled with a form of servitude that forces them to work. . . . And so we should find methods of allowing for the expulsion from Spain of the spurious, false, and deceptive poor who, as usurpers of charity and transgressors of good customs, provoke the wrath of God against the whole people, . . . and in stealing charity . . . they harm those who deserve and need it. . . . It would be good to take steps affecting all the vagabonds and idlers, even the lame and crippled. . . . Of the many thousands who live this kind of life, only a very few are legitimately poor. We saw this in our city last year, when out of five thousand beggars gathered here only six hundred were found to be real. There are so many of this kind of people in our republic, those who are so keen to show off their poverty and their injuries so as not to have to work, that we have seen in them great fictions of lameness and poverty designed to acquire more alms. . . .

As a solution, we could create workhouses in the big cities and towns . . . *Solutions>*
where those who lead this life can work off whatever term their demerits
call for, as if in a prison. . . . It would also be good if each city had houses
designated to teach poor children various trades. . . .

What has done the most to distract our people from the legitimate
occupations that are so important to this republic has been the placing of so
much honor and authority on the avoidance of work, and the disdain, contrary to all good sense, for those who pursue agriculture, commerce, and all
kinds of manufacturing. . . . And if it is true, as it is, that our Spaniards are
all so concerned about honor, and that they care more about their reputation
than about the wealth they can acquire, what can one expect of such people
other than that they will disregard their material affairs? . . . It is obvious that
the reason why our kingdom is in trouble, why royal revenues have fallen,
why the vassals have been ruined and the republic finished off, is the abusive
and depraved tradition that has been introduced in this kingdom that holds
that whoever does not live off of rents is not noble, and that all other forms
of income, whether from agriculture or commerce or any other equally good
and just trade, prevent one from being noble. . . .

[Farming] is so honorable and noble that there is no office or occupation that equals it, and this has been true since the beginning of time. . . .
Among the kings of Persia, Cyrus the Younger prized farming so much that
he planted many trees with his own hands, and among the many words
of praise uttered about [Roman] Emperor Antoninus Pius, the greatest was
that he had been a farmer. . . . For a man to work on inherited lands of his
own, even with his own hands, not only does not prevent him from being
noble or holding any dignity or honorable office, but indeed it is a trait of
kings, great princes, and noble lords. . . .

A republic . . . is like a musical instrument, which requires proportions among
all its parts in order to produce the harmonious sweetness of music. . . . If
republics are arranged this way, they are firm and stable, but if the king and
the kingdom are in discord, and the vassals [in discord] among themselves,
there cannot be the harmonious concert that the government of states
requires. . . . Hence we say that there is nothing more necessary for the
endurance of states than for the king and the kingdom to be in such proper
correspondence that upon the just petition of the people, the king offers a
fitting response, and when the king asks for necessary support, . . . the
prince's orders are quickly obeyed. . . .

As Plato said, what disrupts republics is their poverty and wealth,
because of the harm that either extreme can do. If one looks at the harm that

the poverty in a kingdom can do, one will see that there is no greater plague, nor any that depopulates it more [than extreme inequality]; this is even more true if that kingdom was once rich and powerful and then declined. . . .

Our republic has come to the extremes of rich and poor, without there being any middle to moderate them; so we are either rich people who do nothing or poor people who ask for things; we lack those in the middle who, being neither rich nor poor, remain in the just occupation that natural law obliges them to hold. And it is the cause of this evil that our people do not take up in proper proportion the things necessary to the kingdom, with the ability and the desire to do so going together; as a result . . . those who want to cannot, and those who can, do not want to; and so the lands remain unworked, the crafts not pursued . . . and many projects necessary for the public good remain undone. . . .

In former days, [the high nobles], together with rich and noble hidalgos, were not so numerous. . . , and they were in proper balance with the number of the others, the poor and those in the middle. . . . Since then, [those in the middle] have been moving either to the side of the rich or to that of the poor, so that instead of being the most numerous, that group has come to be the smallest and the most abandoned. To the side of the rich have come some of the middle sort through censos, dowries, and *mayorazgos*. . . . To the side of the poor have come many others from the middle, who wished to jump into the group of the rich but fell into the void and ended up poor. . . . Much harm is done as a result, because . . . they are the ones who support the rich and the poor, the monks and the clergy . . . and the king, and who pay the taxes.

32. Magdalena de San Jerónimo,
Vagabond Women (1608)

Given the ease with which a woman might be considered to have transgressed the strict norms designed for her in early modern Spain, it is not surprising that there were many women who were either disowned by their families or who left them for some reason. Such women might find refuge in a convent, but those who would not or could not do so often found themselves with few other options. Some, of course, turned to prostitution or petty crime.

Among those who devoted themselves to disciplining such women was Magdalena de San Jerónimo. Historians know little about her, but records indicate that by 1588 she was the administrator of a house for "penitent" women in Valladolid, and in 1605 she founded a convent in Madrid. In 1608 she published a book describing the Galera, a women's institution that she administered in Madrid. The following text is from that book.

SOURCE: Magdalena de San Jerónimo, *Razón y forma de la galera y casa Real, que el Rey, Nuestro Señor, manda hacer en nuestros reinos, para castigo de las mujeres vagantes, y ladronas, alcahuetas, hechiceras, y otras semejantes* (Valladolid: Francisco Fernández de Córdova, 1608); the text also appears in A. María Aguado et al., eds., *Textos para la historia de las mujeres en España* (Madrid: Cátedra, 1994), 298–300.

On the Importance and Necessity of This House for Wayward Women

There are many young vagabond and idle women, including some girls sixteen and younger, who are supported by nothing other than a bad life. And thus, when night falls, they go out in search of prey like wild beasts from their caves; they set out from these places, through the streets and the gates of houses, inviting those wretched men who go about carelessly, and they cast the nets of Satan, and they fall and cause men to fall in extremely grave sins. They go to the houses of the gentlemen where there are pages and other young servants, they even go to the lords and weak men, offering the opportunity, and they fall miserably; and then, having spent the whole night out, or most of it, they retire with their lewd earnings to their inns and houses, and there they spend the day sleeping, eating, and lazing until night returns. . . .

There are many others who, being sound and good and with the strength to work or serve, go about begging for alms, going from house to house where alms are usually given; and normally many of them have men, and they bring the men with them to gather alms; and although some have never had children, they bring with them two or three young creatures to elicit pity, and in this way they shamefully take alms away from the real poor and those who out of real necessity cannot work. And as these lazy women find sustenance in this way, they do not wish to work or serve.

There are others who take a little house for themselves, setting up shop sewing and doing alterations and mending trousers and doing needlework, or other similar lines of work, and under this pretense their house is a house of offenses to God, sometimes sinning themselves and other times getting other women to do the same.

There are many others who serve as go-betweens and procuresses. . . .

There are many women, especially older ones, who as a way of making money have two or three girls who, under the pretense of seeking alms, go to many places where there are offenses against God, and other times the same women take them and sell them . . . and from this line of work these bad women make a living. . . .

No less serious has been . . . the evil and the damage that has been seen for the last twenty years among these maidens [who are] servant girls, because aside from not having anyone to serve—for having led the life of urchins—those who manage to serve do this so badly and are so full of vices (because either they have boyfriends or they are thieves or procuresses) that a great deal of trouble is incurred with them. . . .

To solve . . . such a great problem . . . in whole or in part, an effective remedy is needed; and for this, the main one is to attack the problem at its roots; for this reason, in all the cities where this is possible, there should be houses or schools where all orphan girls are gathered, so that they can be taught virtue, Christianity, and decency, taking them away from the danger of ruin and from the disreputable singing and dancing and many other evil inclinations and customs that have been created, making them practice Christian virtue and doctrine, and learn work, decency, and good habits, so that in due time they may serve in proper and honest houses, where after a few years they may be put right and rescued. . . .

On the Form and Outlines of This House for Wayward Women

A house should be chosen in a very appropriate site, but not one that is too isolated or distant from a town, because of the great disadvantages that could derive from that. This house must be strong and well locked, having no window or opening facing in any direction and cannot have access to any other adjoining house. . . .

In this house there needs to be very little: because there does not need to be anything but a room that serves as a dormitory, with cots made of boards without any ropes. . . . In each one of these beds there should be a mattress of straw with a pillow of straw, and one or two dark blankets, where each one sleeps. There should be another room where they work, each one doing what they know how to do; if they know nothing, then they should be taught.

33. Francisco Bermúdez de Pedraza, The Moriscos of Granada (1638)

In 1491, on the eve of the Christian conquest of Granada, the last Muslim-ruled territory in Iberia, Ferdinand and Isabella had made many concessions to the Moors, allowing them to keep their religion and much of their culture. By 1499, however, the Spaniards had gone back on their word and forced the Muslims, now known as Moriscos, to convert to Christianity or leave Spain. Most reluctantly converted, but Christians harbored grave doubts about the authenticity of their conversion, and strong pressures persisted within Christian society to deal more harshly with the Moriscos. After a long series of conflicts, including more than one major uprising, the Crown finally chose to expel the Moriscos from Spain in 1609. In the following text, written in 1638, a Spanish chronicler presents a list of the kind of complaints—some true, some false—commonly heard from those Christians who long demanded their expulsion.

SOURCE: Francisco Bermúdez de Pedraza, *Historia eclesiástica, principios, y progresos de la ciudad y religión católica de Granada* (Granada, 1638), chap. 82, folio 238.

The monarchs, being such Catholic Christians, valued the spiritual benefit of their vassals more than their own worldly interests. They wished to see the Moriscos adhere to the Catholic religion, so they graced them with many favors and kind treatment and spoke on their behalf with the ministers of justice, but it was all sowing in sand, and even in stone. It was soon realized that these works were all futile. They were apparent Christians and real Moors. They cared more about the rites and ceremonies of their sect than about the law of Christ our Lord, and being treated better by our kings than by their own, and also less burdened by taxes and tributes, they abused this good treatment, longing for the ways of Egypt, for its sheep and goats, for their traditional prayers and festivals. They were not declared Moors, but rather secretive heretics, in whom faith was lacking and baptism was superfluous. They practiced good moral works, were truthful in their business and contracts, showed great charity toward the poor, were not lazy but all hard working, but showed little respect for Sundays and Church holidays and even less respect for the Church's sacraments. They went to mass out of fear of paying penalties, they worked on holidays behind closed doors, with more enthusiasm than on other days, and they observed Fridays more than they did Sundays. They bathed even in December, and did their traditional prayers. They baptized their children to satisfy the requirements, but they then washed the sacramental oils off them with hot water when they got home, and, carrying out their ceremonies, they circumcised them and gave them Moorish names. Their brides went to church to be blessed in borrowed

Christian clothing, and then returning home, they took off those clothes and dressed as Moors, celebrating their weddings with Moorish instruments and songs. They learned the wedding prayers because the priests tested them, but once they were married they no longer remembered them. They confessed during Lent simply to fulfill the letter of the law, and their confessions were very brief. . . .

When a Moor was stricken with illness, a priest would go to hear his confession and to administer communion as well; then he would tell him that if he needed sacred oil for the sacraments, he could go ask for it at the church. The Morisco, feeling more afflicted by this than by the illness, would say: "So there will be three tortures in one day: confession, communion, and the oil?" In the farmhouses and villages of the Alpujarras region and the coast, they welcomed Turks and Moors from the Berber country, who kidnapped children at night, and the Moriscos would steal the Christian children from the houses and then send them off to the Berber lands at night. They taught them their law and they circumcised them and made them Moors, something that was very damaging for the kingdom, but something that was very useful for them and their farming.

The priests told all of this to the archbishop and the king, who deliberated upon it and decided to take away from them their Moorish clothing so that they would begin forgetting it. He gave them six years to break with the habit of dressing in Moorish clothing, and he waited another ten years hoping to see some improvement, until the Honorable Pardo Abad . . . [and others] informed the king that they were still adhering to the rites of Mohammed, and not one of them was Christian.

34. Philip III,
Decree of Expulsion of the Moriscos (1609)

Ever since the defeat of the last Muslim kingdom at Granada in 1492, a country increasingly devoted to the ideal of religious uniformity had faced the problem of a religious minority remaining inside the country's borders. In 1492, the Christians had promised the Moors the right to continue practicing their religion, but soon more zealous Christian leaders had pushed for a policy of forcible conversion, which soon led to a revolt in the heavily Muslim Alpujarras region of southern Spain. When that revolt was defeated, Muslims were forced to choose between conversion and emigration.

Those who stayed, adopting Christianity but retaining many aspects of their Arabic culture, became known as Moriscos. Even more troubling to many Christians than the persistence of Arabic customs and speech was the tendency of these "new Christians" to continue practicing Islam in secret. In part because of the Christians' prejudice and intolerance, and in part because of fears that the Moriscos were conspiring with Spain's enemies, the Turks, pressures for new measures aimed at the Moriscos rose again in the 1560s, and when new decrees demanding the adoption of Christian ways were enacted in 1566, a second revolt broke out in the Alpujarras region. This time the defeated rebels were scattered throughout Spain.

By the early 1600s, however, Christian prejudice and intolerance, combined with economic motives (such as a desire to seize the Moriscos' lands), led to new calls for a total expulsion. In 1609, the Crown, facing the embarrassment of having to admit defeat in its long war with the Dutch rebels, sought to distract people's attention from that setback and to placate popular sentiments by expelling the Moriscos from Spain. Some 275,000 Moriscos, concentrated primarily in Valencia and Aragon, but also found in half a dozen other regions, emigrated. Many of the emigrants soon died of starvation or were killed in conflicts upon their arrival in North Africa. King Philip III (1598–1621) addressed this decree to the entire kingdom.

SOURCE: *Novísima recopilación de las leyes de España* (Madrid, 1805), Book XII, Title II, Law IV, 312–13.

[From] the King . . . to the Grandees, Prelates, Titled Nobles, Barons, Gentlemen, [et al.] . . .

You are all aware of what I have through such long efforts tried to do toward the conversion of the Moriscos of this kingdom . . . and the edicts of grace that have been granted to them and the attempts that have been made to instruct them in our holy faith, and the little that has been accomplished, for we have not seen any of them convert, and they have instead merely increased their stubbornness. . . . A few days ago many learned and holy men addressed me, urging me to take swift measures that good conscience requires to placate our Lord, who is so offended by these people, assuring me that one could without any scruples punish them in their lives and property, for the continuation of their crimes convicts them of heresy, apostasy, and actions of divine and human treason. And though one could justly proceed against them with all the strictness that their faults deserve, nonetheless, wishing to reduce them by soft and gentle measures, I ordered the junta . . . [in] which you, the patriarch, and other prelates and learned persons participate, to meet to see if there was some way to avoid removing them from these kingdoms. But realizing that those of this kingdom [Valencia] and of that of Castile were continuing in their harmful intentions, and given that I have heard on sound and true advice that they were persisting in their apostasy and perdition and were seeking to harm and subvert people of our kingdoms through their envoys and other ways, and wishing to fulfill my obligations to assure the preservation and security particularly of that kingdom of Valencia and of its good and faithful subjects, given that its dangers are more evident, and wishing for the heresy and apostasy to cease, and having had entrusted to our Lord, and trusting in his divine favor concerning matters related to his honor and glory, I have resolved that all of the Moriscos of that kingdom be expelled and sent to the land of the Berbers. And in order to assure the execution and completion of that which His Majesty commands, we have published the following decree:

1. First, that all the Moriscos of this kingdom, men and women, with their children, within three days of the publication of this decree in the places where they live and have their houses, must leave, going to the place to which the authorities . . . order them. . . . They will take with them that movable property that they can carry on their persons in the galleys and ships that have been prepared to take them to the land of the Berbers, where they will disembark, without having been mistreated or personally abused. . . . They will be provided with the necessary provisions for their sustenance during the voyage, and they may also take what they can with them. And he who does not comply and violates any point of what this decree states will incur the death penalty, which will be carried out immediately.

2. If, at the end of the three days after the publication of this decree, any of the said Moriscos are found out of custody and outside of their proper place, along the roads or in other places, . . . then any person can, without incurring any penalty, arrest them and seize their goods, turning them over to the officials in the nearest place, and if they resist, they may kill them.

3. Under the same penalty, no Moriscos, once this decree has been published, . . . may leave their place of residence to go to another, but must remain there until the officials who are to escort them to the point of departure arrive for them.

4. Should any of the said Moriscos hide or bury any of the property they have out of not being able to take it with them, or should they set fire to their houses, fields, gardens, or groves, they will incur the said penalty of death at the hands of the inhabitants of the place where it happens. And we order that this be executed because His Majesty has seen fit to grant the use of this real estate, foundations, and movable property that they cannot take with them from the lords whose vassals they were. . . .

6. No old Christian or soldier, whether a native of this kingdom or not, may dare to mistreat, either by deed or by word, any of the said Moriscos or their wives, children, or any of them.

7. The same may not hide them in their houses, conceal them, or give any of them assistance . . . under penalty of six years in the galleys without parole, as well as other [penalties] we reserve for our prerogative.

8. And so that the Moriscos may understand that His Majesty's intention is merely to expel them from his kingdoms, and not that they should be harassed during their voyage but rather deposited on the coasts of the land of the Berbers, we will allow ten of the said Moriscos who embark on the first voyage to return to give word of it to the rest, and the same may be done on each voyage.

9. The boys and girls under four years of age who wish to stay, and their parents and guardians (if they be orphans), may do so and will not be expelled.

10. Boys and girls under six years of age who happen to be children of Old Christians must stay, along with their mothers, even if they be Moriscos; but if the father happens to be a Morisco and the wife is an old Christian, he shall be expelled, and the children under six years of age will stay with the mother.

11. The same shall hold for those who for quite some time, for example two years, have lived among Christians without attending the council of the *aljama* [community].

12. The same shall hold for those who receive the Holy Sacrament with the permission of their prelates, as attested to by the rectors of the places where they live.

13. His Majesty sees fit and considers it proper if some of the said Moriscos wish to go to other kingdoms, and can do so without passing

through any other of the kingdoms of Spain, leaving for them from their places of residence within the allotted time. Such is the royal and determined will of His Majesty, and also that the penalties specified in this decree be executed without fail. . . .

Valencia, September 22, 1609

35. The Archbishop of Seville,
On the Expulsion of the Moriscos (1610)

Spain's Christians did not react unanimously to the expulsion of the Moriscos. In many areas there was a kind of popular fervor demanding their expulsion, often stirred up by fiery speeches and sermons by zealous monks and parish priests. But many landowners and nobles, particularly in Valencia, depended on the Moriscos for their labor and their agricultural skills, and they lobbied the Crown to try to stop the expulsion. Also opposing the decree, or at least some of its terms, were a few members of the clergy, including the archbishop of Seville, Don Pedro Vaca de Castro.

SOURCE: Antonio Domínguez Ortiz and Bernard Vincent, *Historia de los moriscos: Vida y tragedia de una minoría* (Madrid: Revista de Occidente, 1978), app. VIII, 281–82.

Lord, in this city a decree of Your Majesty for the exclusion of the Moriscos has been published. It has caused grief and compassion and, being such a general decree, it seems to include the innocent, and I fear that it may bring danger to the consciences of some of them. Everything will have to be considered with the usual deliberation. I, as a father of the Church, regret this [decree], and I feel pain, and I would like to assuage the danger of the consciences. This is what gives me the boldness to write these lines.

The aim and principal reason for this decree is not to punish crimes, but rather, with Your Majesty employing his clemency, to remit them and to avoid the danger that there is to be feared from these people. Among the Moriscos who reside in this city, it appears that there is no danger because they are few, they were all expelled from here after the last rebellion, they remain few, and they are humble people; they are not party to anything.

Nor is there any danger from the women of any age, nor from men over sixty or seventy years old, for they are not given to participating in uprisings or taking up arms.

[There are] Morisca women who are married to old Christians and their children are old Christians, like their fathers and grandfathers. . . . And the wives, although Moriscas, must enjoy the privileges of their husbands and fathers. They married in good faith with the permission of Your Majesty and according to your laws and those of the Holy Mother Church. Why must their wives be taken away, and who can do this? If any of them should go away or be absent, even if it be a Morisco married to a woman who is an Old Christian, it would appear that this is dividing a marriage. . . .

There is also no danger from the little children. Where must they go? And especially those who have neither father nor mother. Will they not be

enslaved and lose their faith and religion? They are not of age to be punished, and supposing that the fathers are Moors and their children are baptized, if they have to leave their parents or be taken away from them . . . is
it not wrong?

Among the male Moriscos who are known to be descendants of
Moriscos, there are some who appear to be Christians. Among all of these,
some of them must really be. They receive the sacraments, raise their children
with virtue, and lead them to study, and Your Majesty favors them and
grants them mercy, and allows them to receive positions and benefits in the
churches, and I myself have admitted some to the [religious] orders, first
investigating their upbringing and customs with great diligence, and some
of them hold positions as professors in the university in this city. It does
not appear and is not credible that they have conspired or consented to
rebellion. Now, in this decree, they are punished, exiled, despoiled of their
property. What are we to do with these virtuous members of the orders,
who with God's grace and favor could be useful for the conversion of their
own kind?

There are others who lent service during the last rebellion. They left
their relatives, served Your Majesty with distinction, and for this reason Your
Majesty allowed them to stay in this kingdom and keep their property. These
men have always served and have been faithful when the whole kingdom was
in rebellion, . . . and it does not seem likely, now that they are alone among
us, that they would rebel.

Some of them are needed in this city and kingdom, and from here
they serve all of Spain and other provinces. Given this need for them, Your
Majesty saw fit, even though all the others were removed and taken from this
kingdom because of the past rebellion, for those of them who are officials
and hold public offices to remain in this city, and the Moriscos alone know
them. It is clear that the royal rents and affairs will be badly damaged if they
are removed from here; for those kinds of work that old Christians do not
know and which they do not do will cease. The party most damaged will be
the royal treasury, and only secondarily the others.

Your Majesty's examples of clemency favor them, as was used with those
in the rebellion that took place in this kingdom in 1570, who rose up and
rebelled and took up arms and denied baptism, faith, and religion; they were
defeated by arms and had their property confiscated by the Crown. At that
time Your Majesty acted with clemency toward many of them and showed
them mercy. . . . We all have hope that the same clemency will be used
toward those in Granada.

The time allotted for these men to leave is short, and it does not give me time to fix these ink splotches. I beg Your Majesty to forgive me and to receive my will, which is always to serve well. May God protect and exalt the Catholic person of Your Majesty as I, your chaplain, beg.

Granada, January 24, 1610

36. The Count-Duke of Olivares, Instructions on Government (1624)

Don Gaspar de Guzmán (1587–1645), the count-duke of Olivares, was the son of an ambassador from one of Spain's leading noble families. After completing studies at the University of Salamanca, he spent time at the royal court and became well acquainted with the heir to the throne, who became King Philip IV at the age of nineteen in 1621. Olivares himself was only thirty-four at the time, but he was Philip's closest adviser, and by 1623 he had become the king's "favorite," or chief minister.

In Europe in these years, monarchs and their ministers (most notably France's Cardinal Richelieu) were seeking to free royal authority from the interference of rival powers such as the Estates General in France and the Parliament in England, and Olivares sought to govern Spain in that same vein. The traditional system of political autonomy in regions such as Catalonia struck Olivares as outdated and contrary to Spain's national interests, and he resented resistance from the nobility and the Cortes in any part of Spain. His efforts at economic reform, however, proved largely fruitless in a country of strongly entrenched interests and privileges and deeply rooted cultural attitudes, and his military and diplomatic policies also fell well short of their objectives. In 1640, resistance to his policies culminated in revolts in both Catalonia and Portugal, and in 1643 Philip finally gave in to the many pressures inside and outside the royal court and removed Olivares from power. The bouts of depression that had long troubled Olivares then worsened, and he died within two years of his ouster.

Though this document, sometimes referred to as the Gran Memorial, gives the impression that Philip is about to take the reins of government in hand, Olivares continued to govern. Yet in offering the young Philip confidential advice on a range of basic issues, Olivares reveals central elements of his political philosophy.

SOURCE: *Memoriales y cartas del conde duque de Olivares*, ed. John H. Elliott and José F. de la Peña, vol. 1, *Política interior, 1621 a 1627* (Madrid: Ediciones Alfaguara, 1978), 49–53, 55–63, 86–88.

Considering how young Your Majesty is—and may the Lord grant you a very long life—I believe it is my obligation to provide Your Majesty with instruction on some general principles concerning the government of Castile and of Spain. . . . I hope that Your Majesty will be pleased by this brief work, and that many years from now, when I am no longer alive, Your Majesty will find in these brief lines certain true principles and signs of the fidelity, zeal, and love of this humble servant and slave of Your Majesty. . . .

Lord, the ecclesiastical estate, which because of its religious piety may be considered the first estate, is, I suspect, that which, without a doubt, is currently the most powerful in wealth, revenues, and properties. And not only do I fear that it is the richest, but also that it is completely reducing all the substance of these kingdoms and drawing it toward itself, and although it is, as one may imagine, such a grave and potentially problematic matter, in light of the caution and great care with which one must proceed in matters concerning the Church, it remains the most important and delicate domestic matter facing Your Majesty, for its implications concern the preservation of everything there is within these kingdoms, and because of the circumstances I have mentioned, it is a very difficult matter to resolve. . . .

It is also true that Your Majesty cannot resolve this matter without the wise counsel of great, learned, Christian ministers, so I will be content with the role of advising Your Royal Majesty of the great harm that might possibly be done and the not inconsiderable harm that is already being done today, to the chagrin of those who seek the public good of these kingdoms and the greater service of Your Majesty.

Given what I have said, Your Majesty will surely be aware of how powerful this estate is in these kingdoms, and Your Majesty must also understand how important it is to deal very carefully with its members, striving to keep them happy and content, since they are people who are and see themselves as so dependent on the high pontiffs [popes] even in temporal matters. And if it is true that they make important [monetary] contributions both to Your Majesty and to the general good, both having been authorized by concessions from the high pontiffs, there is still more in that estate, in terms of resources, that could go a long way toward meeting Your Majesty's needs, should the high pontiffs wish this and should they not oppose it. . . .

Appointments [to Church positions] should be made with even greater attention to the candidates' intrinsic virtue than in any other appointments Your Majesty makes given how much greater their influence is, and this applies even to lesser positions. . . .

And so, my lord, what I see fit to advise Your Majesty is that this ecclesiastical estate is the richest in Your Majesty's kingdoms, and it is on the path toward being the owner of everything, which is the source of great problems today, and henceforth it should be recognized that it could become the ruin of these kingdoms. . . .

Having no more specific points concerning Your Majesty's government in mind, and lacking others' distinction on this topic, I will not go into any more detail on it. . . .

The governance of these kingdoms depends on many different matters with which one must deal carefully, given the present state of things, which, because of our sins, is perhaps the worst that has ever been seen.

The nobility is composed of infantes [princes of the royal family], grandees, titled lords, knights, and hidalgos.

It is very important that the infantes be greatly esteemed and respected by all the other vassals, grandees and others alike. And although in these kingdoms they have never been treated as they are today, it is to Your Majesty's benefit that it be this way, for this offers a good and unobjectionable pretext for the humbling of the grandees, an order that in other times could barely be made to submit even to kings, but at the same time great care must be taken that [the infantes] submit to the kings, just as any other individual vassal must do. . . .

It would be wise to restrict their movements completely and prohibit their communication with the grandees and ministers of importance other than the confidants and favorites of Your Majesty, remaining highly attentive and vigilant that this communication not take place even through third parties among those who serve their lordships the infantes, and it would be wise to give the significant positions in their house to persons who are totally dependent on Your Majesty or your favorite ministers so that they cannot attempt to promote favor through other paths. . . . In granting them estates and properties, Your Majesty must do so within limits, though not leaving them in poverty, while always ensuring that no one else aids them, and this should be prohibited very forcefully in the instructions given to their servants.

Of all these means, which are those prudence requires, the best and surest for the security and service of Your Majesty will be to seek to establish them, in the proper style they deserve, in other provinces and kingdoms that do not belong to Your Majesty through the means of marriages [to foreign princesses], while in the meantime keeping them under the tightest possible control. . . .

Lord, the second rank of the nobility is occupied by the grandees of Castile and those treated as such. . . . It is good for Your Majesty to honor them and preserve their high places and for them to see that Your Majesty is pleased with them and welcomes them, when there is no particular reason for anger with them. . . . As the highest persons in Castile after their lordships the infantes, it would be wise to treat them in the same way, favoring them, but keeping them under control and keeping a firm grip on the reins while never letting any one of them grow too mighty. . . . For these reasons, I consider it unwise to place them in high offices, whether those of justice, the royal household, or the royal treasury, though this rule does not need to be so strict that exceptions are impossible. . . .

Lord, the third rank of the nobility is occupied by the titled lords, a dignity so great in Spain that it has been given to the sons of kings. . . . These are much more numerous than the grandees, and though each individual has less power, all of them together undoubtedly have more power than the grandees, and so, as I said to Your Majesty in my comments on the grandees, it is very advisable for the good governance and the tranquility of these kingdoms to preserve a rivalry between the titled lords and the grandees, and, without showing great effort, it would be wise if Your Majesty discreetly made it clear that you esteem some of the titled lords as much as the grandees. . . .

Our lord, King Philip II used this class of persons for positions in his household and in other positions in the councils and offices, for, as I said earlier, because the power of these individuals is more limited and because they have smaller entourages, he believed they would be more attentive to their conduct and more punctual in the execution of their orders, given the greater ease of removing them when they did not follow their orders, in comparison with those who were more powerful and had more illustrious relatives. . . . Your Majesty should order the presidents of [the Council of] Castile and of the orders to treat the titled lords with special respect, provided they have done nothing to deserve otherwise, because in light of the stated considerations, it would be wise not to lower their status, but rather to maintain them as a counterweight to the other power. . . .

The fourth class of the nobility consists of the individual knights, among whom I do not count the brothers of grandees or the first, second, or third sons of the titled nobility. . . . I also divide the knights into two classes, one being the knights who are lords of manors and estates, a very small group ever since titles have been given out so liberally, and the other class being knights without manors. . . . The second class, lord, is by far the largest one [of the two] in the kingdom, and the one Your Majesty should use, . . . [by] seeking to send most of them to war, where they are very useful; in this profession . . . they may believe and hope that their conduct will allow them to rise, securing the highest military honors by their courage and service. . . .

The hidalgos make up the lowest grade of the nobility, for it is from that rank that one ascends to all the others. . . . This nobility is the most numerous, just as it is the lowest. Within this group there are three great distinctions, even if all are called by this name of hidalgos, for some are manorial hidalgos and their descendants, and this is the old and esteemed nobility of Castile of whom I have spoken, and who are undoubtedly very worthy of great respect. Another group is that known as hidalgos by privilege. This is of extremely low quality and much lower in reputation, for many of these acquired hidalgo status by purchasing it, or by other ways. There is a third group, hidalgos well known to be such, but who lack manors and whose status as nobles rests merely on being widely considered and respected as such. These make up a category of nobility that is more esteemed than the hidalgos by privilege, but less than the manorial hidalgos. . . .

The people, lord, occupy the third rank, and the lowest in quality, even if one can and must consider them the greatest power, not only in comparison with the other two estates, but even compared with those two combined. Therefore Your Majesty's first concern must be the government of this estate. . . . It is essential for justice to remain infinitely vigilant over them, punishing them with penalties and intimidating them so that they do not get out of control, a means that works better on them than any other, and [this is] something to which they are very attentive. . . .

The people will not put up at all with a lack of bread and sustenance, and so the first concern must be that these things are never lacking, but rather, one must expend great efforts to see that these things are abundant, and this is, without a doubt, the matter requiring the most attention, seeking to guarantee that all possible means are used to ensure not only abundance but also low prices. . . . Theirs is not a judgment to which Your Majesty must always be resigned, but it is always wise to pay attention to the voice of the people. . . .

Those who govern must be very careful not to permit them to have noble leaders, whether high-ranking or low, who make themselves popular; this calamity must be prevented by keeping them separate or using other means that seem appropriate, in light of the great harm that can come from that, as experience has shown. In the cities it is infinitely important to punish severely those who would attempt such a thing and thus do great harm to the collection of Your Majesty's taxes. . . . Whenever the people get out of control, the prince would be very wise to use severe means of control and punishment, but if they do not give in to these, then there is no other way but to loosen the reins and work discreetly, for their confusion and lack of leaders and their disorderliness will soon reduce them to a state in which one can easily and safely mete out the necessary punishments and lessons they deserve. . . .

Great and varied are the matters of government and state that arise in these kingdoms of Castile, as in all the other kingdoms of the world, and to hope to understand them by fixed rules would be a vain ambition and an unwarranted presumption. . . . I will simply say to Your Majesty that it should be your royal ambition to be greatly loved by your vassals, but I also warn Your Majesty that it is impossible for a king to be loved without being feared and considered just as well, and without making sure that the kingdoms are well governed in matters of religion, state, and justice.

In order to achieve this, it is necessary to have upright, learned, impartial, and completely independent ministers.

It is necessary to watch closely over the religion, behavior, lives, customs, and learning of the ecclesiastical estate and of its prelates and leaders.

It is necessary to distribute favors and administer distributive justice with great temperance, moderation, and care.

It is necessary to close the door to the granting of patrimonial favors, even if Your Majesty should find himself with a great patrimony, . . . for there is no greater discredit nor any comparable problem than that which causes the vassals to become lazy and wasteful; even those who benefit from these favors grumble about what others are given, and while no one ends up satisfied, the royal treasury is destroyed and with it, the republic.

One should seek to increase the royal revenues by all just means possible. . . .

Your Majesty should keep all the ministers dependent on your royal approval, and let no one assume that he will enjoy tolerance from Your Majesty, nor that he will be able to conceal any grave error committed out of malice, presumption, or self-interest. . . .

The navy should be maintained and the maritime profession greatly favored. . . .

Commerce should be favored and unburdened as much as possible, and foreign merchants should be well treated and favored.

Mercantile companies should be created everywhere.

37. Consell de Cent,
Catalan Grievances (1640)

For years, the count-duke of Olivares, Philip IV's chief minister, had been seeking a "Union of Arms," under which all the parts of the monarchy would contribute troops and money for use anywhere the king saw fit. That idea angered many in Catalonia (as well as in Portugal, which was still under Spanish rule), and it did not help that Olivares was also pushing through a series of new taxes in the region. The combination of these measures, in short, led many to perceive a broad assault on the region's *fueros*, the traditional charter of rights and privileges guiding relations between Catalonia and the Crown. When war with France broke out again in 1635, Olivares expected the Catalans to help with troops and money, but the resentful province resisted his entreaties. Olivares sought to punish the province by stationing troops there (at the locals' expense), worsening tensions in the region. In 1640, Olivares planned a new meeting of the Catalan Cortes—which had not granted the king a subsidy for three decades—at which he intended to revisit the old constitutional arrangements that gave Catalonia so much autonomy.

Before that Cortes could meet, however, a peasant rebellion broke out in Catalonia. Royal troops sent to quell the rebellion dealt very severely with local villages and towns, provoking even more rebellion, and in June 1640 a mob entered Barcelona and rioted, murdering the king's viceroy. Among the upper classes there was certainly deep resentment at the Crown's actions but also fear of a rebellion that targeted the rich as well as the Crown and its Castilian forces. In September, Barcelona's Consell de Cent, a municipal council composed mostly of urban aristocrats but also of some artisans and merchants, issued the following letter to the king.

SOURCE: Fernando Díaz-Plaja, ed., *Historia de España en sus documentos: Siglo XVII* (Madrid: Cátedra, 1987), 180–82.

This province was filled with a universal joy upon the fortunate advent of Your Majesty to the monarchy [in 1621]. But then uneasiness arose with the granting of privileges of Your Majesty's representative to the duke of Alcalá and the bishop of Barcelona before Your Majesty had sworn in Barcelona to honor the customs and constitution of Catalonia and the privileges of the city. . . . Your Majesty came to hold a Cortes in 1626, and as the ministers sought to pervert the form of the Cortes by dealing with the matter of tax payments before establishing laws and satisfying grievances, the agreement was spoiled, to the great disservice of Your Majesty and the harm and consternation of the province and of universal opinion.

The principality rendered a service to Your Majesty in the year 1632 with the authorization of the princely Lord Ferdinand by the Cortes, and this was celebrated with words of esteem and very distinguished service; dissension was then created over the prerogative of remaining covered, which the members of the Council of Barcelona alone enjoyed. And with the city being thrown into this dissension it was not possible to choose judges as justice demanded, . . . and Your Majesty was unable to collect the taxes that could be expected from this province, and it was not possible to assure the public good, which is the main purpose of the Cortes. The gentlemen of Catalonia raised many troops for duty in Italy; they contributed quantities of money to the universities on many occasions; but despite this, Your Majesty's representatives continued to seize people without notifying the prisoners of why they were being arrested, within the thirty-day period prescribed by the Constitution; and they were held for many months without their being told why they were being held in jail against all justice. . . .

After this came the changes to the *audiencia* of Barcelona, to the notable detriment of litigants. Its judges were occupied in various commissions, . . . [securing] supplies of weaponry, foods, fodder, transportation for soldiers, baggage, billeting of troops and other similar tasks, more suited for commissars and policemen than for such important ministers. All of this was upsetting to the inhabitants, between these things and the lack of respect that the soldiers had for them and the license with which they spoke to them; gradually the natives began to do the same, and those who had previously been respected for their positions thus came to be disliked and detested.

Lord, from the decrees and announcements Your Majesty has seen fit to have published, this, your most faithful city, has understood that, with the motive and good reason of wishing to restore justice in this city and province, Your Majesty wishes to honor them by coming to it with a large number of infantrymen who have already come marching, announcing to these soldiers and also the *tercios* [military units] that are in Rosellón [in northern Catalonia, now part of France] that they have to stop killing, devastating, robbing, and taking away honor, lives, and property from its provinces. They have caused so much unrest that all the people of the provinces have taken up arms to resist such wicked people. . . . [This is] a province that has always been, is, and will be so loyal and faithful to its lord, and one that has never failed in its royal duties . . . [that we ask] that Your Majesty remove from here certain ministers who have so greatly offended this province. . . .

We inform Your Majesty that in some of the vassals of his royal monarchy fidelity is no longer firmly implanted the way it is in the hearts of these your faithful vassals, who have always obeyed and served with our lives and property. And we can only think that Your Majesty has not been properly informed of our inborn fidelity and the things we have always done in your royal service, and for this reason there is no cause for displeasure with this province; but negative reports drawn up by the count-duke [Olivares] and Lord Jerónimo de Villanueva, Your Majesty's protonotary, who have always been ill-disposed toward this province, have led Your Majesty to be angry at your faithful and to order what has been done. . . .

It is of very great importance to your royal Crown not to lose this province, as it would certainly endanger the entire kingdom, being that it is the natural defender resisting hostilities that threaten Your Majesty's soldiers who are in Rosellón and on the boundaries of Aragon. We have first-hand knowledge of what the *tercios* have done there with those of the ever-faithful town of Perpignan, treating them worse than slaves, especially with the burning of the Holy Sacrament (may it ever be praised). . . .

We beg Your Royal Majesty, prostrate at your loyal feet and with tears in our eyes, to order that these things be considered, and as a kind and merciful father, to look upon us, your vassals, with pitying eyes, liberating us from the acts of the soldiers, since there is no reason for us to suffer in this way, ordering them . . . not to enter these principalities and counties, and removing those who are in them . . . so that we may return to the enjoyment of the desired justice and peace that were previously enjoyed, for this is the will of Your Majesty. May God guard your royal person for long and happy years, as Christianity requires.

Barcelona, September 18, 1640

38. Philip IV,
Decree Pardoning the Catalan Rebels (1644)

At the same time that Philip IV was facing rebellion in Catalonia, he was also fighting a revolt in Portugal. These simultaneous events, combined with Spain's other costly military obligations, placed the Crown in a very difficult situation. In 1643, Philip had dismissed his longtime chief minister, the count-duke of Olivares, who had been widely hated in Catalonia. This document represents part of a continuing approach to ending the crisis.

SOURCE: *Colección de documentos inéditos para la historia de España*, vol. 95 (Madrid: Imprenta de Rafael Marco y Viñas, 1890), 364–67.

Because we desire so greatly that our vassals in our principalities of Catalonia and the counties of Rosellón and Cerdaña return to a state of obedience to us and to a state of calm, and that they remain free of the oppression they are suffering from French troops, living in peace and keeping themselves clear of the error and confusion that today disturbs those provinces, and for whose good alone we have formed the armies that have entered that province, it is our will and royal intention to use means of clemency and kindness with them, to oblige them to follow their own best interests and to recognize the errors into which they have fallen and the great benefits that will follow for them if they return to their obligations and obedience, living under the peaceful government that they are accustomed to enjoying, as is fitting for the service of God and the common good of all.

And in light of these considerations we have declared through various means our desire and determination to pardon them and to receive them in our good graces, as long as they, as good and worthy vassals, have been deserving of this. And so . . . we offer a general pardon to all the vassals and inhabitants of those provinces of any estate, grade, condition, age, and quality, and we assure them, under our good faith and royal word, that if they return to obedience to us as they were previously, we will consider them pardoned of any and all charges, crimes, and punishments that they may have incurred by their rebellion and sedition. . . . And we promise to forget all of the past and to treat them like good and loyal vassals, allowing them to keep their estates, privileges, usages, *fueros*, ranks, chapters of the Cortes, laws, and constitutions of our said principalities and counties. . . .

Under this general pardon, it is not our will, nor do we want it to be understood, that it include Lord José Marguerit, Doctor Fontanella, José Rocabruna, and Francisco Bergos, nor those who participated in the killing of the count of Santa Coloma [the viceroy killed by rebels in 1640]. . . .

And we serve notice publicly that . . . for those who do not wish to enjoy our benevolence and paternal love, persisting in their disobedience, . . . we will order that they be pursued with all hostility, as the laws of war permit, until we have reduced them to obedience to us as their natural lord and sovereign prince with a title of succession that is as ancient as everyone knows.

39. Juan de Solórzano y Pereyra, *Indian Policy* (1648)

Juan de Solórzano y Pereyra, born in Madrid in 1575, earned degrees at the University of Salamanca before setting out for a seventeen-year stint as an official of the *audiencia* of Lima in Peru in 1609. Soon after his return to Spain in 1627, Solórzano was named to the Council of the Indies, and he later served on the Council of Castile as well. One of Spain's leading legal scholars, Solórzano participated in the drafting of the colonial legal code, the *Recopilación de leyes de las Indias*, and he also published a major treatise on colonial law, *De Indiarum jure et gubernatione*, in the late 1620s.

After retiring from government service, Solórzano chose to write *Política indiana*, a Spanish-language book aimed at a larger readership than his massive *De Indiarum* had reached. In this excerpt from that work, Solórzano considers the grounds for Spain's authority in the New World. He rejects the idea that Christians could conquer and enslave non-Christians simply because they were "infidels," citing arguments by Pope Innocent IV (1243–1254).

SOURCE: Juan de Solórzano, *Política indiana* (Madrid: M. Sacristan, 1736–39).

The opinion of [Pope] Innocent is supported by passages in the Scriptures and canonical texts and the authority of very serious doctors [of the Church]. . . . [He argues] that the first governor, whom God installed over his creatures after the flood, was Noah, and that in this authority he was succeeded by patriarchs, judges, kings, priests, and others, who for some time were entrusted with the government of the Jewish people, which lasted until the coming to the world of Christ, who was our natural Lord and King . . . [and] Jesus Christ chose Saint Peter and his successors as his Vicar, when he handed over the keys to the kingdom of heaven and told him to watch his sheep. With those words, he meant it to be understood that Jews, as well as Saracens [Muslims], Gentiles, schismatics, and any other infidels of any kind had to be under the jurisdiction of the Church and the Roman pontiff. . . .

There are few Catholics who fail to agree to the concession [of temporal authority] to the Roman pontiff, instead considering it well established; for although some deny him full temporal authority even in the kingdoms of the faithful, others, who see more clearly, admit this, and most, taking a middle way, agree that although he does not possess it directly—for we find that these two jurisdictions [the spiritual and temporal worlds] are different—there is no doubt that he has that authority indirectly, namely, when he uses it in relation to the kings and temporal kingdoms when it is a matter of pursuing some spiritual objective, in matters relating to their government and jurisdiction, health, and the security of the souls of the human race, which is the flock that God entrusted to their responsibility and care.

And in such a case, and even absolutely, many are those who feel that [the pope] can rule over the kingdoms and lands of the infidels, even if they have never been within the fold of the Church. For it must seek to attract them and to gather them all to it in whatever way it finds most appropriate.

And the way it favors is the preaching of the faith and propagation of the Gospels, something all Christians, and especially princes . . . must seek to do among those very infidels; and the Roman pontiff, who in this matter that is so much in his purview, is seen as and has the role of the prime mover, or motor; and not being able to execute this task himself, he generally entrusts it to someone he chooses to execute it. And as a reward, he grants supreme authority over the people and provinces that are to be brought under the Church's governance. . . .

I do not feel . . . nor will I say that it is legitimate absolutely to force the infidels to receive the faith that is preached to them, nor to make war on them or to despoil them of their lands and properties for this reason, for I know well that this is not permitted; but rather because there are cases in which those who are legitimately engaged in this very preaching make themselves worthy of this reward. And there are also other cases in which those to whom one is preaching commit excesses, for which they deserve to be punished, despoiled, and deprived [of their authority and property], as plainly happened in many of the provinces of these barbaric infidels of the New World of whom we are speaking, as they did not want to hear or peacefully welcome our people, who were bringing them this evangelical gift; many times they tried to kill them or did kill them, after having already welcomed them, or they denied them passage to other countries, where they were perhaps better received, and where their zeal and their preaching had greater success.

This all shows very plainly that one cannot work in the same way in all times and all places and with all peoples, and those who were found to be so uncivilized, barbaric, or wild often had to be tamed to be able to reduce them and persuade them to believe, or at least to hear and understand or pay attention to what was being preached to them. All of these points have been dealt with and analyzed by very serious authors, and here I content myself simply with having noted them.

And I will add, to support all this, speaking specifically of the conquest of the Indies . . . that although there are some heretics who write freely and audaciously about this, and other Catholics who do not consider the papal grant very binding, the opposite opinion has others in its favor, and they are much more numerous and have greater authority, and they base their view on very convincing reasons.

And it appears that to call this into question is to wish to doubt the greatness and power of the one we call the Vice-God on the earth. And it is also to say that the Church has erred in making so many grants, as it has done for many centuries, such as the grant that [Pope] Alexander VI made to the Catholic monarchs. . . .

Martha cites many of these [grants], and I will add that of Pope Adrian VI, who granted the kingdom of Hibernia [Ireland] to Henry II, king of England, and his successors, with the task of converting it to the faith. . . .

After citing various papal grants and presenting the text of the papal bull in which Pope Alexander VI granted Ferdinand and Isabella authority over most of the New World, Solórzano then proceeded to answer accusations against Spain's conduct in the New World.

The heretics and other rivals of the glories of our Spanish nation, having seen the strength and validity of its titles and the great increase that its monarchy secured through the conquests and conversions in the New World, seek to discredit or weaken them. They say, first of all, that greed for the gold and silver of their provinces did more to attract us there than the zeal for preaching and the propagation of the Gospels, and that because one must always judge actions by their purpose or intention, . . . and because in this case it was corrupt or erroneous, one cannot produce a title that must be considered valid and legitimate.

And in support of this they argue that those who seek to preach and spread the gospels in a Christian and apostolic way must think more about the profits or gains for the souls of the infidels than about those of their states, persons, or properties. And that greed, according to the doctrine of the glorious apostle Saint Paul, is the trap of the devil, the incentive for harmful desires, and the root of all evils. . . . And in regard to our conquest . . . [they say] that our first concern was to ask the Indians for gold and silver. . . .

If we grant that greed for gold and riches, whose power is so ancient . . . has prevailed in some, this does not negate the merits of so many good people who are sincere in this and have acted apostolically, nor the zeal and concern of our kings to secure it, as demonstrated by so many wise decrees and instructions, . . . which can be seen in many printed volumes. . . .

In the second place they charge that from this greed came a lack of peace and benevolence shown toward the Indians . . . [and] that for the conversion of souls no means are required, nor can be used, other than gentle, peaceful, and soft ones, like those, for example, of our Lord Christ and his sacred apostles. . . .

But although I do not wish to, nor can I, excuse everything in the wars
that had to be waged against the Indians in some places in the first moments
of our conquests, with limited justification, . . . I nonetheless dare say and
affirm that these excesses could not and cannot cancel out the many good
things that have been done in all places in the conversion and instruction of
these infidels by men who were religious, observant, impartial, and punctual
in the fulfillment of the ministry of evangelical preaching—and much less
the piety and ardent zeal of our kings, or the justification of their titles. For
they have always sought to act in a gentle, religious, and Christian way, with
great care and concern, and without sparing any . . . expense or any trouble
of any kind, ordering everything that could serve this purpose, and preventing, restricting, and punishing abuse and harassment of the Indians . . . looking everywhere and in all states for persons, both ecclesiastical and secular,
who seemed most qualified to carry out this task and to fulfill the duties and
obligations given by the Holy See. . . . [Solórzano then quotes royal instructions to this effect given to various conquistadors.]

It is thus established and proven that . . . the principles and instructions
for these conquests and conversions were always issued with due vigilance and
the humane and Christian prudence that such high purposes required. . . .
So one can clearly see that although there may have been some excesses,
deaths, and abuse of the Indians in the carrying out and execution of these
instructions, as the competitors, heretics, and slanderers charge, they cannot
and must not question the titles and rights of our kings, nor dismiss the
glory and esteem of that which . . . has been achieved in such remote and
vast provinces in the conversion of so many barbaric infidels, and in reducing them to a civilized life, as all serious and Christian authors, not only our
natives but also foreigners, so wisely recognize. . . .

For the purpose and principal object of an action is that which should
primarily be considered in all matters, and when this is basically achieved,
it is never proper to dwell on whether there were errors in the ways and
means. . . . As Tacitus said, there cannot fail to be vices and mistakes wherever men are involved, and this is especially true in such remote provinces
that are so far from their kings, where . . . the orders of princes tend to be
disregarded or to arrive in modified form. . . .

Moreover, if one looks at this impartially, the Indians in many places
gave sufficient grounds for being conquered and abused, either because of
their bestial and savage customs, or for the grave excesses and betrayals they
committed and intended against our people. . . . In other places it was not
the Spaniards who caused their death, but rather their vices, their drunken-
ness, earthquakes, serious diseases, and repeated outbreaks of smallpox and

other illnesses with which God, in his inscrutable wisdom, has seen fit to afflict them. . . . And in all places it seems that these travails are destined for them, . . . for no matter what is ordered, decreed, or attempted for their health, usefulness, or preservation, it ends up causing greater damage, harm, and desolation among them. . . .

It seems that this must all be attributed to the wrath and punishment of heaven, rather than to the tyranny and oppression that some say we inflict on them. God acts in this way because of their grave sins, and their ancient, abominable, and stubborn idolatries. . . .

Be that as it may, I would like those who slander us to look into their own hearts and say whether there would not have been even greater damage and excess had they had the fortune of carrying out those conquests. . . .

But if they will not say this, the total destruction of the islands and other lands that they have tyrannically and unjustly occupied and sacked give ample testimony; and others that they have populated, treating them with great cruelty and insatiable greed until they are completely used up, without their being able to show that they have taken any care to indoctrinate them, but rather they have perverted them with their despicable errors, nor have they founded any church, nor founded any bishopric, whereas those found in our lands are almost innumerable. . . .

To conclude this chapter, I will repeat . . . that I do not wish to excuse the past excesses, much less those that will in the future be committed against the Indians, for the principal profit and wealth that we can find and get from them must be that of their conversion, instruction, and preservation. Indeed, we were entrusted with this task, and it is more easily carried out by gentleness and piety than by abuses and atrocities.

40. Francisco Pacheco,
The Art of Painting (1649)

Perhaps better known for his writings on art than for his paintings, Francisco Pacheco (1564–1654) also made his mark on the art world by serving as Diego Velázquez's teacher (and later, his father-in-law). Pacheco was born in Andalusia, and when his father died at a young age, he was adopted by his uncle, a canon of the Seville cathedral. After serving an apprenticeship as a painter, Pacheco worked in that profession for many years in Seville, painting competent but conventional religious works. At the same time he also headed an academy in which theologians, nobles, and others gathered to discuss the ideas of the time. In this excerpt from his most important book, Pacheco discusses the artist's place in society, revealing prevailing concerns over social status and attitudes toward manual labor, which Castilians of that era generally considered incompatible with noble status.

SOURCE: Francisco Pacheco, *El arte de la pintura, su antigüedad y grandezas*, vol. 1 (Madrid: Imprenta de Manuel Galiano, 1866), 166–73, 183–89.

Legal scholars . . . say that the nobility of a thing must be judged in two ways, one that derives from the approval of men, and which thus depends on another's judgment; this is called extrinsic or contingent nobility. The other consists of the very nature and perfection of a thing, and is called intrinsic nobility because it derives from the thing itself. . . . But in my view both kinds of nobility apply to the art of which we are speaking, because the first, being born of the clarity with which one perceives the quality of things, acquires its dignity from the esteem and repute with which it is regarded. . . . Legal scholars have determined that one should call noble anything that is considered to be noble in its own country.

If it should seem strange for the people to be the judge of the dignity of an art they judge blindly, one can reply that this simply distinguishes this kind of nobility from intrinsic nobility (about which we will speak later). Yet this first kind of nobility, though it may seem uncertain, is generally just, for we see from experience that the difference in how greatly painting is esteemed from one place to another is not primarily based on the ignorance of the people, but rather on the quality of those who exercise it and on that of the works they produce. So it is with the rest of the arts and sciences that when they are carried out by learned and excellent subjects they are greatly esteemed, whereas when they are carried out by the lowly and ignorant they are considered despicable and vile. And so it is with painting, that it tends to be esteemed according to the knowledge and skill of its practitioners. . . . Hence we can infer that painting acquires more or less respect based on the quality of the artists, as there is great difference among them not only in terms of their genius and competence but also in terms of their creativity and the subjects they select. . . . And so we turn to the second kind of nobility, known as intrinsic.

I say that this kind also attests to this art, for being similar to poetry in certain ways, it takes its rule from it, following Aristotle, who wrote that "excellent painters should imitate excellent poets." And as poetry is among the noble arts, so should painting be. And just as poetry, in describing the illustrious feats of men and women, gives examples of how to live a good life and is thus a noble and moral art, by the same token, painting, by placing before the eyes those who have shown excellent virtue, teaches and incites souls to imitate them. Just as all the professions of study and knowledge are honorable, the same is true of the painting of images, which serve to teach the people (in accordance with their rank) and must be considered noble and worthy of esteem. . . .

But if anyone should object, saying that painting should be considered a mechanical trade in that it uses paints and brushes, which are material things, one can answer that just because these instruments are necessary to the art, they do not take away its value, in the same way as with the paper and ink a lawyer uses to write his briefs and opinions; or the theologian to communicate his homilies and sermons; or the astronomer uses the ruler, compass, and astrolabe, for none of this obscures the excellence of those professions, and they all need instruments to achieve their purposes. . . .

Therefore bringing together the two kinds of nobility we say that if the value of a thing, the difficulty of doing it, the usefulness it has, the honor that great persons attribute to it, its role in inspiring virtue, its ability to instill discipline and to educate the people are all things that make an art or an artist truly noble, then there is no doubt that with all of these things being found in the art of which we are speaking it is worthy of appreciation, dignity, and splendor. . . .

In addition to the two kinds of nobility (referred to above), there remains the Christian kind, which is even more illustrious and sublime, given that the evangelical law is more perfect than any others that have ever existed. And I say that this kind of nobility justly applies to the art of painting. But I do not say this because God invented it . . . because it would follow that everything in the world would be equally noble, being made by the same author. For although God made all things, He made them all in different ranks, some superior and some inferior, some more and some less perfect. And similarly He has created diverse orders of persons, and higher and lower professions, as is appropriate to the beauty and perfection of the universe. We can see this with the parts of the body, in that some are more noble than others. . . .

Hence we can see that our sacred religion measures things differently from other laws, for it does not content itself with the external form nor the intrinsic quality, nor other circumstances under which things are made, if they are not accompanied by the concern and the pure intention to serve God, being offered to him as a sacrifice from our hands. Because when they are guided by this purpose, he adorns them and imprints them with the character of heavenly nobility, as the supreme artisan. And on the other hand, all other things, even if they should seem great and made by illustrious persons, are vile and without value if they are not accompanied by his grace. . . . From all of this we can infer that since God can ennoble all things, even be they small and lowly, it is all the more true that he can ennoble painting carried out by Christian rules. . . .

In speaking of the aim of painting . . . it is necessary to borrow a division used by scholars, which will serve to clarify things; they distinguish between the aim of the work and that of the worker. And following this doctrine, I distinguish between the aim of the painter and that of the painting. The painter's aim . . . may be to earn a living, or fame, or respect, to render a service or create pleasure for another person, or to work for his own enjoyment or other such things. . . . But considering the aim of the painter as a Christian artist (which is what we are speaking about), he may have two objects or aims—one primary one and one that is secondary or contingent. This less important aim must be to practice his art to earn a living or to gain the respect of others. . . . The more important one must be to achieve a state of blessedness through the study and practice of this profession, enjoying God's grace. For the Christian, raised for holy things, does not content himself in his daily acts with looking at lowly things, caring only about the rewards of men and earthly comforts, but rather, raising his eyes to the heavens, sets himself a higher and more excellent goal, one found in eternal things. . . . Therefore . . . painting . . . raises itself to a supreme aim, looking toward eternal glory, seeking to keep men away from vice, and leading them toward the true worship of our Lord God.

We can also see that Christian images are not only directed toward God, but also toward us and toward our fellow man. For there is no doubt but that all virtuous works may at once serve the glory of God, our own education, and the teaching of our neighbor. And the more something serves these three elements, in which the sum of Christian perfection consists, the more it should be esteemed. . . .

One cannot fully say how useful Christian images are. They guide the mind, move the will, and refresh the memory of divine things. They produce the greatest and most useful effects imaginable in our souls. They place heroic and magnanimous acts—acts of patience, acts of justice, acts of chastity, gentleness, mercy, and disdain for this world—before our eyes and imprint them on our hearts. And so in an instant they give us desire for virtue and hatred for vice, which are the principal paths that lead to blessedness.

41. Pedro de Zamora Hurtado, The Situation in Seville (1652)

Full-scale food riots were uncommon in early modern Spain, but a series of them broke out in Andalusia in 1652. At first, the uprisings caught the authorities unprepared, and in many towns they were forced to grant the crowds' demands, but once the movements dissipated, the authorities quickly withdrew the concessions and arrested the ringleaders. But if the uprisings ultimately accomplished little, these two letters from the head of the *audiencia* of Seville, Pedro de Zamora Hurtado, to King Philip IV (1621–1665) nonetheless offer a glimpse into the world of the urban poor, their demands, and their modes of collective action during times of economic crisis.

The seventeenth century was a time of recurrent economic crisis throughout Europe, but food-supply problems were particularly severe in southern Spain in the late 1640s and early 1650s. The Crown's finances were also in dire shape throughout most of the seventeenth century, and one consequence of that situation was the debasement of the coinage. The *vellón* mentioned below was a copper coin whose value was plummeting in relation to silver coins; workers were generally paid in the increasingly worthless copper coins.

SOURCE: Antonio Domínguez Ortiz, *Alteraciones andaluzas* (Madrid: Narcea, 1973), 207–10.

Most Excellent Lord,

I send this dispatch urgently to inform you of the unfortunate state Seville has been in since half past eight this morning. Because of the bread shortage, the people have rioted, and there are no forces capable of calming them. They have seized the arms that the city had, including muskets, rifles, pikes, swords, and other weapons, dividing themselves up into squads throughout the city; it is estimated that there must be as many as ten thousand men who are going around rioting in this way.

All the judges and officials, including the archbishop, have come in person to try and calm them, and we have all gone about on horseback, visiting the houses of those the crowd suspected of hiding wheat. They have visited more than three hundred, but in no house have they found more than twenty bushels, and in most of them they did not find a single grain, and in some only two or three bushels. So it is certain that inside Seville there is not enough wheat to feed the city for a day.

And the worst of it is that it is lacking throughout the entire district, though all that can be found is being brought in. Until today it had not run out, and when the uprising began there was bread, with much more coming, but when the uproar broke out the bakers became terrorized and did not dare to come in to work. Nevertheless we have sent men to look for them, and as I have said, the riot did not occur because of a lack of bread but rather because of the excessive price. Still, I fear that as a result of the tumult there will be neither bread nor wheat, because those who do not live here will flee Seville, and with bread lacking the riot will only get worse, and even greater excesses will be committed. So far no one has been murdered or injured and no houses sacked because we officials have always been in view, scattered among the troops, seeking to calm people.

On two occasions I prevented the crowd from going to the Alcázar [a government building], and at one point I came across a band of two hundred men who said they were going to go hang Lord García de Porras. I told them that first they would have to cut me to pieces, and I said that if they wanted wheat they should go to a particular neighborhood where two officials had gone to get some. Once again they headed off to visit another house, but again I stopped them.

In short, things are in bad shape here, and there are fears of great disorder this evening. At noon I went to his lord the archbishop's house, where I gathered various officials, and all recognized the bad state of things. His lord the archbishop offered five hundred bushels of wheat and two thousand *ducados* in money, and each man present sought whatever money he could come up with so that they could buy wheat and sell it at moderate prices, but I fear that wheat will not be found. Therefore, the situation is worse than that in Córdoba, where the people calmed down when they found wheat.

The same official sent the following letter on the next day.

The problems here have been growing excessively, as the number of people in rebellion is now greater and the excesses they are committing are worse, as they are losing all respect. When a large amount of bread was brought in and offered to them at four *cuartos* [a copper coin] per pound, the commotion that the bakers had to endure was so great that almost all of it was taken violently, with some carrying away a lot and others nothing, and without paying for it, accomplishing all of this and everything else while bearing arms. Several times they have entered my house, placing weapons against my chest, and one of these times the cardinal was with me; hearing the tumult that was coming up the stairs, we both went out into the corridors to stop them, and they showed disrespect toward the cardinal, and all of them were clamoring for the exchange rate of the *vellón* to come down; and in order to calm them, the monks and priests took their hands and told them that everything they demanded would be done. They then called for a town crier to announce the reduction in the exchange rate. Not content with this, they violently forced the cardinal and me, as well as some other officials, town governors, and other gentlemen to mount our horses, and they led us throughout the city to hear the announcements, and they had the cancellation of the *millones* [tax] and the pardon of any crimes they had committed included in the announcements.

After that they went to the jails and had the prisoners released, and in the afternoon they broke down the doors of the criminal records offices and brought out the trial records and other papers and burned them in public, without there being anything that the ministers could do to resist these violent actions. And I was in such a state that for two days I neither ate anything nor slept for even a moment. The gentlemen and all of the nobility are fully united with the ministers of Your Majesty, wishing to be able to subdue these people, and the Inquisitor Lord Pedro Manjarrés is also helping us.

42. The Velázquez Investigation (1658–1659)

Diego Rodríguez de Silva Velázquez, the most famous Spanish painter of the seventeenth century and one of the greatest painters of any time, was born in 1599 in Seville. At the age of twelve, Velázquez was apprenticed to Francisco Pacheco, and at twenty-four he obtained a position as a painter at the royal court of Philip IV (1621–1665) in Madrid.

Enjoying Philip's favor for many years, Velázquez wished to crown his career with an appointment to the noble Order of Santiago, but that required an exhaustive investigation of his personal background. This reading contains the following documents from that investigation:

(1) the king's decree calling for an investigation into Velázquez's personal and family background;

(2) excerpts from the questionnaire the investigators were given;

(3) excerpts from one of the 146 witnesses' answers;

(4) a passage from the Council of the Orders' report to the king; and

(5) the king's final decree granting Velázquez membership in the Order.

The nature of the investigators' concerns, the answers obtained, and even the very existence of the application all cast light on important aspects of Spanish culture and society in that era. Velázquez died in 1660, a year after the investigation was completed.

SOURCE: *Varia Velazqueña: Homenaje a Velázquez en el III centenario de su muerte, 1660–1960*, vol. 2 (Madrid: Ministerio de Educación Nacional/Publicaciones de la Dirección General de Bellas Artes, 1960), 303–6, 339–40, 371–73.

Royal Decree Calling for the Usual Investigation for the Granting of Membership in the Order of Santiago, Sought by Velázquez, and Designating Those Commissioned to Investigate, September 27, 1658

Lord Philip, by grace of God king of Castile, . . . perpetual administrator of the Order and Knighthood of Santiago by apostolic authority, to you, the noble and religious members of the same order. . . .

Know that Diego de Silva Velázquez has informed us that he wishes to enter said order and live under its observance, rules, and discipline, because of the devotion he has toward the blessed apostle Lord Santiago, begging us that we order him to be admitted and to grant the habits of that order, given that he is a hidalgo . . . both on his father's and his mother's side, as called for by the ways and *fueros* of Spain, and that the qualities that the rules of said order call for are all present in him. It was agreed that we should order that this, our letter, be sent to you for this reason, and we have considered it proper to entrust you with being the ones who will do this service. . . . [You will do] properly and faithfully, with all due care and diligence, what we have asked you and ordered you to do, and you will keep this secret. . . . And you will swear that . . . none of you is a relative within the fourth degree of Diego de Silva Velázquez, nor of his wife if he is married. . . .

You will go to any place you see fit, and you will take testimony in due form from any witnesses you consider necessary, if they be persons of good reputation and conscience who know the said person and his ancestors. And you will ask them the questions contained in the inquiry enclosed with this letter we are sending you. . . . And with any witness who says he knows the answer to the question, you will ask how he knows it . . . and with those who say they saw and heard things said, ask how and when, and how long ago, so that each witness gives sufficient reason for his statement and deposition. . . .

The investigators were to ask the following questions:

1. First, whether they know Diego de Silva Velázquez, and how old he is, and where he is from, and whose son he is, and if they know or knew his father and mother; and what their names were, and where they resided, and where they were from, and whether they knew the father and mother of the father of said Diego de Silva Velázquez, and the father and mother of his mother, and what their names were, and where they were from, or where they lived, or where they were born. If they respond that they know them or knew them, they should declare how . . . they knew that they were his father, mother, and grandparents, specifying that for each one.

2. They should be asked if they are relatives of said Diego de Silva Velázquez, and if the witnesses state that they are, they should declare in what degree; and if they are related by marriage, or friends, or enemies of said person, or his servants . . . and whether he has spoken to them, or threatened them, or bribed them, or given or promised anything if they should lie for him.

3. Whether said Diego de Silva Velázquez and his father and mother and grandparents have been and are . . . born of legitimate matrimony . . . and if any of them is or has been a bastard, and if the witnesses say that they were and are, they should state specifically who is or was and the nature of this bastardy, and how . . . they know this. . . .

4. Whether they know, believe, have seen, or heard say that the father and mother, grandfathers, and grandmothers of said Diego de Silva Velázquez . . . [are] commonly reputed to be pure, old Christians, free of any race, without any mixture of Jew, Moor, or *converso* in any degree, no matter how remote and distant. . . .

5. Whether they know, believe, have seen, or heard say that the father and mother, grandfathers, and grandmothers, paternal as well as maternal . . . have been . . . commonly considered to be hidalgos, according to the customs and fueros of Spain, and not by privilege. . . . And they should state and declare the reputation and general opinion that the said candidate and his parents and paternal and maternal grandparents have, and have had, regarding their nobility and status as hidalgos.

6. Whether they know if said Diego de Silva Velázquez, his father, and his paternal and maternal grandparents have been or are merchants or traders, or have carried out any low or mechanical occupation, and if so what occupation it was. . . .

7. Whether they know if said Diego de Silva Velázquez knows how and is able to ride a horse, and whether he has one, and how they know.

8. Whether they know if said Diego de Silva Velázquez has ever been challenged [to a duel]; and if the witnesses say that he has, they should declare how they know this, and how he was saved from the challenge. . . .

9. Whether they know if said Diego de Silva Velázquez has had his reputation questioned with any serious and ugly charge, such that his reputation is tainted among hidalgos. . . .

10. Whether they know if said Diego de Silva Velázquez or his father, mother, grandfathers, grandmothers, or any other relatives to the fourth degree . . . have been condemned by the Holy Office of the Inquisition as heretics, or for any type of heresy, whether turned over to the secular authorities or reconciled, or as being suspect in their faith, or publicly punished on the gallows, or in the Church, or any other place. . . .

The following is one of the 146 interview summaries:

Witness 104: In said city [Seville], on said day, month, and year, Juan Manuel de Dueñas, a scribe in this city and a resident and native of it, was received as a witness, swearing as duly required. . . . He said that he knows Diego de Silva Velázquez, . . . a resident of the palace and a chamber aide of His Majesty, who must be more or less fifty-eight years old, and a native of this city, as were his parents. . . . He said that he did not know the paternal grandparents but that he considers it well known that they were called Diego Rodríguez de Silva and Lady María Rodríguez, and that they had been natives of the city of Oporto in the kingdom of Portugal, whence they came to this city of Seville, where they lived and died. He also said that he did not know the maternal grandparents, but that he also heard of them, and that they were called Juan Velázquez and Lady Catalina de Çayas [Zaias] and that they were natives of this city of Seville. . . . He considers the said candidate Diego de Silva Velázquez and his parents and paternal and maternal grandparents to be legitimate and of legitimate matrimony, without bastardy or illegitimacy, and this has been and is their reputation and general opinion. . . . He considers said candidate, his parents, and his maternal grandparents to be old Christians, without any stain of Jew, Moor, or *converso* in any degree no matter how remote, because he has always heard people speak well of the purity of the candidate's lineage. . . . The witness stated that he considered said Diego Rodríguez de Silva Velázquez, the candidate, and said parents . . . and grandparents . . . to be nobles and hidalgos by blood, according to the practices, *fueros*, and customs of Spain. . . . He said that he does not know nor has he heard that said candidate Diego de Silva Velázquez, or his father Juan Rodríguez de Silva, or his paternal or maternal grandfathers . . . had exercised any vile, low, or mechanical trade, nor any other included in this question, but rather that he had heard from those who managed to meet them that they were seen to comport themselves very illustriously, living off their estates and possessions. . . . That the candidate, although they commonly call him a painter, since he paints for His Majesty, . . . resides in his palace and is his chamber aide; and as declared in the first question, during the time he spent in this city he did not know him to have any public or secret store or shop as other painters do, nor to have sold paintings either directly or through a third person, and that the painting he does in the town of Madrid is in the service of His Majesty, and he has often heard it said that he takes care of the decoration and adornment of his royal palace, and that he has been sent several times to Italy to purchase paintings and statues with His Majesty's funds, but that it has never come to his attention that he has had or has any store or shop in said town of Madrid. . . . He stated that said candidate and his parents and grandparents are of the quality mentioned, both in terms of nobility and purity [of blood], and that neither he nor any of his relatives has been tainted with any public or secret penitence by the Holy Inquisition, nor by any other tribunal, for any crime of heresy committed against our holy Catholic faith. . . .

Report of the Council of the Orders, April 11, 1659
In the council on February 26, 1659, the lords President [et al.], . . . having seen the evidence of the qualities of Diego de Silva Velázquez, candidate for membership in [the Order of] Santiago, native of Seville, stated that in regard to the purity of all lineage, they approve and approved, and in regard to the nobility of Lady María Rodríguez, the candidate's paternal grandmother, and that of Juan Velázquez and Catalina de Zaias, maternal grandparents,

they reject and rejected it, because it was not fully proven in accordance with the regulations of the order. . . .

After the rejection, the king wrote to Rome seeking papal dispensation, which was granted. The king then granted Velázquez both hidalgo status and membership in the order.

Royal Decree Granting Membership in the Order of Santiago to Diego Velázquez, July 29, 1659

From Lord Philip, by grace of God, king of Castile, . . . perpetual administrator of the Order and Knighthood of Santiago by apostolic authority, to you [blank space], know that Diego de Silva Velázquez . . . informed me of his desire to enter said order and to live under its observance and discipline because of the devotion he has for the blessed apostle Lord Santiago. . . . Recognizing his devotion and the services he has rendered to me and to the order, . . . I have granted said subject membership in said order, in light of the qualities he possesses, and which the regulations require, . . . despite the unproven nobility of María Rodríguez, his paternal grandmother, and of Juan Velázquez and Lady Catalina de Çayas, his maternal grandparents.

43. Treaty Between Spain and Portugal (1668)

After sixty years of living under the rule of the Spanish Crown, Portugal rebelled in 1640, taking advantage of a simultaneous revolt in Catalonia and Spain's ongoing conflict with France. In 1652 Catalonia's rebellion against Spain collapsed, and in 1659 Spain ended its war with France, so there were now grounds for Spanish optimism in the struggle to control Portugal. Yet Portugal could draw on the wealth of its Brazilian colony and the aid of both England and France, while Spain's finances were still in crisis. Three years after several important defeats in 1665, Spain finally accepted the loss of Portugal.

Overseeing the negotiations on the Spanish side was a regency government, for Philip IV (reigned 1621–1665) had just died, and the new king, Charles II, was still a child. On the Portuguese side there was also a regency, for real power was in the hands of Prince Pedro (reigned as Pedro II, 1683–1706). Despite winning its independence, however, Portugal remained under English hegemony for many more years.

SOURCE: Esteban de Ferrater, *Código de derecho internacional*, vol. 1 (Barcelona: Imprenta de D.R.M. Indar, 1846), 398–99.

Treaty Between Spain and Portugal, Made in Lisbon on February 13, 1668

Article 1. A perpetual, firm, and inviolable peace is established, with all acts of hostility now being ended.

Article 2. Places occupied by each side during the war will be returned, except for that of Ceuta, which will remain in the power of the Catholic king [of Spain]. The inhabitants will be able to leave freely with all their possessions, and they will be able to dispose freely of the property they possessed by other rights than those of war. . . .

Article 7. And so that this peace will be observed properly, the kings of Spain and Portugal promise to give free and safe passage to all commerce, by sea or by navigable rivers, guarding against the invasion of any pirates or other enemies, whom they will arrest and punish. . . .

Article 9. And if some inhabitants, opposing the terms of this treaty, cause any damage without orders or mandates from their respective kings, this damage will be repaired and those responsible will be punished once they are apprehended. But no one will be allowed to take up arms or break the peace based on this cause. And in case justice is not done, it will be possible to issue orders or reprisals against the criminals in the usual manner.

Article 10. The Crown of Portugal, given the interests it has reciprocally and inseparably with England, will be allowed to enter into any offensive or defensive alliance or alliances that the Crowns of England and Portugal will make between them, together with any of their associates. And the conditions and reciprocal obligations that in such case will be adjusted or later added will be maintained and preserved inviolably by virtue of this treaty, in the same form and manner as if they were specifically expressed in it, with the allies already being named.

Article 11. The kings of Spain and Portugal promise to do nothing against or prejudicial to this peace, nor to consent that such be done, and if necessary to repair it without any delay. And for the observance of all of it they are obliged, with the king of Great Britain as a mediator and guarantor of this peace, and for the security of all they renounce any contrary laws and customs.

44. The Marquis de Villars,
Memoirs of the Court of Spain (1678–1682)

Foreign observers had been pointing out problems in Spain for many years by the late seventeenth century, but these memoirs from the years 1678 to 1682 suggest, as do many historians, that the situation had reached new lows during the reign of Charles II (1665–1700). The precise authorship of these memoirs remains in question, as the French ambassador to Spain, the Marquis de Villars, probably did not write all, or even part, of them himself, and the observations on which they are based probably came from others. Regardless of their author, however, they attest both to the deteriorating situation in the final years of the Habsburg dynasty in Spain and to the kinds of perceptions of Spain that French and other foreign observers held at the time.

SOURCE: Marquis de Villars, *Mémoires de la cour d'Espagne sous la regne [sic] de Charles II, 1678–1682*, ed. A. Morel-Fatio (London: Imprimerie de Whittingham et Wilkins, 1861), 3–4, 82–83, 92–93, 95–97, 153–58, 185–89, 290–91.

The idea that these memoirs may give of the present state and the government of Spain will undoubtedly have little relation to that which the power and the policy of the Spaniards had formerly projected throughout the world. Yet no one can be unaware that since the beginning of this century, the one and the other have been in a state of steady decline. This change has become so rapid that in recent times it has become perceptible from one year to the next.

I have seen this court and most of Spain. Fifteen years ago, one still found ministers of great reputation in the councils; one still found enough money in the king's finances and the subjects' commerce to remember the riches that the Indies provided under a better government. But during a second stay, during which, for two years, I had the opportunity to observe the court and the ministers continually, I found few remaining traces of the old Spain in either the public or the private realm. This is what led me to write these memoirs, in order to reveal in detail the change that has taken place in this monarchy. . . .

A few days after [the queen's] return, there was in Madrid the most magnificent bullfight that had been held for a long time. The duke of Medina-Sidonia [and other nobles] . . . were the combatants, and they showed great skill, especially the duke of Medina-Sidonia. They entered the plaza followed by lackeys dressed in the Turkish style, and the others also had a sumptuous livery, with each one representing the dress of a given nation.

This spectacle is a legacy of the Moors, whose spirit and manners did not entirely disappear from Spain when they were expelled. It has an air of barbarism about it, since one sees men expose themselves to danger fighting wild bulls in order to entertain the public, and since there are few bullfights in which someone is not killed, but the show is quite grand, the combatants appear on the noblest horses in the world, and nothing is more impressive than the plaza where this combat takes place. That plaza is extremely vast, surrounded by buildings six or seven stories high, with equal-sized balconies adorned with rich fabrics and filled with an infinite number of spectators. . . .

During [factional] agitations in the palace, the government fell into a feeble state that finished the ruin of a Spain that had already been overwhelmed for a long time. All the affairs that concerned the state or its individuals were equally put on hold, and they languished in the hands of advisers who examined them extraordinarily slowly; if anyone brought them to the king's attention, they did so without finding any resolution.

Foreign ambassadors complained of the way in which their countries' interests were being handled. Several of them, who had long given up seeking the payment of sums owed to Spain's allies, were upset at having received no responses or at having been deceived by false promises. The envoy of the elector of Brandenburg went away quite unhappy at seeing all the promises about what was due his superior broken. . . .

The state's affairs were in no better shape, as the money from the galleons and the fleet was used up without it being clear how. Expenses could not be met in Flanders or anywhere else for lack of funds, and the lenders ruined by the loss of their previous loans were no longer in a position to make new loans; one could not even find the money to pay for regiments of Spanish infantry one wanted to send to Milan in preparation for supposed French designs there, and the exhaustion was so severe that funds were lacking for the ordinary expenses of the king's household.

The depth of the disorder was the debasement of the coinage, which had gone so far that a copper coin whose real value was only forty-eight *reales* reached a nominal value of one hundred ten, and the piasters or *patacones* that should only have been exchanged at twelve per royal *vellón* traded publicly at thirty. The cause of this disorder was that more than three quarters of these [copper] coins were false. . . .

Formerly, this coinage was pure copper, of no more value than its weight [in copper]. Toward 1660, it was decided to give it more value by adding a trace of silver, but in 1663, one proposed to do away with that silver because of the excess of value and the ease of counterfeiting. This proposition, then so necessary for the state, was rejected by private interests, covered by some alleged small harm it would do to the king.

The great profit one could make by counterfeiting this money, which filled all of Spain, made the prices of gold and silver soar, and the difficulty of distinguishing this false money from good, or rather the corruption of those who should have kept watch over the coinage, led to the continuation of the abuses. . . .

As the high cost of living persisted in Madrid, there was at that time grumbling and even agitation among the people. The masons, who make up a large part of the city, and who are people accustomed to the thefts and murders that are so common and so rarely punished in Madrid, began assembling for several days in outlying neighborhoods and came up with the plan to pillage the houses of some magistrates who had reputations for enriching themselves from public misery. This plan fell apart on its own, but it happened at the same time that the city's shoemakers presented a petition that complained about a regulation lowering the price of shoes, pointing out that one could not lower their price while allowing food and other merchandise to remain at their current high prices; the shoemakers were sent to see the president of the Chamber of Alcades [sic], whom they went to see as a group. He abused them with his words and threatened to punish them as instigators of disorder, so, realizing that they could hope for nothing from him, they headed off to the plaza in front of the royal palace, where they stood under the king's windows and cried, as the custom was, "Long live the king, down with bad government!" The King, surprised to see people gathered in this way, sent them to go see the president of [the Council of] Castile, who calmed then down at first with soothing words, invited some of them to come in to speak with him, and, upon their request, authorized them to sell their shoes at the same price as before, ignoring the new regulation.

They would have gone away happy had they not run into the president of the Alcades, who threatened them again; some of them followed him with swords drawn, intending to kill him, while others went to speak with the president of Castile and forced him to revoke the regulation by a signed order that they had proclaimed publicly in the plazas of the city.

A few days later, there was an investigation into this incident, and a few of the ringleaders were arrested, but they were allowed to go after a few days in jail, and calm also prevailed among the people who had not done much to mutiny and among the magistrates who did not dare punish the first insolence.

Another affair that happened at the same time made the government's lack of authority even more apparent. Every year in Madrid, during the Holy Week, one can see a number of people disciplining themselves in the streets, their faces showing less piety than caprice and excessive religious fanaticism.

It happened that some of those who went about disciplining themselves at night caused a commotion, and there was a decree of the king expressly prohibiting such disciplining by torchlight. The ban was scarcely published when Don Antonio de Leyva, a relative of the duke of Medinaceli, gathered some young people like himself, and all of them went out together at night in great numbers and with torches and attendants.

The president of Castile, who had just been appointed, wished to make an example of them, but several high-ranking persons became involved, and the prime minister himself objected on behalf of a relative. The president went to the king and declared to him that he would be forced to resign if he were unable to implement policy on such a just matter. He was given the freedom to act as he saw fit, and he condemned all these young men to banishment, but Don Antonio de Leyva, who stayed in Madrid in violation of the judgment, absconded with a woman who had been placed in a convent by her husband, and went away with her to Aragon, and from there to France, thus avoiding punishment by this insolence.

The [newly named] president of Castile, being the head of the kingdom's justice system and police, . . . soon had occasion to find out about corruption among several magistrates, whose greed and whose monopolies were among the main causes of the high cost of living and the public misery. He learned that some members of the royal council were, under borrowed names, involved in the sale of meat, as well as coal, oil, and other necessities, and, being the superiors of the police, were able to raise the prices as high as they wanted. The *corregidor* and the officers of the city government did similar things with the sale of grains, which made bread sell for double what it should have, and the burden on the public was a consequence of its powerlessness and the way in which the magistrates had long been robbing the king and the people. The president at first seemed to want to find some solution to these outrages, but, not being backed by the minister, he was forced to leave things as they were. . . .

The provinces were so exhausted that in some parts of Castile people had to resort to bartering merchandise, because there was not enough money to buy things. In Madrid itself there was almost none left, and one could easily see the consequences of the change in coinage that had been carried out so suddenly. People of quality, whose expenses had doubled because of this change, could not pay their merchants, and the bankers had no more funds and could not find any more deposits; nothing was being paid in the royal household, and things reached such an extreme point that most of the servants turned in their things in preparation to leave, and one had great difficulty in finding ways to get them to stay. . . .

The crisis went on, nonetheless, and although there was a large harvest of grain, the price of bread did not come down in Madrid, where the magistrates' monopolies still prevented the abundance from the countryside from having any effect.

At the same time, plague began spreading through Andalusia. The year before, it had depopulated Granada and the coast from Alicante to Málaga; it now spread to the area around Seville, toward Cordoba, and to the frontier with Estremadura. . . . It was a great obstacle to commerce and a new calamity added to Spain's other miseries.

On the last day of June, something happened in Madrid that had not been seen for forty-eight years. A great auto-de-fe of the Inquisition took place, in which there was a very ceremonial public account of the trial and sentencing of several people guilty of crimes against religion, gathered from Inquisitions from all parts of Spain. For this occasion a grand stage was set up in the Plaza Mayor in Madrid, where from seven in the morning until nine at night criminals were put on display, and their confessions were heard. Eighteen obstinate Jews, men and women alike, two backsliders, and a Mohammedan were condemned to the flames, while fifty other Jews and Jewesses, first-time offenders and repentant, were condemned to several years in prison and to the wearing of what is called a *sanbenito*, which is a yellow garment with a red cross of Saint Andrew in the front and back. Also appearing were ten others, guilty of double marriages, of casting spells, and of other evils, who appeared with dunce caps of cardboard, with a rope around the neck, a candle in one hand; the punishment for these is normally to be whipped, sent to the galleys, or exiled.

On the following night, those who were condemned to the flames were burned outside the city, in a specially constructed site, where these miserable wretches suffered a thousand tortures before being executed. The very monks who attended burned them with small flames from torches in order to convert them; several people who were at the site gave them blows with their swords, and the people rained stones upon them.

Those who have not been raised amid Spain's anxieties, which lead people to watch these ceremonies with veneration, may find it strange that in this session, the Inquisitor was on a higher level than the king, on something that looked like a throne, and that from morning to evening the king had criminals in front of him, viewing torture as a form of entertainment, and that in his presence one abused some of the criminals, whom the monks struck several times at the foot of an altar in order to force them to kneel. . . .

On the kingdom's frontiers, the few remaining troops could barely get by. On the Estremadura frontier, a crucial one given that the Portuguese have several strong points there and could quickly put ten or twelve thousand men into the field, the Spanish bases were ruined and dilapidated, having long been guarded by two weak and incomplete infantry regiments. The cavalry was almost completely disintegrated, often without fodder for the horses, and all of the soldiers had received only a month's pay over the last year.

The frontiers of Navarre and Vizcaya were hardly better guarded, and at the end of 1680, the governors of San Sebastián and Fuenterrabía came to the court to complain that they and their garrisons were dying from their poverty, if one can call a garrison the few old and married soldiers who were remaining in these two places, where all the young and unattached men had deserted. After several months of solicitations, these governors were sent back with promises that were not kept.

45. Alexander Stanhope,
Spain Under Charles II (1696–1699)

Charles II inherited the throne in 1665 at the age of four. For most observers, his reign marked the low point of Spain's fortunes, as Charles, stricken with a variety of physical ailments, presided over a country in chronic economic crisis and one in which the nobility managed to wrest real political control from the Crown. In 1690, Charles married for second time (his first wife having died in 1689), this time to Mariana of Neuburg, a princess related to the Habsburgs. Yet before long, it became clear that this marriage, like the previous one, would produce no offspring, and Charles had no brothers to succeed him either. With the prospect of the end of the Habsburg dynasty in Spain, the great powers began positioning themselves to place their favored candidates on the throne of Spain.

There were three main contenders to succeed Charles; the French candidate was Louis XIV's grandson Philip, duke of Anjou, but the idea of France and Spain being united under one ruler alarmed both England and Austria as well as many Spaniards; the Austrian candidate was Archduke Charles, the favorite of Queen Mariana, but the prospect of a son of the Holy Roman Emperor joining Austria and Spain under one crown disturbed England and other powers; a third candidate, Joseph Ferdinand of Bavaria, was more acceptable to England, among others, but he died in February 1699.

In the following letters written to various government officials and relatives, the English ambassador, Alexander Stanhope, offers a portrait of Charles, the royal family, and life in and around the court in Madrid.

SOURCE: Alexander Stanhope, *Spain Under Charles the Second, or Extracts from the Correspondence of the Honorable Alexander Stanhope, British Minister at Madrid, 1690–1699* (London: John Murray, 1840), 59–60, 79–81, 100–102, 104, 106–8, 110, 120–21, 141, 143, 147, 150–51.

February 22, 1695

I can inform you little more of the affairs of this court than by my last [letter], only that it is agreed on all hands that the young queen carries all before her, since His Majesty's confessor has told him he is obliged on conscience to do whatever she will have him, which [the confessor] proves thus: upon the satisfaction of her mind depends the good disposition of her body; upon that the hope of succession; upon that the happiness of the monarchy, which His Majesty is obliged in conscience to do all things to procure.

September 16, 1696

His Catholic Majesty has been extreme[ly] ill these seven days, which has stopped all couriers and expresses; but, thanks be to God, [he] is now much better by taking the quinquine [cinchona], yet not so safe as his good subjects wish him.

September 19, 1696

The king's danger is over for this time, but his constitution is so very weak, and broken much beyond his age [thirty-five], that it is generally feared what may be the [result] of another attack. They cut off his hair in this sickness, which the decay of nature had almost done before, all his crown being bald. He has a ravenous stomach, and swallows all he eats whole, for his nether [lower] jaw stands so much out, that his two rows of teeth cannot meet; to compensate which, he has a prodigious wide throat, so that a gizzard or liver of a hen passes down whole, and his weak stomach not being able to digest it, he voids in the same manner. The king's life being of such importance in this conjuncture as to all the affairs of Europe, I thought might excuse these particulars, which otherwise would seem impertinent.

November 14, 1696

The grandees and foreign ministers were admitted into the king's bedchamber on his birthday, His Majesty being in bed. The ceremony passed in a low bow, without a word on either side, which is represented to the people as if he were so well as to receive the compliments as usually. To the same purpose, they sometimes make him rise out of his bed, much against his will, and beyond his strength, the better to conceal his illness abroad. He is not only extreme[ly] weak in body, but has a great weight of melancholy and discontent upon his spirits, attributed in great measure to the queen's continual importunities to make him alter his will.

March 14, 1698

Our court is in great disorder. . . . The king is in a languishing condition; not so imminent a danger as last week, but so weak and spent as to his principles of life, that all I can hear is pretended amounts only to hopes of preserving him some few weeks, without any probability of a recovery. The general inclination as to the succession is altogether French; their aversion to the queen having set them against all her countrymen; and if the French king will content himself that one of his younger grandchildren be king of Spain, without pretending to incorporate the two monarchies together, he will find no opposition either from grandees or common people. . . .

March 14, 1698

The king is so very weak, he can scarcely lift his hand to his head to feed himself; and so extremely melancholy, that neither his buffoons, dwarfs, nor puppet shows, all which have showed their abilities before him, can in the least divert him from fancying every thing that is said or done to be a temptation of the devil, and never thinking himself safe, but with his confessor and two friars by his side, whom he makes lie in his chamber every night.

May 28, 1698
Their Majesties are expected here the beginning of next month, the queen being very uneasy at the impudent railleries of the Toledo women, who affront her every day publicly in the streets. . . .

June 11, 1698
What I can discover of these people's inclination is for a French prince, provided they can be assured the same shall never be king of France. By that choice, they think they shall secure peace and quietness at home; but they would rather have the devil than see France and Spain united. It is scarce conceivable the abhorrence they have for Vienna, most of which is owing to the queen's very imprudent conduct. . . . They have much kinder thoughts for the Bavarian, but still desire a French prince.

June 25, 1698
Our gazettes here tell us every week [that] His Catholic Majesty is in perfect health, and it is the general answer to all who inquire of him. . . . His ankles and knees swell again, his eyes bag, the lids are as red as scarlet, the rest of his face a greenish yellow. His tongue is *travada*, as they express it, that is, he has such a fumbling in his speech, those near him hardly understand him, at which he sometimes grows angry, and asks if they be all deaf.

July 9, 1698
His Majesty has had no sensible alteration since his great fit I wrote you by the last express. He is made to go abroad [out] every day, though he looks like a ghost, and moves like an image of clockwork. They talk of a diet of hens and capons, fed with vipers' flesh.

January 6, 1699
The scarcity of money here is not to be believed but by eyewitnesses, notwithstanding the arrival of so many treasure fleets and galleons, supplies not to be expected again in many years, for the last fleet went out empty. . . . Their army in Catalonia, by the largest account, is not eight thousand men, one half of them Germans and Walloons, who are all starving and deserting as fast as they can. When I came first to Spain, they had eighteen good men-of-war [ships]; these are now reduced to two or three, I know not which. A

wise council might find some remedy for most of these defects, but they all hate and are jealous of one another; and if any among them pretends [out of] public spirit to advise anything for the good of the country, the rest fall upon him, nor is he to hope for any support from his master, who has the greatest facility of any prince in the world in parting with his best friends and dearest favorites. This is a summary account of the present state of Spain; which, however wretched it may seem to others, they are in their own concert very happy, believing themselves still the greatest nation in the world, and are now as proud and haughty as in the days of Charles the Fifth.

June 24, 1699

His Catholic Majesty grows every day sensibly worse and worse. It is true that last Thursday they made him walk in the public solemn procession of Corpus, which was much shortened for his sake. However, he performed it so feebly, that all who saw him said he couldn't make one straight step, but staggered all the way; nor could it otherwise be expected, after he had had two falls a day or two before, walking in his own lodgings, when his legs doubled under him by mere weakness. In one of them he hurt one eye, which appeared much swelled, and black and blue, in the procession; the other being quite sunk into his head, the nerves, they say, being contracted by his paralytic distemper. Yet it was thought fit to have him make this sad figure in public, only to have it put into the gazette how strong and vigorous he is!

July 15, 1699

The doctors, not knowing what more to do with the king, to save their credit, have bethought themselves to say his ill must certainly be witchcraft, and there is a great court party who greedily catch at and improve the report, which, however ridiculous it may sound in England, I can assure you is generally believed here, and propagated by others to serve a turn.

September 9, 1699

People's minds seem as turbulently disposed as I have at any time known them. One night last week a troop of about three hundred, with swords, bucklers, and firearms, went into the outward court of the palace, and under the king's window sang most impudent pasquins and lampoons, and the queen does not appear in the streets without hearing herself cursed to her face. . . . The pasquins plainly tell her they will pull her out of the palace and put her in a convent. . . .

October 21, 1699

They talk of a famous exorcist come from Germany, who has dissolved several charms by which the king has been bound ever since a child; yet not all of them, but that there is great hope of the rest; and then he will not only have perfect health, but succession. Laugh at this as much as you please, I was told it today by a reverend churchman.

In November 1699, with war between Spain and England approaching, the Spanish government expelled Ambassador Stanhope from Spain. Charles died on November 1, 1700 at the age of thirty-eight.

46. Laws of the Habsburg Monarchy

These excerpts from the Spanish law codes offer a valuable glimpse of many different aspects of life in Spain—or at least of the government's desires regarding them. Most of the laws were written during the Habsburg dynasty, although a few of them were older laws that remained on the books. Several of these laws are composites of many separate statutes passed at different times, as indicated by the dates for each law.

SOURCE: *Novísima recopilación de las leyes de España* (Madrid, 1805).

On the Nobility

Book VI, Title I, Law XVI (1586): To remedy the great disorder and excess that has existed and exists in the placing of coronals in the coats of arms used in seals and emblems, we order and decree that no one may put coronals on said seals and emblems or any other place where there are arms, except for dukes, marquises, and counts.

Book VI, Title I, Law XIX (1609–1682): Any official of the court or of the chancelleries or *audiencias* or any other judge who prosecutes any grandee of these kingdoms in any criminal matter shall not pass sentence . . . before consulting . . . His Majesty's council.

Book VI, Title I, Law I (no date): It is among the privileges and franchises of our hidalgos, which we confirm, that for debts they owe, neither the houses in which they dwell nor the horses nor the mules nor their weapons may be pledged, and we consider it proper that they be allowed to keep those things, except for debts owed to us; and we want the same to be extended to all those who maintained arms and horses, even if they are not knights. . . .

Book VI, Title I, Law II (1348): We order that no hidalgo can be arrested or imprisoned for debts owed, unless that person be commissioned or hired to collect our taxes and duties, for in such case that person nullifies his own liberty; and we similarly order that no hidalgo can be subjected to torture, for this was previously granted as a *fuero*.

Book VI, Title I, Law XI (1525): We order the judges of our kingdoms that the hidalgos and knights who have been imprisoned for some crime shall be held separately from commoners and other ordinary people.

On Clothing

Book VI, Title XIII, Law I (1534–1623): In all times one has sought to resolve the abuse and disorder in the matter of clothing and garments, because in addition to leading many to use up their wealth in vain, it has offended and offends good customs, and for this purpose our predecessors, the kings of glorious memory, have published various laws and decrees. And though the damage has still not been completely resolved by these laws, some moderation has been achieved, taking many useless and costly garments out of use. Wishing that this be reduced to the proper state for the good of our subjects and vassals, we order and decree that in the clothing and garments of any person of any estate, quality, or preeminence . . . the following rules shall be observed.

1. We prohibit . . . any person . . . except our royal persons and our children from daring to wear or put on any brocade or fabric of gold or silver, or gold or silver thread, or any silk that contains gold or silver . . . but we declare that . . . for the service of the divine cult . . . one may freely wear all that is appropriate without any limit.

2. We permit, for the honor of the knighthood, that they may wear brocades and cloths of gold, and anything else they wish . . . on their weapons and other effects related to them. . . .

7. In the bedclothing of men and women one may wear any kind of decorated silk . . . and passementerie and fringe, as long as they are of neither gold nor silver; and we declare that in regard to our prohibition on any kind of gold or silver, we mean real as well as false [gold and silver]. . . .

12. We order that what is prohibited regarding clothing . . . also holds for actors and actresses, musicians, and the other persons who assist in their presentations. . . .

13. We order that women who are publicly bad and earn their living that way may not wear gold, pearls, or silk. . . . That which is prohibited for all women regarding their clothing and garments shall not be worn by so-called public women, both in their houses and outside them. . . .

15. We order that those who work in manual trades, including tailors, shoemakers, carpenters, blacksmiths, . . . and other such lower occupations, as well as workers, farmers, and day laborers may not wear any silk, except for caps, hats, or bonnets of silk

Book VI, Title XIII, Law VIII (1586): We order that no woman of any estate, quality, or condition anywhere in our kingdoms may go about with her face covered in any way, but must rather keep it uncovered, under penalty of a fine of three thousand maravedís for each offense. . . .

Book VI, Title XIII, Law IX (1639): We have been informed of the lack of observance of the previous law and its confirming decrees of 1593 and 1610, resulting in certain damage and problems, to God's disservice and ours. And wishing to furnish a proper remedy, we order that in our kingdoms and domains all women of any estate or quality shall go about with faces uncovered, so that they can be seen and recognized, and they shall not cover their faces or any part of them with scarves or other things. . . .

On Servants

Book VI, Title XV, Law I (1565): We order that male or female servants of any condition or quality, in any service or position, who quit the service of their lord or master cannot stay with or serve any other lord or master in the same place or its surrounding areas, nor can any other person take them in or welcome them without the express permission and consent of the lord and master whose service they left. Servants who violate this law . . . shall be imprisoned for twenty days, and shall be exiled from that place for one year. And anyone who hires them shall incur a fine of six thousand *maravedís*. . . . But if said servant did not quit his or her lord's service, but was instead fired, he or she can stay with and serve another in the same place, provided that the person who is to hire the servant first informs the lord or master whose house he or she left, to find out whether he or she was fired or quit, which shall be established by the statement and declaration of the lord whose house the servant left. But we do permit the male or female servant who quits the service of his or her lord to take on work in the towns or in the fields, and also to serve another lord or lords outside the place in question. . . .

Book VI, Title XV, Law II (1565): We order that no grandee or knight, nor any person of any estate or condition and preeminence, whether man or woman, can have or bring along . . . more than two lackeys or personal attendants. Whoever brings along or is served by more than the said two attendants or lackeys, violating this law, shall incur a fine of twenty thousand *maravedís* for each infraction. . . . And the lackey or attendant . . . who knowingly stays with such a lord or serves him shall be exiled for one year from that place. . . .

Book VI, Title XV, Law III (1618): Because we have been informed that the previous decree . . . has not been observed as it should, but rather has been violated and the number of lackeys has been exceeded, . . . using various means and methods to defraud the law, and because the law's observance is very important to public government, for whose cause it was promulgated, we order that from now on it shall be observed, fulfilled, and executed inviolably in all ways . . . except in relation to the grandees, any of whom may have or bring along four lackeys or attendants. . . .

On the Assistance and Regulation of the Poor

Book VII, Title XXXIX, Law I (1523–1558): Given that when the poor move about throughout our kingdoms it follows that there are many loafers and vagabonds, we order that inhabitants or natives of other areas cannot and will not wander throughout our kingdoms, but rather, each one must beg in his native area; and our district magistrates and judicial officials and mayors will be given the necessary resources by our court to carry this out. . . .

Book VII, Title XXXIX, Law III (no date): So that it can be known which persons are really poor, and so that each one will only be able to beg for alms in one's native area, we order that no one shall be able to beg for alms without a certificate from the priest of his parish. Along with that same certificate, the judges of the city or town where a person lives or was born shall give approval and license for it, . . . declaring where the person's home town is, and his name, and some other indication by which he can be known. No one shall beg with someone else's license. And we authorize said priests, and we order said judges to give these certificates and licenses to those persons who are truly poor and who cannot work, and not to anyone else. And prior to and at the time of granting those certificates and licenses, they should inform themselves very carefully and diligently so that the alms that should go to the needy poor will really do so, and will not be given to those who are not really poor. These certificates and licenses shall be granted on Easter Sunday each year, good for one year. . . .

Book VII, Title XXXIX, Law IV (no date): As one takes care to maintain the bodies of the poor, it is even more just to take care of their souls, in light of some disorder that has existed in this area among those who beg for alms. We authorize the priests and order the judges not to grant certificates and licenses to those poor people until they have first gone to confession and taken communion. . . .

Book VII, Title XXXIX, Law VI (no date): Given that when fathers and mothers bring their children along when begging for alms they demonstrate that they are vagabonds and are not learning trades, no one . . . may bring either their own children over five years old, or anyone else's, with them. . . . And we authorize the prelates and ecclesiastical judges, and we order our judges and the councils of the cities and towns to take great care to see to it that those children serve someone, or learn trades, . . . and that they be fed in the meantime without having to go about begging for alms.

Book VII, Title XXXIX, Law VII (no date): Students can beg for alms with the permission of the rector of the school where they are studying. . . .

Book VII, Title XXXIX, Law VIII (no date): Those who are truly blind can beg for alms without any license in the places where they are natives or inhabitants, . . . if they have gone to confession and taken communion.

Book VII, Title XXXIX, Law IX (no date): The poor who have licenses to beg for alms may not do so inside the churches and monasteries during the time when mass is being said.

On Books and Printing

Book VIII, Title XVI, Law II (1554): We order that from now on the licenses that are given for the printing of . . . books of any kind shall be given by the president and members of our council, and nowhere else. We authorize them to look at and examine them with due care before granting such licenses; for we have been informed that with such licenses having been given easily, useless books with no redeeming value, in which impertinent things are found, have been printed. And so we order that in works of importance, when the license is granted, the original should be placed in said council, so that nothing can be added or altered during printing.

Book VIII, Title XVI, Law III (1558): We order and prohibit any bookseller or any other person from bringing into this kingdom novels printed outside it, even if they are printed in the kingdoms of Aragon, Valencia, Catalonia, and Navarre . . . if they are not printed with a license signed in our name and attested to by the members of our council, under penalty of death and the loss of property. . . .

And because once the presentation and inspection in our council has been carried out and the license granted, there can still be alterations or changes or additions made, . . . we order that the original book presented in our council, having been seen and inspected and appearing worthy of license, be marked on each page by one of our chamber scribes . . . , who will place at the end of the book the number and total of the pages. . . . Once this is done, the printer shall bring to our council the original along with two or three of the printed volumes, so that it can be seen and verified that the printed works are identical to the original that remains in our council's possession. . . . He who prints, or has printed, or sells printed material without having received said authorization shall incur the penalty of the loss of property and perpetual exile from these kingdoms. . . .

And because we are informed that in these kingdoms there are books written by hand and not printed, and that these are possessed by some persons, who communicate, publish, and share them with others, the reading of which has caused problems and harm, we prohibit anyone . . . from possessing, communicating, sharing, or publishing any new works or books written by hand, if they deal with matters of doctrine, the Holy Scriptures, and things concerning the religion of our holy Catholic faith, if it is not presented to our council to be seen and inspected, . . . under penalty of death and the loss of property, and the public burning of those books and works. . . .

And in order for these laws to be observed, . . . it is appropriate to visit

and see the books that are in the possession of booksellers. . . . We order and
authorize the archbishops, bishops, and prelates of these kingdoms . . . to see
and visit the bookshops . . . and any other ecclesiastical or secular individuals they see fit; and if there are books they find suspect or prohibited, or in
which there are erroneous or false doctrines, or which contain indecent
material of poor example, . . . they should send signed reports of them to our
council. . . .

And we order that the penalties collected . . . be divided in this way: one
third for our chamber, another third for the sentencing judge, and the final
third for the person who denounced the crime.

On Diviners, Sorcerers, and Augurs

Book XII, Title III, Law II (1410–1604): No persons of any estate or condition whatsoever shall dare to use these techniques of divining, including
augury by birds, or sneezes, or words that they call proverbs, or fortune-
telling, or sorcery, or gazing into water or crystal balls or swords or mirrors,
nor in anything else translucent; nor may they make amulets of metal or anything else, or use as tools of divination the skulls of men or beasts, nor read
palms of children or virgins, nor cast spells . . . or other such things . . .
under penalty of . . . being exiled from the land forever. . . . And in order for
this to be all the more closely obeyed, it is ordered that the judicial authorities should have this ordinance read in public council, summoned by the
ringing of bells, once a month, on a market day. . . .

On Blasphemers

Title V, Law VII (1566): We order that in addition to the corporal punishment that the laws and decrees of these kingdoms impose upon those who
blaspheme against our Lord God, they also be condemned to ten years in the
galleys. . . .

On the Gypsies, Their Vagrancy, and Other Excesses

Book XII, Title XVI, Law I (1499–1534): We order that each of the Egyptians
who wander through our kingdoms and domains with their women and children must, within sixty days from the day when this law is announced, . . .
begin living by known kinds of work . . . remaining fixed in the places where
they agree to establish themselves, or else earn a living as servants of lords,
who will supply their needs. And they may no longer go wandering together
throughout our kingdoms, as they do, or else within another sixty days they
must leave our kingdoms and not return in any way, under penalty that if
they are found or arrested without a job or without masters, . . . they shall,

for the first offense, be given one hundred lashes and exiled forever from these kingdoms; for the second offense their ears shall be cut off and they shall spend sixty days in chains before being exiled again; . . . for the third offense they may become captives for life of anyone who arrests them. . . .

Book XII, Title XVI, Law III (1586): We order the observance of the laws and decrees of these kingdoms, which prohibit Gypsy men and women from wandering as vagabonds, and which order them to live in a fixed place with a job or employment. . . . And in the same way, we order that none of them be allowed to sell anything, either in markets or outside of them, without the signed testimony of a public scribe, attesting to their residence and the place where they are employed, and of the horses, cattle, clothing, and other things, and evidence of their origins . . . under penalty that anything otherwise sold shall be considered stolen goods, with them being punished for this as if they had really and truly been proven stolen.

Book XII, Title XVI, Law IV (1619): In the Cortes held in the town of Madrid last year, among other things the public prosecutors informed us of the great damage that results to our kingdoms from the deaths, robberies, and thefts that the Gypsies cause as they wander through the kingdom; [the prosecutors] also proposed to us the means available for resolving these problems and damages. And because we wish to offer relief in all things for our subjects and vassals, . . . we order and command that all the Gypsies currently found in our kingdoms leave them within six months of the publication of this law, and that they not return under penalty of death. And those who wish to remain must take up residence in cities, towns, and places in our kingdoms of one thousand residents or more. And they cannot use the clothing, name, and language of Gypsies, but rather, because they are not part of a nation, this name should be forever forgotten. . . . And we also order that under no circumstances shall they deal in the buying and selling of large or small livestock. . . .

Book XII, Title XVI, Law V (1633): Having learned from various reports and accounts by some prelates, district magistrates, and other judicial officials of my kingdoms of the great problems created by the Gypsies, in spiritual as well as temporal governance, and [having been informed] that this damage is increasing every day, to the detriment of peace and public security, with the laws that have been passed since 1499 not sufficing, . . . and wishing to offer a lasting remedy for such an important problem, it was agreed that those who call themselves Gypsies are not that by origin or nature, but rather have taken up this way of life, with the negative effects that have been experienced, and with no benefit to the republic. Therefore from now on neither those people nor anyone else, whether men or women of any age, shall wear . . . Gypsy clothing, nor use the language, nor practice the kinds of work that they are forbidden from doing and that they generally do, nor frequent markets, but rather must speak and dress like the other inhabitants of these kingdoms, and occupy themselves in the same lines of work, so that there will be no difference between the one group and the other. A penalty of two hundred lashes and six years in the galleys for those who violate any part of this, with the penalty of the galleys being commuted for women to exile from the kingdom.

Under the same penalty, they must leave the neighborhoods in which they live by the name of Gypsies, dividing up and mixing among the other inhabitants, and not coming together either in public or in secret. . . .

On Insults, Affronts, and Obscene Words

Book XII, Title XXV, Law I (1566): Anyone who insults anyone else, calling him or her leper, or sodomite, or cuckold, or traitor, or heretic, or—for a married woman—whore, or other such insults should be denounced before the mayor and before decent men . . . and fined three hundred *sueldos* . . . half going to our chamber and half going to the plaintiff. . . . And if a man of another religion has converted to Christianity, and someone calls him a turn-coat or a Marrano [a derogatory term for Jews converted to Christianity but secretly adhering to Judaism], or other similar words, he shall be fined ten thousand *maravedís* for our chamber and another ten thousand for the plaintiff. . . .

Book XII, Title XXV, Law VI (1564): We order that from now on no one shall dare to say or sing any dirty or indecent words, which are commonly called taunts, nor any other songs that are dirty or indecent, in the streets, plazas, and roads, at night or during the day, under penalty of one hundred lashes and exile for one year from the city, town, or place where the person was convicted.

On Concubines and Public Women

Book XII, Title XXVI, Law I (1387): We order that no married man shall dare to have a public concubine, and whoever would have one, no matter what his estate or condition, shall lose one-fifth of his property, up to the quantity of ten thousand *maravedís* for each offense noted.

Book XII, Title XXVI, Law III (1387–1502): It is an indecent thing, con-demned by the law, for clergymen and ministers of the holy Church, who are chosen by the grace of God, . . . to soil the sacred temple with bad women, having public concubines. . . . We order that any woman who is found to be a public concubine of a clergyman, monk, or married man shall, on the first offense, be fined one silver mark and exiled for one year from the city, town, or place where she lives; and for the second offense the penalty shall be one silver mark and two years of exile; and for the third offense, one silver mark and one hundred public lashes and exile for one year. Anyone may accuse and denounce her, and the fine shall be divided, with one-third going to the accuser and the other two-thirds to our chamber. . . .

Book XII, Title XXVI, Law V (1503): Given that it often happens that some clerics have some women as public concubines, and they seek to cover up the crime by having them marry their servants and other such people who are willing to be in the houses of the clergymen, . . . we order that each and every one of these women . . . shall be penalized and punished in accordance with law III of this title. . . .

Book XII, Title XXVI, Law VI (1575): Women who are publicly bad persons and who earn money this way in our kingdoms may not wear scapulars or any other religious clothing. . . .

So that their example may not easily create others like them, we order that such women may not have maidservants under forty years of age, under penalty of the mistresses being exiled for one year and paying a fine of two thousand *maravedís*. . . . And we also want the servants to be exiled . . . for one year. . . .

Book XII, Title XXVI, Law VII (1623): We order that from now on in no city, town, or place in these kingdoms shall any concubinage or public house where women earn money with their bodies be permitted.

Book XII, Title XXVI, Law VIII (1661): By different orders I have commanded that lost women should be gathered up. . . . And because I am informed that the number of these women is increasing every day, causing many scandals and much damage to the public good, you shall give the mayors orders to gather them up, visiting the inns where they live. And those who are found without husbands and without employment in those inns, and all those who may be found in my palace and in the plazas and public streets in the same condition shall be rounded up and taken to the women's jail, where they will stay as long as it seems appropriate. . . .

On Adulterers and Bigamists

Book XII, Title XXVIII, Law I (no date): If a married woman commits adultery, she and her fellow adulterer shall both be under the power of the husband, and he may do whatever he wishes with them and their property, though he cannot kill one and spare the other; but if both or one of them should have legitimate children, they shall inherit their property. And if by chance the woman was not guilty, but was forced, then there is no penalty.

Book XII, Title XXIX, Law III (1565): We order that any servant or person who serves in any capacity or position who becomes involved with and has carnal relations with any woman or female servant of the house of his lord and master shall, if he is not a hidalgo, be given one hundred lashes publicly and shall be exiled for two years, with the same penalty being given to the female servant or woman. But if he is a hidalgo, he shall be shamed and exiled from the kingdom for one year, and for four years from the place where it happened. But if this happened with a relative of the lord or master, or with a young lady he is raising in his household, or a nursemaid who is raising his child, in that case one should proceed and exact justice more rigorously, as the nature of each case dictates, with the same penalties being inflicted on those male or female servants who are proven or noticed to have been third parties or intermediaries. . . .

On Sodomy and Bestiality

Book XII, Title XXX, Law I (1497): Given that among the various sins and crimes that offend our Lord God and shame the land, there is one that is especially committed against the natural order; against which the laws must act to punish this wicked crime that is not worthy of being named, destroyer of the natural order, punished by divine judgment; for which nobility is lost and the heart cowers, engendering little firmness in the faith; and which is an abomination in the eyes of God, and which brings down pestilence and other torments upon man. . . . And because the penalties previously decreed have not sufficed to eradicate and definitively punish such an abominable crime, and wishing, in order to render accounts to our Lord God and thus to ourselves as well, to restrict such a cursed blemish and error; and because the laws previously passed have not provided a sufficient remedy, we establish and order that any person of any estate, condition, preeminence, or dignity who commits the wicked crime against nature, being convicted by that manner of proof that according to the law is sufficient for proving the crime of heresy or treason, shall be burned at the stake in that place . . . and similarly shall lose his movable and landed property. . . . And to better avoid said crime, we order that if it should happen that it is not possible to prove said crime with perfect and complete evidence, but if very close and related acts can be found out and proven . . . the delinquent shall be considered truly guilty of said crime, and shall be judged and sentenced and suffer the same penalty as those convicted by perfect evidence. . . . One may prosecute based on an accusation by . . . any member of the town.

47. Philip V, Decrees on Political Centralization (1707, 1716)

When the last Habsburg king, Charles II, died childless in 1700, there were three main contenders to inherit the Spanish Crown, one each from Bavaria, Austria, and France. The French candidate, Louis XIV's grandson Philip, prevailed, becoming Philip V of Spain (1700–1746), but that led to the outbreak of a European war, known as the War of the Spanish Succession, in 1701. In Catalonia many feared that Philip would create a centralized, absolutist regime like that of Louis XIV—thus threatening Catalan liberties and institutions. In 1701, Philip sought to reassure the Catalans by coming to meet with the Catalan Cortes, but by 1705 tensions had worsened, and the Catalans joined the war alongside Spain's enemies, England and Austria. In 1707, Philip V issued this decree in response to the Catalan rebellion, confirming Catalan suspicions about the Bourbons.

SOURCE: Fray Nicolás de Jesús Belando, *Historia civil de España y sucesos de la guerra y tratados de la paz,* vol. 1 (Madrid: Imprenta y Librería de M. Fernández, 1740), 316–18.

Considering that the kingdoms of Aragon and Valencia and all their inhabitants have through their rebellion completely broken the oath of fidelity they swore to me and lost all the *fueros*, privileges, exemptions, and liberties that they enjoyed and that had been so liberally granted to them by me as well as by the lord kings, my predecessors, thus setting them apart from the other kingdoms of this Crown; and affecting the absolute dominion of the said kingdoms of Aragon and Valencia, for . . . the right of the conquest that my armies have just won because of their rebellion is now added to the rest [of the rights] I so legitimately possess in this monarchy. And considering that one of the legitimate attributes of sovereignty is the imposition and repeal of laws, which I may alter with the fluctuations of time and the change of customs, even without the great and well-founded motives which now come together in relation to those of Aragon and Valencia, I have judged it proper . . . to reduce all my kingdoms of Spain to the uniformity of one set of laws, usages, customs, and tribunals, with all being governed equally by the laws of Castile, which are so reasonable and praiseworthy throughout the whole universe.

[I have also seen fit] to abolish and repeal entirely . . . all the aforementioned *fueros* and privileges, practices, and customs that have been observed in the said kingdoms of Aragon and Valencia, given my will that these kingdoms be reduced to the laws of Castile and the custom, practice, and form of government it has in it and in its tribunals without any difference in anything. Because of this change my most faithful vassals, the Castilians, will be able to obtain offices and positions in Aragon and Valencia, just as the

Aragonese and the Valencians will from now on have the ability to enjoy these in Castile without any distinction, as in this way I thus give the Castilians new reasons for them to believe in the affection of my gratitude, dispensing to them the greatest favors and services, so well deserved by their time-tested and proven fidelity, while also equally and reciprocally giving the Aragonese and Valencians greater proof of my benevolence, enabling them to do things they could not do amid the great liberty of the *fueros* they enjoyed and that are now abolished.

I have thus resolved that the *audiencia* of ministers that has been formed for Valencia, and that I have ordered be formed for Aragon, govern and take charge of everything as in the two chancelleries of Valladolid and Granada, literally observing the same rules, laws, pacts, ordinances, and customs that are kept in these, without the slightest distinction or difference in anything except in controversies and points of ecclesiastical jurisdiction. . . .

In 1711, with war still going on over the Spanish succession, the Austrian candidate, Archduke Charles, became heir to all of the Habsburg possessions. The British, not wanting a single ruler to control both Spain and the Habsburg lands, decided to withdraw their support for the archduke's candidacy in Spain. After British diplomats were able to secure the Bourbons' assurances that France and Spain would not be joined under common rule, Britain and France ended their war and signed the Treaty of Utrecht in 1713 [see reading 48]. Yet the now-abandoned Catalans fought on against Philip's troops, holding out in Barcelona until 1714. Whether it was an act of punishment for the Catalans' rebellion or the fulfillment of prior intentions to impose a new political centralization on Spain, Philip V did indeed impose a new system of rule in Catalonia after the war. The Catalan movement that emerged in the nineteenth century and continued throughout the twentieth was essentially an attempt to recover linguistic, political, and other rights and powers lost at this time.

SOURCE: *Novísima recopilación de las leyes de España* (Madrid, 1805), Book V, Title IX, Law I, 405–9.

By a decree of this October 9 [1716], it pleases me to say that with my armies having entirely pacified the principality of Catalonia with divine assistance and the justice of my cause, it was the prerogative of my sovereignty to establish its government and to see to it that its inhabitants live in peace, quiet, and abundance. For their good, having proceeded with due deliberation and the consultation of ministers in whom I have the greatest confidence, I have resolved that in said principality an *audiencia* shall be formed, over which the captain general or commanding general of my armies shall preside, so that the dispatches I dictate shall be given in his name. That captain general or commander need only be devoted to matters of government, the latter being located in the *audiencia*, and with the regent having, in serious matters and affairs, to inform it one day ahead of its considering those matters. . . .

2. The *audiencia* must meet in the houses that were previously used for the *Diputación* [a Catalan political institution whose task included guarding Catalan liberties] and must be composed of a regent and ten ministers for its civil branch and five for its criminal branch, plus two public prosecutors and a high constable. . . .

4. Cases in the royal *audiencia* will be argued in the Castilian language, and in the interests of attaining the greatest possible satisfaction of the parties involved, the petitions, presentations of instruments, and the rest will take place in the rooms; public matters will be heard in public on Mondays, Wednesdays, and Fridays of each week. . . .

11. The *audiencia* will apprise me of the holidays that existed in Old Catalonia, in order to establish those that there should be, and until this is resolved, the previous ones will be observed. . . .

31. In the city of Barcelona there have to be twenty-four magistrates, whose appointment I reserve for myself, and in the other places eight, who will be named by the *audiencia* at the appropriate time, of which I will be informed. Those named by the *audiencia* will serve for one year. . . .

35. Finding myself informed of the legality and the skill of the notaries of the number of the city of Barcelona, I order that their college be maintained. . . .

36. Neither in the chancellery nor in the office of the so-called brief judge, nor in the courts will any novelty be introduced by my royal jurisdiction, nor in the resources that are used in ecclesiastical matters in Catalonia. . . .

37. All of the other offices that previously existed in the principality . . . and all of the municipal governments not expressly mentioned in this, my royal decree, are suppressed and abolished. That which had been entrusted to them, if pertaining to matters of justice or government, will from now on be within the purview of the *audiencia*, and if pertaining to revenues and the economy shall be entrusted to the intendant or the person or persons I shall name for this purpose. . . .

39. Concerning the inconveniences that have been experienced in the volunteer militias and military juntas, I order that there no longer be such volunteer militias or other military juntas, under pain of being treated as subversives. . . .

40. Prohibitions based on foreignness must end, because my royal intention is that in my kingdoms the dignities and honors should be conferred

equally to my vassals based on merit and not based on birth in one or the other of the provinces. . . .

42. In everything else that is not specified in the preceding chapters of this decree, I order that the constitutions that previously existed in Catalonia be observed, with it being understood that they are newly established by this decree and that they have the same force and vigor as the individual points decreed here. . . .

43. And it is my will that the same be executed in relation to the Consulate of the Seas, which must remain so that commerce will flourish, for the greater benefit of the country.

48. The Treaty of Utrecht (1713)

The War of the Spanish Succession broke out in 1701 largely because of concerns over the balance of power in Europe. England feared that the placing of a French Bourbon on the throne of Spain would amount to Louis XIV acquiring Spain and its colonies, so England supported the Austrian candidate, Archduke Charles. Yet in 1711, the archduke's brother, Joseph, who was Holy Roman Emperor, died, raising the prospect that Spain and the Holy Roman Empire could once again be joined under the Austrian Habsburgs. That prospect seemed worse to Britain than that of having both Spain and France under one ruler, so British diplomats began negotiations with the Bourbon king of Spain, Philip V.

Once Philip agreed to renounce any future claims to inherit the throne of France upon the death of Louis XIV, the British were ready to end the war and accept a Bourbon dynasty in Spain. The treaty signed in the Dutch town of Utrecht, however, shows that Britain did not limit its demands to Philip's renunciation of the French throne.

SOURCE: Fray Nicolás de Jesús Belando, *Historia civil de España y sucesos de la guerra y tratados de la paz*, vol. 1 (Madrid: Imprenta y Librería de M. Fernández, 1740), 650–55.

A Treaty of Peace Between the Catholic Monarch Lord Philip V and the Most Serene Princess Anne Stuart, Queen of England. . . .

[The parties agreed to the following articles.]

1. That there is a firm peace between the sovereigns and their successors, with each one of Their Majesties seeking to have their subjects preserve it.

2. That, wishing to remove suspicions of the union of the kingdoms of Spain and France from men's spirits, and to establish peace and tranquility with a fair balance of powers, His Catholic Majesty renews and confirms his renunciation of the Crown of France. . . .

3. That both sides should perpetually forget the hostilities that have occurred as part of the war.

4. That after the ratification of this treaty, all prisoners should be released. . . .

6. The Catholic king promises not to bother the queen of Great Britain, nor the successors of her line. . . .

8. That the rights of navigation and commerce in the two nations should be free, as in times of peace and in the reign of [Spain's] King Charles II, and in the trade in Negroes, as expressed in article 12. . . .

10. The Catholic king cedes to the Crown of Great Britain the property of the city and the castle of Gibraltar, but this is without any territorial jurisdiction and without any open communication with the surrounding areas,

with Her Majesty agreeing not to allow either Jews or Moors to live or own property in that city of Gibraltar for any reason, nor to allow access to or use of the port for Moorish warships, and allowing the inhabitants of the city the free practice of the Roman Catholic religion.

11. The Catholic king also cedes to the Crown of Great Britain the island of Minorca, the port, the city and fortress of Port Mahón, on the same conditions as those for Gibraltar, and in the case of its alienation, it shall be offered first to the Crown of Spain.

12. His Catholic Majesty concedes to that of Great Britain and to the [South Sea] Company of her subjects the [exclusive] right to import Negroes into his domains in America for a period of thirty years, beginning the first of May 1713, under the same conditions that the French enjoyed, and with the provisions explained in the Treaty of the Asiento [slave trade] concluded in Madrid on 26 March of the present year of 1713, a treaty that is understood to be part of this treaty as if it were inserted word for word.

13. That the queen of Great Britain insists that the natives of the principality of Catalonia be granted a pardon and the possession and enjoyment of their privileges and properties, and His Catholic Majesty not only concedes this, but also that they may henceforth enjoy those privileges that the inhabitants of the two Castiles enjoy.

14. His Catholic Majesty also agrees, in response to the petitions of Her Britannic Majesty, to cede the kingdom of Sicily to His Royal Highness Victor Amadeo, duke of Savoy, with Her Britannic Majesty promising that in the absence of male heirs of the house of Savoy she will take care to see that the kingdom returns to the Crown of Spain, and Her Britannic Majesty also agrees that said kingdom may not be alienated, under any pretext or any other way, nor given to any other prince or state, but only to the Catholic king of Spain and to his heirs and successors.

15. Their Royal Majesties both renew and confirm all the treaties of peace, confederation, and commerce already made between the two Crowns, which are not contrary to this one, and Her Britannic Majesty agrees that the Vizcainos and other peoples of Spain who claim a certain right to fish in waters of Newfoundland shall have their privileges preserved. . . .

17. That if any subject of both Majesties should violate any part of this agreement, the peace will not therefore be broken, but they will instead be punished according to the existing laws.

18. That if by some accident (may God forbid) this peace should be broken, the subjects of each party may, within six months, withdraw or sell their interests. . . . . .

This express treaty of peace was confirmed by the queen of Great Britain at Kensington on July 31 of this year, and His Catholic Majesty did so in Madrid on August 4, and in this way the peace between the two Crowns was carried out, to the great benefit of all the subjects. July 10, 1713.

49. Benito Feijóo,
In Defense of Women (1737)

Benito Jerónimo Feijóo y Montenegro (1676–1764) was a Benedictine monk and a professor of theology at the University of Oviedo, but despite his membership in a religious order he was a pioneer in bringing Enlightenment ideas into Spain. Feijóo often subjected popular conceptions to critical scrutiny, as this essay demonstrates, and his wide-ranging works often proved controversial in the deeply traditional world of Spanish scholarship.

SOURCE: "Defensa de las mujeres," in *Obras escogidas de Fr. Benito Jerónimo Feijóo* (Barcelona: Biblioteca Clásica Española, 1884), 61–85.

It is a serious matter that I am taking up here. I am not only taking issue with an ignorant populace: to defend all women is ultimately to offend all men. . . .

The common opinion deriding women has gone so far that it hardly accepts that there is anything good in them. That common opinion sees women as morally full of defects and physically full of imperfections; but what is mainly emphasized is the limits of their minds. For this reason, after defending them rather briefly, . . . I will expound at greater length on their aptitude for all kinds of sciences and higher knowledge. . . .

Very often the duller parts of the common people see in women a horrible collection of vices, as if virtue resided only in men, [but] very strong opinions of this sort can also be found in an infinite number of books.

I do not deny the vices of many women. But ah! if we looked into the causes of their transgressions, we would certainly find their origins in the stubborn impulses of individuals of our own sex! Whoever wishes to make all women good, start by converting all men [to virtue]. . . .

Moving from moral to physical questions. . . , the advantage of the robust sex over the delicate sex stands as well established, so much so that many see no problem in calling the female animal imperfect, and even monstrous, claiming that the design of nature, in the work of procreation, always intends to create a male, and only produces females . . . by error or defect. From the same physical error that condemns the woman as an imperfect creature another theological error was born, . . . the authors of which said that when the universal resurrection occurs, this imperfect work will have to be perfected, as all women change over to the male sex. . . . All of this is false. . . .

And yet I do not approve of the boldness of Zacuto Lusitano, who . . . for frivolous reasons wished to put women on a higher level, asking us to believe that they are more physically perfect than men. . . . My goal is not to argue for any advantage, but rather for equality. . . .

There are three areas in which men are generally believed to have an advantage over women: physical strength, perseverance, and prudence. But even if women conceded that men have advantages in these areas, one could still argue that there was a tie, by pointing out three other qualities in which women prevail: beauty, gentleness, and simplicity. . . .

I think I have noted those advantages that women have, which offset and perhaps even exceed those that men can claim. . . . Yet one can reply on behalf of men that the good qualities I attribute to women are common to both sexes. I admit this, but the same is true for the good qualities that men have. . . .

As for political prudence, there are thousands of examples of princesses who are extremely skilled. . . .

Of economic prudence it is not necessary to speak, since every day we see households that are very well governed by women and those that are very poorly governed by men.

And moving to the subject of strength, a quality that men consider essential to their sex, I will admit that the heavens gave them an advantage. . . . Yet it did not give them a monopoly on strength. . . .

We now come to the main matter, which is the question of understanding, . . . because the authors who deal with this issue (with rare exceptions) are in favor of the opinion of the populace, which almost always speaks with disdain about women's understanding. . . .

The fact is that it was men who wrote those books condemning women's powers of understanding as very inferior. Had women written them, we would be on the bottom. . . .

These arguments against women are made by superficial men. They see that normally women only know those domestic skills to which they are destined, and from that they infer . . . that they are incapable of anything else. The most basic logic would tell us that we cannot deduce a lack of potential from a lack of actually doing something, and so one cannot infer from the fact that women do not know how to do something the idea that they have no talent for it.

50. Benito Feijóo,
Causes of Spain's Backwardness (1745)

The Benedictine monk and professor of theology Benito Jerónimo Feijóo y Montenegro (1676–1764) spent much of his career in conflicts with his colleagues in Spain's universities. Many of Spain's university professors continued to favor traditional intellectual methods and outlooks such as scholasticism, and far from promoting the spread of Enlightenment ideas in Spain, the universities often served as focal points of opposition to them. Feijóo published this letter, entitled "On the Causes of the Backwardness from which Spain Suffers in the Natural Sciences," in his *Cartas eruditas y curiosas* (1742–1760); this letter, which does not name its recipient, appeared in volume 2 of that work, published in 1745.

SOURCE: *Cartas eruditas y curiosas*, vol. 2, letter 16 (Madrid: Imprenta Real de la Gazeta, 1773), 215–34.

My very dear sir,

In response to the expressions you offer in your letter about the limited and slow progress that physics and mathematics are making in our Spain, even after foreigners have presented in so many books the great insights they have acquired in these fields, I have a curious desire to know the cause of our nation's scholarly backwardness, . . . and I will tell you frankly what I have discovered.

My dear sir, there is not just one cause of the very limited progress of the Spaniards in the fields mentioned, but rather many, and although each one by itself would do little damage, the combination of all of them forms an almost insurmountable obstacle.

The first is the limited reach of some of our professors. There is a certain kind of men who are persistently ignorant, ever determined to know very little for no other reason than that they think there is nothing more to know than the little bit they do know. You must have seen more than four of such men, as I have seen more than thirty, who without having their knowledge adorned with more than the logic and metaphysics that are taught in our schools . . . are so satisfied with their knowledge, as if they possessed all the knowledge of an encyclopedia. It is enough simply to mention the new philosophy to turn their stomachs. They can barely hear the name of [French philosopher René] Descartes without laughing and sneering. And if you ask them what Descartes said, or what new opinions he proposed to the world, they do not know and have no idea what to say, for they do not even have the roughest idea of his maxims. . . . The maxim that no one can be condemned without being heard is very broadly accepted. But the scholastics of whom I speak not only pass sentence without hearing from the defendant, but even without having any sense of the body of evidence. . . .

The second cause is the consternation with which all novelty is viewed in Spain. Many say that in the matter of doctrines, the title "new" is grounds enough to condemn them. . . . New doctrines in sacred fields of knowledge are suspicious, and all those who have rightly reproached doctrinal novelties have spoken of this. But to extend this disdain to anything that seems new . . . is to indulge in a stubborn ignorance. . . .

No one should be condemned on mere suspicion. So these scholastics cannot help but be unjust. Suspicion calls for examination, not decision; this is true in all fields, with the sole exception of faith, in which the object of suspicion is hateful, and as such, worthy of damnation.

And so be it; if we are to believe these Aristarchs, we can neither accept Galileo's four moons of Jupiter, nor Huygens's and Cassini's five moons of Saturn, nor Viète's algebra, nor Napier's logarithms, nor Harvey's circulation of the blood; for all these are novelties in astronomy, arithmetic, and physics, of which antiquity was unaware, and are no older than the new philosophy. For the same reason one would have to condemn the immense number of machines and instruments useful to the perfection of the arts that have been invented in the past century. If only these men could see the excesses to which their unlimited aversion to novelties leads them.

They do not even admit that an absurdity follows from this aversion when it falls on their heads like lead. In the arts and sciences there is no discovery or invention that was not once new. Let us apply this point to Aristotle. He invented that system of physics (if it can still be called physics) that these enemies of novelties now follow. Was this system not new at the time of its invention? . . .

The third cause is the mistaken concept that what the new philosophers present us can be reduced to a few useless curiosities. . . . There is no kind of truth whose perception is not useful to the understanding, because all help satisfy one's natural appetite for knowledge. This appetite came to the understanding from the Author of nature. Is it not a grave insult to the Deity to think that He has placed in the soul an appetite for something useless?

But is it not odd that the philosophers in our lecture halls disdain the investigations of the moderns as useless? Which is more useful: to explore the works of the Author of nature through the examination of the physical world, or to investigate the fictions of human understanding through long reasoned treatises containing logical and metaphysical abstractions? The former naturally elevates the mind to contemplate with admiration the greatness and wisdom of the Creator; the latter keeps the mind locked in labyrinths that that same mind creates. . . .

Lord Jean d'Elgar, an excellent French anatomist who now lives in this city, once brought to my study a sheep's heart, so that all the professors of this college could learn of the admirable machine. At inevitable length he set about showing us, part by part, all the visible components that make up the whole, explaining their uses as he went. I can assure you with certainty that it was not just admiration, but even astonishment, that the knowledge we achieved from that prodigious demonstration produced in us. What a variety of instruments! How delicate some of them were, and yet how strong they were together! What a variety of departments, working together toward the same end! What harmony! What a clever combination among all the parts and the uses of them! . . . In the end, we all agreed that we had never seen or considered anything that gave us such a clear, such a perceptible, such a vivid and effective idea of the power and wisdom of the Supreme Artisan.

These and other similar matters make up the studies of the moderns; while those of us who call ourselves Aristotelians break our heads and engulf the classrooms in cries over "whether an entity is univocal or analogous; whether it transcends differences; if the relationship is distinguished from the foundation," etc.

The fourth cause is the diminished or false notion that many here have of modern philosophy, together with the well-founded or baseless concerns against Descartes. They are almost completely ignorant about what the new philosophy is, and what they do understand under that name they consider a creation of Descartes. Since they have formed a sinister idea about this philosopher, they apply this bad concept to all modern learning.

The excellent critic of Cartesian philosophy, Father Daniel, speaks very well in his fine and insufficiently praised work, *Voyage to the World of Descartes*, that those scholars who curse this philosopher's doctrine without having learned about it sufficiently deserve to be called ridiculous. . . .

Descartes was endowed with a sublime mind, prodigiously inventive, of great resolve and extraordinary subtlety. As he was both a soldier and a philosopher, he joined the boldness of the soldier to the speculations of the philosopher. Yet this lively spirit degenerated into rashness in him. He took on projects that were too vast. His investigations into received doctrines did not stop at some of the margins. Hence some of his opinions arose in which he views philosophy as strange and views religion with mistrust. His efforts are of an extremely magnificent quality, but they are not equally solid. . . . His ideas about the essence of matter and space conflict . . . with what faith teaches us about the creation of the world. . . . Finally, he did not manage to reconcile his way of philosophizing with the mystery of transubstantiation.

Nevertheless, although Descartes sometimes argued in error, he taught countless philosophers to argue correctly. He opened a legitimate path for discourse, leaving certain stumbling blocks along that path, it is true, but stumbling blocks that can be avoided or removed. With less genius than Descartes one makes better philosophers than Descartes; with less genius, yes, but with more circumspection. It is easy to make good use of his enlightenment while avoiding his excessive boldness. . . .

What we call "new philosophy" does not depend in any way on the Cartesian system. It can be said that Cartesianism is new philosophy, but not that new philosophy is Cartesian; just as one rightly says that man is an animal, but not that animals are men. . . .

The fifth cause is a zealousness, pious, it is true, but indiscreet and poorly founded; a vain fear that the new doctrines of philosophy will do some damage to religion. Those who are dominated by this religious fear are afraid that the damage will occur through two ways; either that certain maxims, which either on their own or through their consequences are opposed to what faith teaches, will arrive hidden inside foreign philosophical doctrines; or else, that as Spaniards grow accustomed to the liberty with which foreigners (the French, for example) discuss matters of nature, they will begin relaxing their restraints and reasoning with the same freedom about supernatural matters.

I say that neither of those seems likely to happen. The first will not happen because we have plenty of subjects who are skillful and well educated in dogma, who can distinguish what is opposed to faith from what is not, and who will alert the Holy Tribunal that watches over the purity of doctrine so that it will separate the liquor from the poison and throw the chaff into the fire, leaving the wheat intact. This remedy is always available to reassure us, even with respect to those philosophical opinions that come from countries infected with heresy. Beyond this, it is ignorance to believe that its venom is transmitted to all learning in all kingdoms where error reigns. In England, Newtonian philosophy reigns. Isaac Newton, its founder, was just as heretical as the rest of the inhabitants of that island generally are. And yet in his philosophy there has yet to be found anything that either directly or indirectly conflicts with true faith.

To assuage all reasonable fears on the second point, it is enough to note that theology and philosophy have their limits well marked out, and that no Spaniard is unaware that revealed doctrine has superior rights over human discourse, of which all the natural sciences are lacking. And consequently, one can argue freely in the latter field as in one's own territory, while one merely bends one's knee with veneration [in matters of religion]. But let us suppose that some person gets out of control and rashly seeks to tread across the sacred limit that the Church places against the excesses of human understanding. Isn't the remedy already available? Nowhere should one fear this problem less than in Spain, because of the vigilance of the Holy Tribunal, which can not only cut away the branches and the trunk, but can even rip out the deepest roots of the error. . . .

To close the door to all new doctrines . . . is a remedy that is, above all, unnecessary and very violent. It is to place the soul in a very hard condition of slavery. It is to tie down human reason with a very short chain. It is to place an innocent mind in a very small jail cell, simply to avoid a remote possibility that some will eventually commit some excesses.

The sixth and final cause is the resentment (perhaps we could give it a worse name) that is personal, national, and factional. If you examine some men's hearts . . . among those who denounce the new philosophy, or generally, to be more precise, all literature that is different from what they studied in the classroom, you will find in them some motives that are different from what they say. Listen to them denounce it either as useless or as dangerous. This is not really what is going on inside them. They do not disdain or hate it: they envy it. It is not the literature that displeases them, but rather the author who shines with it. . . .

This resentment in a few men is purely nationalistic. Spain has still not recovered in all its parts from its hatred of France. There are still very noticeable remains of this ancient ailment in some men. These men wish that the Pyrenees reached to the heavens and that the seas that wash upon the shores of France were filled with reefs so that no one could go from that nation to our own. This can be accepted among common people, and such attitudes can be tolerated among idiots, but it is insufferable in learned professors, who must be aware of the motives we have in common with other nations, especially with Catholics.

I recall having read in the *Causas célebres* by Gayot de Pitaval that a Spanish lady killed some parrots of Queen María Luisa de Borbón . . . out of indignation at hearing them speak French, so those miserable animals paid with their lives for having been taught a few words of French in Paris. Such anger and simplemindedness is not surprising in an ignorant woman. But not far from her is that irritating and fastidious disapproval with which some who should know better react to any citation from a French book, pretending to believe, and urging others to believe, that there are nothing but useless things in books written in that language. A few years ago a priest, a fine scholastic who had earned the highest honors of his religion, and a gentleman of this city did this, . . . saying that there could not be anything of any importance printed in the French language that was not printed in Latin or Spanish.

51. José Campillo y Cossío,
A New Economic Policy for America (1762)

The advent of the Bourbon dynasty in the eighteenth century led to important changes in the theory and practice of government in Spain, eventually affecting the colonies as well. By this time, Spain had lost its European possessions, making the American colonies all the more crucial, but Spain's control over the American empire had long been eroding, as Spain's rivals took over commerce with those colonies. At this point, old rules such as those restricting areas of Spain other than Castile from trading directly with America, and those requiring all goods to sail in annual convoys known as the fleets and galleons, made less and less sense.

As reformers envisioned changes, they often looked to policies enacted elsewhere, particularly Spain's dynastic relative, France. Spanish reformers particularly admired the steps Louis XIV had taken to make France a dominant power, steps that included the appointment of royal agents in the provinces, known as intendants. The most influential reformer interested in colonial affairs was José Campillo y Cossío, and many of the ideas presented here were indeed put into practice. Campillo's manuscript was circulating informally by the early 1740s, but was first published in 1762 as part of Bernardo Ward's *Proyecto Económico* (which seems to have plagiarized Campillo's manuscript). Campillo's work echoes the philosophies of various Enlightenment economic theorists as well as the mercantilist outlook of Louis XIV's chief minister, Jean-Baptiste Colbert (1619–1683).

SOURCE: José Campillo y Cossío, *Nuevo sistema de gobierno económico para la América* (Madrid: Imprenta de Benito Cano, 1789), 1–3, 8–14, 16, 19–21, 36, 38–49, 52–55, 60, 63–64, 68, 70–71, 73, 83–88, 93–95, 112–13, 115–16, 119, 175–76, 178.

Everything we see in that great part of the Spanish monarchy is demonstrating through cries of reason the need to introduce new methods in the governance of such a rich possession and such vast domains, full of such precious resources. This is the sole purpose of this work. In order to reveal more clearly the need for this important remedy, we will compare our Indies with foreign colonies, and we will see that the two islands of Martinique and Barbados alone bring more benefits to their owners than all the islands, provinces, kingdoms, and empires of America bring to Spain.

If the paucity of what the Indies produce for Spain derived solely from the kindness with which the Indians were treated, [the Spaniards] not wanting to burden them too heavily with tributes, that would be something tolerable. But the fate of those unfortunate people is quite the contrary, with their misery and oppression bringing no benefit to the sovereign. . . .

Mexico and Peru were two great empires in the hands of the natives, despite their barbarism. [Now] under a prudent and civilized nation, those provinces, which could be the richest in the universe, are uncultivated, un-populated, and almost totally destroyed. What is the source of this enormous contradiction? It derives, undoubtedly, from the fact that our system of rule is totally rotten, so much so that neither the skill, zeal, and effort of various ministers nor the vigilance and authority of all of the kings have managed, in this century, to repair the damage and disorder of the preceding century, nor will it ever be possible to do so until the governance of those domains is based on new principles. . . .

We have the largest market in the world within the confines of the king's domains. But it does us little good, since Spanish products account for scarcely one-twentieth of what is consumed in our Indies. The same is true regarding the population, cultivation, commerce, and other interests in which there could be improvements. Commerce is what maintains the body politic, just as the circulation of the blood maintains the human body, but in America . . . commerce is broadly obstructed. . . .

The treasures Spain possesses in America now do more harm than good. For nine-tenths [of the proceeds] go to foreign nations. And given that countries are only rich or powerful in comparison to each other, each million that goes to another nation without a corresponding million return-ing to Spain amounts to putting that nation on a higher level than ours and lowering ours in the process.

There are two main causes for this: the violation of the laws and the fail-ure of the government to enact policies suited to the changing circumstances of the time.

As for the first, which is so well known that it needs no explanation, I will simply note here the great distances involved; the ease of deceiving with false reports [and] finding friends when one has money; the oppression of the Indians, who lack the means to bring their complaints before the throne; the lack of punishment for these crimes, despite their being public; and the rarity of reward for those who arrived poor and worked hard; all of this has caused such monstrous harm in that new world that the powerful hand of a monarch such as ours is needed to solve the problem.

There have been occasions and moments when policies have been suited to the circumstances of the times. In the time of Philip II, all sorts of work-shops flourished in Spain and in the Low Countries under our rule, while neither France nor England had them, and there was no Dutch republic in the world. Spain was then the greatest naval power in Europe. The European nations did not have colonies in America, or else they were so weak that they were like scraps that Spain had thrown away.

At that point the rules excluding foreign goods had their full effect.

Spain supplied the Indies with its products, and the products brought back were all hers. At that time it was possible to impose rather high tariffs and place restrictions without thus impeding their ordinary circulation. But when all these circumstances favorable to Spain then changed, Spain . . . [should have] enacted new measures suited to the time. With foreigners having opened free and unencumbered paths to our Indies, the way to preserve that commerce was to facilitate the export of our products and goods in every way, placing low tariffs on them, or none at all. In this way, the products that would have gone from Cantabria, Galicia, Catalonia, and other low-cost provinces in the absence of high tariffs would have sold at the same prices, with little difference from foreign goods. And with the smuggler unable to make profits, the illicit commerce would not have materialized. The preservation of that consumption would have supported our workshops and agriculture in their previous flourishing state, and the products brought back from the Indies, which would have remained in the kingdom, would easily have made up to the royal treasury any amount lost through freeing Spanish exports from duties.

The opposite of all this is what actually happened, and with the new circumstances having been overlooked, . . . the old system is still carried on, taking into account neither the distance and extent of those domains, nor the proximity of the foreign colonies, nor the needs of those vassals [in the colonies], nor Spain's current inability to supply them or to prevent others from doing so openly. We have established, though neither intentionally nor knowingly, a system that has annihilated Spanish interests. . . .

Our American [subjects], finding such advantage in trading with foreigners, have made such mutually beneficial arrangements with them that even if the king spent everything the Indies produced in an effort to shield the colonies, he would still not succeed in keeping the foreign goods out, so long as Spanish goods are not available at more or less the same price. . . .

With the uncivilized Indians an equally mistaken system has been carried on. Were we to imitate the conduct of the French in Canada, who do not seek to subdue the natives but rather enjoy their friendship and commerce, we would experience the consequent effects, but we are always going about with arms in our hands, and the king spends millions to maintain an irreconcilable hatred with several nations, which, if dealt with properly and amicably, could bring us endless benefits. . . .

[There are] other abuses, such as trading through the system of fleets and galleons, and the charging of duties by the *palmeo* [with goods taxed based on their cubic volume]. In wartime it may have been necessary to use the fleet system, but in peacetime that only serves to impede that commerce.

It is no less useful to smugglers, giving them more than a year's advance notice, and allowing them to take their steps in time. . . .

The method of charging duties by the bundle, without opening them or assessing their value, has also contributed greatly to the ruin of Spain's commerce, for with this system, goods of great bulk and low value are excluded, and a package worth two pesos pays the same amount as one worth twenty. As a result, there being in America twenty poor people who need ordinary inexpensive goods for every rich person who wants fine goods, only the latter are supplied; one has not realized that in any country there must be many workshops making ordinary goods, for in addition to being those that employ the most people and account for the most consumption, they also extend their benefits more than the others, affecting the whole of the nation. So this policy is only useful to the foreigner, which is who makes these fine goods, while the Spaniard is excluded from a large part of this market, which could be the richest in the world. With these policies of such high duties and tariffs, . . . it can be said that we have closed the door to the Indies to the products of Spain while inviting the other nations to carry away their products. . . . As a result of all this, among the many abuses, two main ones stand out, which alone make the Indies useless to Spain. These are the allowing of smuggling and the creation of many workshops in Peru and New Spain [Mexico].

The use of a *visita general* [in which royal agents would investigate local conditions] will serve to give the king and his ministers the reports they need for two goals: to restore the governance of those domains and the prevailing order to their original state; and to prepare things for the establishment of the new system of economic policies. . . .

The lack of observance of some excellent laws has been the source of the spread of the evils that have wiped out those natives and made an entire world of riches useless to Spain. It is mainly for this reason that we must demand that the implementation of the perfectly fine laws must be the sole purpose of the visita. . . . We are not arguing that the original laws must all be observed strictly, nor that all practices contrary to them must be reformed; because of the normal passage of time, a law that made sense when created may become contrary and harmful to the very purpose it once had. . . . Even the viceroys and governors have had . . . to set aside their orders and follow what their own experience and judgment dictated, but at the same time, . . . this generally opens the door to all sorts of abuses.

Aside from this, in two and a half centuries, the variety of circumstances and cases that have occurred has made it necessary to make policies conform to specific events, and it is not surprising that amid so many royal decrees and policies, some are, or at least seem to be, contrary to others; that has left the king's good ministers in confusion and the bad ones free to do as they please.

This can be resolved by the *visita*, for when the king gets solid information about everything reform requires, he will be able to entrust the task to wise ministers who care passionately about the fatherland. . . . This investigation does not need to be carried out with such excessive meticulousness that it demands too much time. . . .

Concerning the clergy, . . . it seems that the size of the bishoprics has been decided not out of attention to the spiritual needs of the faithful, but in order to supply the bishop with sufficient revenue, for some of them are hundreds of leagues in size, where, because of a lack of roads, inns, and population, and the great distances involved, the bishop never visits his diocese. There is no need for the bishop to have fifty thousand pesos in income, but there is a need for the priests and other ecclesiastics to have an immediate superior who watches over their conduct.

The reason I speak of this matter is that I have heard a thousand times about the missionaries tyrannizing the poor Indians terribly. . . . These things might not happen, or would be reduced in many places, if the ranking prelate could see what was going on. . . .

The great number of both sexes who enter the ecclesiastical estate, both as secular and regular clergy, is a subject that demands the sovereign's full attention. No one can prohibit one from entering the estate to which God calls one, but a good government must take away the motives that might incline a person to enter the ecclesiastical estate without a true calling.

The immunity [from taxation] that this estate enjoys for its goods—even if they do not belong to the Church—is very harmful to the Crown, given the great wealth that the religious orders and other institutions possess. . . . In America, the son of a man of substance, not being inclined [by his social status] to go into commerce, has no career available to him, which leads to the foundation of too many religious bodies simply in order to be sure of having bread, and when there are men who do not marry, there are women who cannot find anyone to marry. . . .

The great and principal purpose of the *visita* being the establishment of a new economic policy, the commissioners . . . will take note as quickly as possible of the population of each district; of the inhabitants' inclinations; of the way in which men and women occupy themselves; of their ways of living and dressing; of their inclination toward or against industriousness; of the products indigenous to each province; of the means of increasing and improving those exported to Europe; of the workshops that exist in both kingdoms [Peru and Mexico]; of the number of looms; of the goods on which they work; of the class of people they supply with them; and of the price at which each item is sold.

They will examine with the greatest care all that concerns commerce, and they will expound at length on the means of increasing the consumption of Spanish products in each of those provinces. They will take note of the consumption of unnecessary items, of tobacco, sugar, liquor, cocoa, spices, tea, etc., as well as the prices of necessities, of foods, things used for clothing, and how much artisans and laborers earn each day. . . .

Concerning tributes and royal tariffs, they will look into the nature of each one, the means of collecting them, and whether there is fraud, abuses, or excessive expenses in their collection. . . .

The Indians themselves are the great object upon which the commissioners carrying out these visits must focus their attention, efforts, love, and undertakings. This is the great treasure of Spain; they are the essence of the Indies and the richest mine in the world, and they should benefit from the most scrupulous economic policies. Everything else pales in comparison with this, a matter that is in such a state of neglect. Twelve or fifteen million rational vassals of the king, the most submissive in the universe . . . needlessly bear the heaviest burden in the land. . . .

If we want to have a clear concept of what should be done, . . . we should look for a moment at what France or England would do if they possessed our American empire, for one can easily infer what they would do from what they do in their colonies and European states. . . . But although we can generally study their example, there are nonetheless various points on which our interests differ from theirs . . . and though we may find some part of their method that is not relevant or applicable to our circumstances, we can still use the main spirit of their system, which consists, first, of preferring the preservation and good use of men over new conquests . . . ; second, of giving the vassals all the ways and means of enriching themselves, as the only sure way to make the royal treasury and state rich; third, of considering those who cultivate the land . . . ; fourth, of substituting for the unbearable weight of taxes and tributes the voluntary contribution of commerce and consumption . . . ; fifth, of viewing liberty as the soul of commerce. . . . Commerce is no mystery. Natural enlightenment, which is common to everyone, shows us the principles on which it rests. . . .

Since the sole object of this work is to deal with everything that can . . . turn some men, who have scarcely been considered rational, into an industrious nation dedicated to agriculture and the arts, the key to all this . . . is to place intendants in those provinces. . . . The intendants' first task must be to carry out the *visitas* of their respective departments in the terms described [above]. . . .

The good of the republic resting mainly on the cultivation of the land and the useful employment of its men, who constitute the true power and the solid wealth of all nations, these are the two matters that merit most attention. And it is a rule without exception that the land will never be well cultivated [if those who work it do not own it], nor will a man do as much working for another as he would if the product of his labor were his. . . .

England has something like six thousand square leagues of terrain and five and a half million inhabitants. These inhabitants are all free in their persons and properties. . . . The Russian empire must contain more than one hundred thousand square leagues, more or less, with almost twenty-five to thirty million souls, and the sovereign is the owner of lands, lives, and properties. Now the six thousand leagues of England, cultivated . . . by five and a half million free, property-owning men, produce for their sovereign four times as much as the hundred thousand leagues and the thirty million Russian serfs do for theirs. This, if I am not mistaken, seems to be sufficient proof to know how important it is that lands be given as property to our Indians and, consequently, that they be allowed full and peaceful possession of all the fruits of their labor. . . .

As for the Indians' [supposed] incapacity, I cannot believe that it is as bad as many think it is, even denying that they are rational beings. If we look at what they were before meeting the Europeans, they must have had some enlightenment in order to found great cities, construct great buildings, found powerful empires, live under fixed civil and military laws, and have their own sort of religion and ideas of divinity. . . . Even if I admit that they are as some portray them, that is either because long years of oppression have reduced them to barbarism (as happens with the modern Greeks, descendants of those great captains, philosophers, and statesmen of antiquity, who were masters of the world), or else because they really do have less natural abilities; yet even that would not undermine what we are saying, which is to make useful vassals out of them, for we see here in Europe, among the most civilized nations, that the most useful men are those who have the least enlightenment: namely, country people, farmers, herders, et al. It is not necessary in a monarchy for all to engage in discourse or to have great talents; it is enough that the greatest number know how to work, while those who rule, who are the ones who need superior enlightenment, are few in number. The many need only bodily strength and the docility to allow themselves to be governed. . . .

[Therefore] any lands that the kings have not already granted should be given to the Indians to cultivate, with royal dispatches assuring them and their descendants the possession of the lands, which should remain rent-free for fifteen or twenty years on the condition that after that period they will pay the king an amount deemed fair. But the clause should be added that if the land is not placed in cultivation within those fifteen or twenty years, it will revert to the Crown to be given to other, more industrious vassals.

What causes notable damage is that very large pieces of land are granted to Spaniards who cultivate them only using the labor of Negroes and Indians; and naturally, . . . those groups do not apply themselves to the work, since neither the produce nor the lands belong to them. It has already been observed in Europe that where the land is distributed in small plots and cultivated by the landowners' own hands, they produce four times as much as lands that are in the hands of administrators or serfs. . . .

As for workshops, though they are generally desirable and consistent with other nations' practice, they must in no way be permitted in America. . . . Not allowing workshops, which do harm to the few that exist in Spain today or the many that there could and should be, . . . conforms to all reason and good policy. . . . It will also be possible to reserve for Spain certain arts that use materials that we have within the kingdom, such as iron, copper, tin, brass, and any kind of hardware. . . . The arts that should be permitted in America are, first, those that Spain does not have nor should have in the future; second, those whose materials are found in good quality and low price in America, and which we do not have in Spain; and third, those arts and manufactures for which there is a market so large that Spain could never supply it. . . .

If all who want to are allowed to trade freely and go to the Indies, many will undoubtedly go, the goods will become cheaper, merchandise of all kinds for all classes of buyers will be taken, and from all of this will come great consumption, giving employment to the vassals, promoting industry, and enriching the nation. . . . In this way smuggling will also be wiped out, particularly in all those classes of goods that will be made in Spain, since, although the smugglers do not pay tariffs, they must pay many other expenses, and if they have to sell more cheaply than we do, they will not make much money, and so for such little profit they will not take the risk of falling into the hands of our coastal guards.

52. Laws of the Bourbon Monarchy

When the Bourbon dynasty came to Spain in 1700, it kept many of the existing laws on the books, but many of the new laws passed after 1700 reflect the spirit of enlightened absolutism that marked much of Europe in that era. What follows is a selection of the new laws added by the Bourbons and published along with the older laws in a comprehensive collection in the first decade of the nineteenth century. Note that a serious rebellion, known as the Esquilache rebellion, broke out in 1766. A new regulation freeing the grain trade from price controls had already caused considerable unrest—spurred on by nobles and other powerful groups resentful of the Crown's authority and actions—and against that background new regulations restricting the use of capes and hats that concealed people's identities triggered serious outbreaks of violence and public protest. As for the regulations on bullfighting, it should be noted that this piece of legislation was part of a long series of largely ineffective decrees against the activity.

SOURCE: *Novísima recopilación de las leyes de España* (Madrid, 1805).

On Clothing

Book VI, Title I, Law XIV (1766): I [Charles III] have found it undesirable that the subjects who are employed in my royal service and offices wear the broad cape and round hat, clothing that serves for disguising and concealing persons in Madrid and the roads surrounding it, to the dishonor of those very subjects, and in addition to exposing them to many problems, it is improper for the resplendence of the court, and of the very persons who should present themselves everywhere with the distinction I have bestowed upon them. Wishing to end these abuses, which are also harmful to good politics and government, I have resolved that orders should be given to the commanders of the troops . . . and other officials, to inform all individuals that under no conditions may they wear the broad cape, the round hat, or any other disguise. They should instead . . . go about in appropriate dress, wearing a short cape or riding coat, a wig or their own hair, and a three-cornered hat . . . so that they will always go about uncovered.

On the Theater

Book VII, Title XXXIII, Law IX (1753, 1763): In order to avoid the disorders created by the mixing of the sexes in the darkness of night, plays will begin . . . at four o'clock sharp in the afternoon from Easter until the last day of September, and at two-thirty from October 1 until Lent, and the appointed hour cannot be postponed for any reason or pretext, even on the orders of persons of authority. Authors shall take care not to render this decree ineffectual by using lengthy and bothersome interludes and supporting performances, tailoring the entertainment and limiting it to three hours, . . . so that it ends before sunset.

The troops that serve the mayor, deployed at the gates of the theaters, shall not allow coaches to linger after their owners have gotten out, but shall instead make them leave the street to wait in the usual places. . . .

Before the play begins, as well as after it ends, idle men hidden in capes shall not be allowed to loiter, as if planted, on the street corners and near the doors of the theaters and especially near those where women are exiting the upper galleries.

No one hidden beneath a cape shall be allowed to enter the theaters, nor shall anyone with a hat, cap, or other disguise that hides the face, for all must go about uncovered so that they can be recognized, thus avoiding the problems that the opposite situation would cause.

In the doors and entryways of the theaters, water and fruit vendors shall not be allowed; inside the theaters, only men of good reputation and customs, as established by the officials in charge of the theater, shall be allowed to sell these items.

Both during the play and before it, no one shall light tobacco cigarettes, nor smoke a pipe, because of the risk of fire and because of the offense that the smoke and the odor causes for the other spectators.

No man shall enter the galleries reserved for women under any pretext, nor shall they speak with the women in those galleries from the other galleries or from the patio. And at the end of the play, men in capes shall not be allowed in the aisles, with officials and soldiers being stationed there to prevent this and the unfortunate incidents that could otherwise occur there. . . .

In the box seats and booths on all levels, there shall be no blinds drawn, and the people occupying them shall show the appropriate decency, with men not wearing hats and with women not covering their faces with scarves. . . .

It is not allowed to present plays, interludes, dances, one-act plays, or songs without first obtaining permission from the ecclesiastical judge of the town, and also presenting them at the city hall. . . .

In the presentation of the works, and especially with interludes, dances, one-act plays, and songs, the authors will show great concern to preserve the appropriate modesty, . . . not permitting indecent and provocative dances and songs that could cause the slightest scandal.

The authors will be equally responsible for anything done by any actor in the troupe who might come out on the stage dressed indecently. . . .

Book VII, Title XXXIII, Law XII (1801): The censorship of plays, in terms of their appropriateness or inappropriateness, assumes the approval of the ecclesiastical vicar, along with the subdelegate censor. . . .

In no theater in Spain may one present, sing, or dance any work that is not in the Castilian language or [is not] acted by actors or actresses who are natives or are naturalized in these kingdoms. . . .

Prohibited from now on are so-called traveling theater companies, whose mobility is generally prejudicial to good customs, and whose members are composed of corrupt persons, full of misery and vices, discrediting the theatrical profession. . . .

Just as the subdelegate censors must watch over and correct all the imperfections of the art in the theaters and companies, the local committees will watch carefully to see that proper decency, composure, and decorum are maintained, with their presiding officers correcting or punishing any actor or actress who violates said decorum.

On Bullfighting

Book VII, Title XXXIII, Law VIII (1790): Considering the bad consequences that have been and will always be caused by the abuse, which is frequent in many towns of the kingdom, of running bulls . . . through the streets in either daytime or night; and in light of the news given to my royal person of the unfortunate events that recently occurred in some of these entertainments; and wishing to stop this pernicious abuse that produces deaths, injuries, and other excesses to which the vassals would be exposed were it continued and tolerated, I prohibit . . . the abuse of running bulls . . . through the streets both in daytime and night. . . .

Book VII, Title XXXIII, Law VII (1804, 1805): I have chosen to completely prohibit the fighting of bulls to the death, anywhere in the kingdom, including the capital. . . .

On Girls' Education

Book VIII, Title I, Law X (1783): Given the good effects that we have seen from the establishment of a school for the education of poor girls from the Mira el Río neighborhood of Madrid, . . . I have ordered . . . that other such schools be established in the rest of Madrid. . . .

Article I. This establishment's goal and principal objective is to help promote throughout the entire kingdom the proper education of young girls in the rudiments of the Catholic faith, in the rules of good behavior, in the exercise of the virtues, and in the labors appropriate to their sex, guiding the girls from their infancy, . . . as it is the fundamental root of the preservation and growth of religion, and the matter that most interests the good policy and economic government of the state. This instruction . . . has the most exceptional usefulness for the public good; . . . not only does it allow for the raising of diligent young ladies, but it also grants them security and direction for the future. . . .

Article V. 1. The first thing that the teachers will teach . . . will be the prayers. . . [and] Christian doctrine, through the method of the catechism [as well as] the maxims of modesty and proper customs; the girls will be obliged to be clean and well groomed. . . and to maintain themselves . . . with modesty and calm.

2. During all the time they are in the school, they must be devoted to their labors, each one in that which corresponds to her and which has been assigned to her by the teacher, who will see to it that it is done properly and that no one disturbs anyone else. . . .

3. The tasks . . . must be the usual ones, beginning with the easiest, such as beltmaking, hosiery, knitting, patterns, hemstitching, sewing, and then moving on to finer tasks such as embroidery and lacemaking; at other times, according to the judgment of the teacher, [they will make] . . . tassels, pockets, various stitches, homemade ribbons of yarn or silk, braids . . . and all kinds of ribbons, or those parts of this work that are possible, or for which the various students show aptitude. . . .

4. The students who advance most rapidly and distinguish themselves by their good conduct and progress shall, on the recommendation of the headmistress, be awarded some prize. . . .

Article VIII. The teachers will use a clear and plain style when explaining things . . . and will not allow the girls to use indecent or improper words, nor those that are said to be used by . . . majas. [A maja was a belle, a fashionable and worldly young woman, and a morally controversial figure.]

Article IX. The teachers and their assistants will be in school, teaching the girls, four hours each morning and four hours each afternoon. . . .

Article X. The girls whose parents have the means to pay for their daughters' education will contribute to the teachers' pay the moderate sums that have up until now been normal; . . . the poor will be taught free of charge.

Article XI. The principal object of these schools must be the labor of their hands; but if any of the girls should wish to learn to read, the teachers will have the obligation of teaching them, and consequently they must be examined in this skill with the greatest diligence.

Considering . . . that these establishments will be able to produce the same advantages in the capitals, cities, and populous towns of these, my kingdoms, I have ordered my council, in conformance with what the aforesaid report proposed, that these regulations be extended to them insofar as it is suitable to each one's circumstances.

On Work and Honor

Book VIII, Title XXIII, Law VIII (1783): Permission for artisans and employees to hold state office on production of evidence of their integrity and respectability.

We hereby decree that the trades practiced not only by the tanner but by the blacksmith, the tailor, the cobbler, the joiner, and all other occupations of that kind are respectable and honorable, that such a trade in no way demeans the family or the person that practices it, and that to practice such a trade in no way disqualifies a person from holding public office, . . . nor does the practice of such arts and trades disqualify a person from the rank and privileges of a gentleman, should he have lawful right to such estate . . . unless such an artisan or workman should abandon his trade and that of his forefathers and not apply himself diligently to some other honorable art or profession to his betterment, unless he does so because his financial state no longer requires him to work at all. In consideration of this our decree, our council shall, in the case of persons whose families have practiced the same trade or profession for at least three generations, through father, son, and grandson, to the benefit and profit of the state, point them out to us, as we have ordered, as being worthy of such a distinction being conferred on that person who can prove himself head and supporter of that family, and we shall grant such an application, including even a claim to nobility, if we judge such persons worthy of it in light of their achievements in the crafts and trades.

On Women's Work

Book VIII, Title XXIII, Law XIV (1779): Having advised my royal council how damaging it was to industry to allow the monopolies and privileges that various guilds had managed, without a proper investigation, . . . to create rules preventing women from doing jobs that are as suitable and proper to their sex as they are to men; and keeping in mind that the guild of the lace makers, passementerie makers, and button makers of the city of Valencia has sought to prevent the girls' school from teaching things concerning the lace-making trade, as the Economic Society of Friends of that city had proposed, it has seemed fitting, in order to avoid similar privileges, to make known what I consider proper. Having followed the recommendation of the council, I had orders sent to the effect that that guild . . . or any other . . . should not under any pretext or motive prevent . . . anyone from teaching girls and women to make buttons, or any other such craft that is suitable to their sex and to women's powers; and that those who know how to make or produce those things should be allowed to sell them on their own freely, and in this way those hands will not be idle. . . .

At the same time my council was asked to continue the inquiry it had begun regarding the ordinances of the guilds . . . , to reform everything they contained that was impeding the promotion of industry; . . . and considering the well-known advantages that are to be had by women and girls being employed in occupations suitable to their capacities, and in which they may have some earnings, which may serve as a dowry for their marriages, and which may help others to support their households and meet their expenses; and that the men who are employed in these lesser kinds of manufacturing should devote themselves to more demanding occupations . . . ; so that this important objective should be met . . . , by a document of December 23, this decree was made.

By that decree I command all of you, each and every one of you in your respective districts . . . that under no pretext may you impede, prevent, or allow your guild or any other person to prevent or obstruct the teaching of women and girls of all those labors and crafts that are suitable to their sex; [nor may anyone prevent] the selling by them of the manufactures that they may have made despite the respective ordinances that the said guilds or their masters have had.

On Games of Chance

Book XII, Title XXIII, Law XV (1771): Having learned with great displeasure that in the capital and other towns of the kingdom various games have been introduced and continue, games in which increasingly large sums are risked, leading to very serious damage to the public good, with the ruin of many households, with the distraction caused for the persons captive to this vice, and with the disorders and disturbances that often follow from this activity, . . . I have ordered the present pragmatic sanction carrying the force of law. [The decree then lists a long series of prohibited games.]

On Riots and Uprisings

Book XII, Title XI, Law III (1766): We declare null and void all the pardons that have been or may be granted by the magistrates, city councils, or other authorities to those who have perpetrated, assisted, or incited riots and violent acts, as this is the prerogative of the supreme royal authority. . . .

Any person who has committed or shall commit the crime of being an agitator, auxiliary, or voluntary participant in these riots, disturbances, mutinies, public outcries, popular seditions, or tumults shall because of that very fact be noted for life (in addition to personally suffering, in their persons and property, the penalties imposed by the laws of the kingdom against those who cause or abet mutiny or rebellion) as enemies of the fatherland, of infamous and despicable memory for all civil purposes, being destroyers of the pact of society that unites all peoples and vassals with the supreme head of state. . . .

Book XII, Title XI, Law V (1774): The repeated experience of the government has demonstrated in all times that one cannot guarantee the happiness of the vassals unless one maintains the authority of justice in all its vigor, securing the necessary observance of the laws and the measures designed to contain unruly spirits, enemies of public tranquility, and defending the worthy vassals from their pernicious mischief. This important goal has always deserved kings' highest attention, leading to the successive promulgation of repeated laws preventing popular uprisings and disturbances. . . .

In that the defense of public tranquility is an interest and an obligation naturally incumbent on all of my vassals, I thus declare that in such circumstances no *fuero* or exemption can have any force, even if it be of the most privileged person, and I prohibit everyone without exception from alleging otherwise. . . .

The premeditated maliciousness of the riotous delinquents is generally prepared with cruel intentions through pasquinades [public political signs] and seditious papers posted in public places or distributed clandestinely. . . . The authorities shall be very attentive and vigilant in order to intervene and preempt their pernicious consequences. . . . I declare to be accomplices in these undertakings those who copy, read, or hear read such seditious papers without immediately informing the authorities; and for their security, if they do not want to be implicated in the acts in question, they must offer their names in secret testimony. . . .

Those who out of curiosity or chance happen to be in the streets for any reason [during a riot] must return to their houses, under penalty of being treated as disobeying the orders that are posted in all public places. . . .

Given that on such occasions the rebels tend to take over the bell towers, creating confusion among their neighbors by ringing the bells and thus profaning the sacred temples with violence and sometimes the spilling of blood, the authorities . . . shall take care to guard the bell towers safely and close the convents and their residences and temples. . . .

I prohibit the judges from using any discretion at all in the sentencing of these cases . . . and I order that in all of them they should proceed strictly according to the laws. In the contrary case, which I do not hope for, I will consider myself disobeyed, and I will order that steps be taken against those who are transgressors of my sovereign intentions. . . .

On the Gypsies

Book XII, Title XVI, Law VII (1695–1726): It being very appropriate to establish a new form . . . to assure the persecution and punishment of those who call themselves Gypsies, who with the frequency and seriousness of their crimes disturb the calm of the towns, the security of the roads, and the good faith of the markets and fairs, where it is so important, it has seemed fitting to order a new law and decree in this area. . . .

The Gypsies who are to remain and be tolerated in these kingdoms . . . cannot have any occupation or way of life other than that of farming and cultivating the fields, in which their women and children of age may also assist them, with no other kind of employment or commerce being permitted for them, which we expressly prohibit, especially blacksmithing. . . .

The Gypsies who remain as fixed inhabitants may not have horses or mares in their houses or outside of them, nor use them in any way; if they are caught or found out to have them, they shall suffer the confiscation of those horses and mares . . . and they will be given a penalty of two months in jail. . . .

They may not have short or long firearms of any kind in their houses or outside them, and if they are found with them . . . they shall incur the penalty of two hundred lashes and eight years in the galleys. . . .

The district magistrates and judicial officials of each place in which Gypsies live have the obligation to visit and inspect their houses personally as often as they see fit, to find out whether they have any of these things prohibited here; and they must also remain well informed about their way of life and customs, in order to apply the appropriate remedies.

The residents may not go to or attend fairs or markets, and if they are found in violation of this . . . they shall incur by that fact a penalty of six years in the galleys; and the same shall be applied even if they are not caught there, but if it is proven that they went to a market or fair. . . .

The residents may not live in neighborhoods separate from the others, nor wear clothing that differs from that which is commonly worn, nor speak the language they call the Gypsy language, under penalty of six years in the galleys for the men, and one hundred lashes and exile from the kingdom for the women. . . .

And we order that if those who call themselves Gypsies are apprehended in bands of more than three, with short or long firearms, on foot or on horseback, . . . they shall incur the death penalty. . . .

On Insults, Affronts, and Obscene Words

Book XII, Title XXV, Law VII (1765): In order to cut the root of the abuse introduced in this capital of playing *cencerradas* ["rough music," taunting by noise and singing] for widows and widowers who remarry, and to end the disturbances, scandals, disorders, and disgraceful acts that may result, it is ordered that no one of any rank or condition shall go about, alone or accompanied, through the streets with cowbells, noisemakers, bells, or other instruments, causing a racket out of this motive. . . .

Book XII, Title XXV, Law VIII (1766, 1804): By this kingdom's laws . . . the composition of pasquinades, satires, verses, manifestos, and other seditious papers insulting to public figures or to any private citizen is prohibited.

Book XII, Title XXV, Law X (1803): The uttering in the streets of blasphemies, oaths, and curses has become too common, and the same holds for the use of scandalous gestures and words even in family conversations, contrary to what is demanded by religion and forbidden by justice, which abhors and detests such language. Neither the laws that proscribe these things, nor the ministers who must execute them, will be able to remedy the evils it causes if fathers, with respect to their children, and masters, with respect to their servants, do not take care to fulfill the duties their position imposes on them, and if they continue to fail to correct and punish [these acts]. . . .

The owners of public houses, such as taverns, billiard rooms, cafés, and other such places shall be held responsible for the lack of observance [of these laws], and as a penalty they will be shut down.

53. The Count of Aranda,
On the Independence of the Colonies (1783)

Pedro Pablo Abarca de Bolea (1718–1798), count of Aranda, was a grandee who held several high government positions during his long career. As Spain's ambassador to the court of France during the American War of Independence, Aranda oversaw Spain's policy of collaborating with France to help the American rebels in their struggle against Britain. This letter, written at the end of the war, presents a thoughtful assessment of the situation in Spain's colonial empire and a useful statement of what at least one important Spanish official considered most important about the colonies. Although Aranda may now seem prescient, his views on the colonies were not widely shared at the time, and the Crown did not attempt to implement his recommendations.

SOURCE: Pedro Pablo Abarca de Bolea, *Díctamen reservado que el Conde de Aranda dio al Rey sobre la independencia de las colonias inglesas* (1783); reprinted in Juan Nido y Segalerva, *Antología de las Cortes de 1879 y 1881* (Madrid: Prudencio P. de Velasco, 1912), 12–17.

A Report Reserved for King Charles III on the Province of America

Lord: The love I have for the august person of Your Majesty . . . and the affection I hold for my country move me to give Your Majesty an account of an idea to which I attach the greatest importance in the current circumstances. In virtue of orders and powers that Your Majesty has seen fit to give me, I have just arranged and signed (September 3, 1783) a peace treaty with England. This negotiation, which, according to the flattering oral and written testimony of Your Majesty, I must believe that I have managed to carry out in accordance with your royal intentions, has left in my soul, I must admit, a painful feeling.

The independence of the English colonies stands recognized, and this is for me a source of pain and fear. France has few possessions in America, but it has had to consider that Spain, its close ally, has many and that from now on they will be exposed to the most terrible disturbances. From the beginning, France has operated contrary to its true interests, aiding and abetting this independence [of England's American colonies], and I have often declared this to the ministers of that nation. What more advantageous event could happen to France than to see the English and the North Americans destroy each other in a partisan war, which could do no less than increase its power by favoring its interests? The antipathy that exists between France and England blinded the French cabinet to the point that it forgot that its interest consisted in remaining a calm spectator of this struggle. And once it launched itself into the arena, it forced us, unfortunately, because of the Family Pact [the alliance between the Bourbon kingdoms of France and Spain], into a war that was completely contrary to our own cause.

This is not the place to examine the opinion of some statesmen, Spanish and foreign, with which I agree, concerning the difficulties of retaining our empire in America. Such vast possessions, located at such great distance from the metropolis, have never managed to be retained for very long. To this general cause affecting all colonies, one must add other causes specific to the Spanish possessions: namely, the difficulty of sending necessary aid; the irritation between some governors and their unfortunate inhabitants; the distance that separates them from the supreme authority to which they can turn when seeking reparation for their grievances, which is the cause for the fact that years sometimes pass without their request being addressed; the vengeance by local authorities, to which they remain exposed in the meantime; the difficulty of really knowing the truth at such a great distance; and finally, the means that the viceroys and governors, as Spaniards, cannot fail to use to obtain manifestations favorable to Spain. Together, these circumstances can do no less than upset the inhabitants of America, moving them to make efforts in order to secure independence as soon as the occasion arises.

So without getting into any of these considerations, I will limit myself for now to . . . the fear of seeing ourselves exposed to serious dangers at the hands of a new power we have just recognized, in a country in which there is no other in a position to clip its wings. This federal republic has been born a pygmy, so to speak, and it needed the support and power of two states as powerful as Spain and France to win its independence. The day will come in which it grows and turns into a giant, even a frightening colossus, in that region. It will then forget the benefits it has received from the two powers, and it will only think of its own expansion. Freedom of conscience, the ability to establish a new population in immense lands, as well as the advantages of a new government, will attract to them farmers and artisans from all nations. And within a few years we will see with real dismay the tyrannical existence of this colossus of which I am speaking. The first step for this power, once it has managed its rise to power, will be to take over Florida, in order to dominate the Gulf of Mexico. After harassing us and our relations with New Spain in this way, it will aspire to conquer this vast empire, which we will not be able to defend against a formidable power established in that very continent and a neighbor of it.

These fears are very well founded, lord, and they will undoubtedly come true within a few years if we do not first witness other, more unfortunate disturbances in our America. What has happened in all centuries and all nations that have begun to grow powerful justifies this way of thinking. Man is the same everywhere; differences of climate do not change the nature of our sentiments, and he who finds an opportunity to acquire power and to elevate himself never disdains that opportunity. So how can we promise ourselves that the North Americans will respect the kingdom of New Spain when they have the means to take over that rich and beautiful country? A wise policy would advise us to take precautions against the evils that could prevail. This thought has occupied all of my attention ever since, as a plenipotentiary minister of Your Majesty, and in accordance with your royal will and instructions, I signed the Paris Peace Treaty, studying such an important matter with all the care of which I am capable. And after great reflection, suggested to me by the knowledge, both military and political, that I have been able to acquire in my long career, I believe firmly that we have no way to avoid the great losses that threaten us, other than the recourse I am going to have the honor to expound to Your Majesty.

Your Majesty must get rid of all his possessions in the continent of both Americas, keeping only the islands of Cuba and Puerto Rico in the northern part and some other that may be appropriate in the southern part, with the object that they serve us as a port of call or a depot for Spanish commerce.

In order to carry out this great thought in a manner suitable to Spain, three princes must be established in America; one as king of Mexico; another as king of Peru, and another as king of Costafirme, with Your Majesty taking the title of emperor. The conditions for this immense cession could be that the three new kings and their successors would recognize Your Majesty and the princes who will later occupy the throne as supreme heads of the family; that the king of Mexico would pay a contribution of a specific number of silver marks as feudal dues each year for the cession of that kingdom, which will be sent in bars to be minted in the mints of Madrid and Seville. The king of Peru would do the same, paying in gold for his possessions. That of Costafirme would remit his contribution in colonial goods each year, above all in tobacco, to supply the government stores of this kingdom. These sovereigns and their sons will have to marry princesses of Spain or its family, and the Spanish princes will marry princesses from the overseas kingdoms. In this way an intimate union will be established among the four Crowns, and before any of these sovereigns can occupy the throne, they would have to solemnly swear that they will observe these conditions.

Trade will have to be carried out under the strictest reciprocity, with the four nations having to be considered united by the closest offensive and defensive alliance for their conservation and prosperity. With our factories not being in a position to supply America with all the manufactures that may be needed there, it would be essential that France, our ally, supply all the articles we find ourselves unable to send, to the absolute exclusion of England. Toward this end, the three sovereigns, upon occupying their respective thrones, would arrange formal commercial treaties with Spain and France, taking great care to exclude the English. As possessors of new states, they will be able to do what they wish freely.

The following advantages would result from the execution of such a plan: the contribution of the three kingdoms of the New World would be much more advantageous for Spain than the assistance in cash that it currently sends to America; the population would increase, ending the continuous emigration to such faraway possessions, and once the three kingdoms of America were closely linked by means of the proposed obligations, there would be no country in Europe that could equal its power, nor any in our continent that could equal that of Spain and France. At the same time there would be the force to impede the rise to power of the American colonies, or that of any other power that might be established in that part of the world. With the union of the new kingdoms and Spain, Spanish commerce would exchange national products for colonial goods that we may need for our consumption. In this way our merchant marine would grow, and our navy consequently would be respected in all the seas. The islands I have cited above, if administered well and placed in a good state of defense, would suffice for our commerce, without any need for other possessions, and, finally, we would enjoy all the advantages that the possession of America gives us, without any of the disadvantages.

Such are, lord, my ideas concerning this delicate point; if it manages to merit Your Majesty's sovereign approval, I will enter into more detailed clarifications, explaining the means of putting them into practice, with all necessary secrecy and precautions, so that England will not notice it until the three princes are on their way and are closer to America than to Europe, thus preventing England from opposing it. This would be a terrible blow for such an arrogant rival; but first we would have to prepare the means we would have to use to shelter ourselves from the effects of its anger. To assure the execution of this plan, it would be wise to reach an accord with France, our intimate ally, which would lend itself to it without difficulty, upon seeing the advantages that would derive from the establishment of its [royal] family on the thrones of the New World, as well as the special protection that will be given to its commerce throughout that hemisphere, excluding England, its implacable rival.

54. Josefa Amar,
In Defense of the Talent of Women (1786)

The daughter of an Aragonese physician and a nobleman, Josefa Amar y Borbón (1749–1833) moved to Madrid as a young girl, when her father obtained a position as one of the king's doctors. There she was tutored by the king's librarian, among others at the royal court, and she also educated herself, learning foreign languages and reading extensively on her own. After marrying in 1764, she returned to Aragon, where she and her husband raised a family. While in Aragon, she continued her scholarship, translating works into Castilian, and eventually receiving the honor of being the first woman elected to membership in the Sociedad Económica de Aragon. Amar wrote this essay and submitted it to the Sociedad Económica de Madrid, which in 1786 was debating whether to admit women as members, and which indeed chose to do so.

SOURCE: *Memorial literario, instructivo y curioso de la Corte de Madrid*, vol. 8, no. 3 (August 1786): 399–430; the text also appears in A. María Aguado et al., eds., *Textos para la historia de las mujeres en España* (Madrid: Cátedra, 1994), 238–40.

When God turned the world over to the disputes of men, he foresaw that there would be infinite points over which people would always quarrel, without ever reaching agreement. It seems that one of these must be the understanding of women. On the one hand men seek their approval and give them some kinds of praise they never give each other; they do not allow them to command in public affairs, . . . they deny them education and then complain that they do not have it. I say that they deny it, for there is no public establishment intended for the education of women, nor any reward that would inspire them in this endeavor. On the other hand, they blame them for almost all the problems that result. If the courage of our heroes is weakening, if ignorance prevails in people's dealings with one another, if customs have become corrupted, if luxury and extravagance are ruining families, women are said to be the cause of all these problems. . . .

In truth, the applause and praise of men, like the charges made against women, are a tacit confession of their understanding, for otherwise they would not seek their approval. . . .

Men not being content with having reserved jobs, honors, and useful positions for themselves . . . , they have deprived women even of the satisfaction that results from having enlightened minds. They are born and raised in absolute ignorance: men disdain them for that reason, women come to persuade themselves that they are not capable of other things, and as if they had their talent in their hands, they do not cultivate other skills than those that can be carried out with their hands. How far behind opinion is in these matters! If opinion sees the principal value in all women in their beauty, in their gracefulness, in their discretion, we soon see them very intent upon acquiring these things, as they are now intent on seeming beautiful and lovely. May men amend their ways first. . . . In the meantime, do not blame women if they only seek to adorn their bodies. . . .

But how can one expect such a necessary change if these very men treat women so unequally? In one part of the world they are slaves, in the other they are dependents. Let us speak of the first part of the world. What progress can they make while surrounded by tyrants instead of companions? Under such conditions it would be better to be completely ignorant, so that women would not fully feel the weight of their chains. If they could want anything, or attempt anything, it should be to become educated and to civilize those men, hoping that the use of reason will break the chains that ignorance now maintains. . . . Violence cannot establish universal laws; but that is indeed how women have been forced into submission, and how tyranny and ignorance have arisen in the land. . . .

The situation in this other part of the world appears to be different. Women, far from being called slaves, are entirely free, and they enjoy certain privileges that come close to being veneration. Both religion and the laws prevent men from having multiple wives, . . . and this contributes to the two viewing each other with respect and esteem. Men have even done more to favor us, for they have almost completely monopolized the authority that comes from having jobs and property, while all men pay tribute to women. What generosity! What magnanimity, . . . and yet what contradiction! This is where the state of dependence, mentioned earlier, begins.

Educated and civilized men do not dare to oppress the other half of the human race so openly, for they do not find such slavery implied in the laws of creation. Yet given that domination brings pleasure, they have managed to arrogate to themselves a certain superiority of talent, or I might say of enlightenment, the lack of which makes women seem inferior. There are few men who, in matters of aptitude and intellectual qualifications, allow women what is needed for the enlightenment of their minds. Women know that they cannot aspire to any public position or honor and that their ideas reach no further than the walls of the home or of a convent. If that is not enough to suffocate even the greatest talent in the world, I do not know what other constraints one could possibly need. The truth is that it would be better to be ignorant of everything and to lack even knowledge than to suffer the state of slavery or dependence. The latter is felt more acutely because of the juxtaposition of praise and disdain, of being raised up and beaten down. . . .

Such great discrepancies have often made me wonder what basis men might have for the superiority they have arrogated to themselves, principally in the endowments of the mind. The creation of one and the other sex may cast some light on this. But what do we discover? That God created Adam, who later felt need of a companion who was similar to him, and then company was granted to him in the form of a woman. Can one hope for more conclusive proof of the equality and similarity of both, in that first state? Is there any hint of subjection in all of this, or of one's dependence on the other? It is true that the man was created first, and created alone, but it did not take him long to realize that he could not live without a companion, the first image of matrimony, and also the first image of a perfect society.

If we now consider what happened in the fall of our first parents, we will not find the woman despoiled of her natural faculties. The abuse she made of them was her sin, but also that of Adam and of all posterity. But without trying to excuse this attempt, who will deny that the woman preceded the man in the desire to know? That fruit that was forbidden to them contained the knowledge of good and evil. Eve did not resist that temptation, but rather persuaded her husband. . . . A despicable curiosity, no doubt, but curiosity is generally the indicator of talent, because without it no one makes any real effort to become educated.

Nor did the fair penalty that was imposed upon both remove her intellectual faculties in any way. If the man can work without thus losing the aptitude for learning, the same can be said of the subjection of the woman. Men should be satisfied with being the head of the family and being in possession of employment without seeking to extend their dominance any further. For even if one accepts those things, it is not conclusive proof of greater talent. Men themselves are not and cannot all be equal. There must be some who rule over others, and it often happens that the one with greater intelligence ends up having to obey and respect the one who has less. So women can be subject to men in certain ways without thus losing their equality in powers of understanding.

If this equality can be seen in the creation, it can be proved even more effectively by the examples women themselves have given. . . . If the examples are not as numerous in women as in men, it is clear that this is because they study less, and men allow them fewer opportunities than they have to prove their talents.

No one who is even partly educated will deny that in all times and in all countries there have been women who have contributed to progress even in the most abstract fields of knowledge. . . . [She then lists famous women writers from various times and places.] If women have distinguished themselves in letters, they have shown just as much skill in government and public affairs. . . . Deborah . . . governed the people of Israel. . . . If we want more modern examples, everyone knows about the wisdom of the Catholic queen, Lady Isabella, who, although she did not govern alone, took part in all the great matters that were carried out in her time; in England, the two queens, Elizabeth and Anne, contributed as much as wise kings . . . did to extending the power of Great Britain. . . . In Russia, the two Catherines have perfected the splendor that began with Peter the Great. . . .

Setting aside what is necessary for public affairs, . . . how many examples could we cite in the republic of the families, where a woman conceals and even hides her husband's defects in management of the household? . . .

Courage is generally held to be a quality specific to and generally possessed by men; and yet it has its exceptions, just as beauty does among women. We see handsome men and ugly women, courageous women and cowardly men, showing that there is no quality that is not common to both sexes. As for bravery, if there have not been as many women as men who have distinguished themselves in this way, one can see that this is because of the different upbringing. . . . If women had the same education as men, they would do just as well or better than men.

But how different this education is! From childhood, girls are only taught to read and write and to develop certain manual skills. Great care is given to adorning them, and as a result, they acquire a certain habit of always thinking about their outward appearance. As for talent, if one speaks to them at all about it, it is considered a superfluous thing, so that it would be no great loss if they gave up any idea of being skilled at anything else. Boys, on the other hand, are taught from the outset to learn and to apply themselves even before they know what studying or knowledge are. They hear that there are universities and schools and that there are fine positions for those who study. And so they grow up with the idea of applying themselves to studies, and they do not take long to reap the fruit of their efforts. . . . If a woman dedicates herself to studying, she necessarily does so only for the personal advantages and pleasure, for she knows she cannot aspire to any rewards. It thus takes a greatness of spirit to undertake and pursue the difficult career of letters merely for the pleasure of enlightening her mind. Nevertheless, we see that some women undertake this heroic task.

55. Joseph Townsend,
A Journey Through Spain in the Years 1786 and 1787

Joseph Townsend (1739–1816) was an English cleric and geologist who traveled extensively throughout Europe, observing nature, especially geology, and writing books recording his observations. In an age when the English were especially interested in books describing agricultural conditions and means of improvement, Townsend wrote a three-volume account of his travels in Spain, offering extensive comments on subjects such as the nature and problems of Spanish agriculture and herding. His outlook reflects the ideas of the Enlightenment, and his specific concerns resembled those of some Spanish reformers of that era.

In these passages he refers to the *Mesta*, an organization of sheepherders that the Crown had had helped form and sustain. (Townsend places the *Mesta's* creation in 1350, but others trace it back to the previous century.) The *Mesta* remained powerful for centuries, promoting its members' interests—and particularly their right to drive their flocks across others' lands as part of the annual migrations from winter pastures in the south to summer pastures in the north.

SOURCE: Joseph Townsend, *A Journey Through Spain in the Years 1786 and 1787*, vol. 2 (London: C. Dilly, 1791), 61–64, 87–88, 282–85.

October 4, as we descended toward León, we overtook a Merino flock, belonging to the monastery of Guadalupe, in Estremadura. These monks have sufficient land near home to keep their flock during the winter months; but in the summer, when their own mountains are scorched, they send their sheep into the north, where, having no lands, they are obliged to pay for pasturage. They were on their return towards the south.

The great lords, and the religious houses, to whom belong these *transhumantes*, or traveling flocks, have peculiar privileges secured to them by a special code, called laws of the *Mesta*; privileges by many considered as inconsistent with the general good.

This institution has been traced back to the year 1350, when the plague, which ravaged Europe for several years, had desolated Spain, leaving only one-third of its former inhabitants to cultivate the soil. But perhaps we ought to look for its origin in more remote and distant ages, when the whole country was occupied by shepherd nations. . . . Occupying the hills with their numerous flocks and herds, it was natural for them in winter to quit a country then covered deep with snow, and to seek the more temperate regions of the south; till these, burnt up by the returning sun, refused them pasture, and drove them back again to the mountains of the north, which, during the summer months are covered with perpetual verdure by the gradual melting of the snow.

The numbers of the Merino sheep are continually varying. Cajaleruela, who wrote [in] 1627, complained that they were reduced from seven million to two million and a half. Ustariz reckoned in his time four million; but now they are near five. The proprietors are numerous, some having only three or four thousand, while others have ten times that number. The duke of Infantado has forty thousand. Each proprietor has a *mayotal*, or chief shepherd, to whom he allows annually one hundred *doblones*, or seventy-five pounds, and a horse; and for every flock of two hundred sheep, a separate shepherd, who is paid according to his merit, from eight shillings a month to thirty, besides two pounds of bread a day for himself, and as much for his dog, with the privilege of keeping a few goats on his own account. . . .

When the sheep are traveling they may feed freely on all the wastes and commons; but, in passing through a cultivated country, they must be confined within their proper limits in a way which is ninety *varas* wide. Hence it comes to pass that, in such inhospitable districts, they are made to travel at the rate of six or seven leagues a day; but where pasture is to be had, they are suffered to move very slow. When they are to remove, either in the spring or the autumn, if the lord has no lands where his flocks are to be stationed, the chief shepherd goes before and engages agistment, either of those proprietors who have more than sufficient for themselves, or of the corporations, who, in Spain, have usually extensive wastes and commons round their cities.

It is to these claims of the Merino stock that some political writers have attributed the want of cultivation in the interior provinces of Spain. . . .

When I express myself satisfied with the husbandry in the neighborhood of Salamanca, it is only so far as it relates to plowing; for in no other respect has it any claim to approbation. The plowman and the grazier, instead of being united in the same person, are here eternally at variance; and as the latter is the best tenant, the great proprietors give him the preference. Hence the country has been depopulated, and the lands, which are in tillage for want of cattle to manure and tread them, produce light crops of corn. This bishopric formerly contained 748 corporation towns; but now it has only 333, the other 415 being deserted, and their arable lands reduced to pasture. . . .

Farmers in this vicinity rent dear, paying commonly two bushels of wheat and one of barley for every bushel of their feed; or if they pay a stipulated sum of money, it is not immediately to the landowner, but, as undertenants, to rich land-jobbers; and therefore they can expect no moderation. Farms, if enclosed, let much higher than those which are open, because the latter are liable to be fed [on] by the Merino sheep; whereas should they enter the former, one-fifth of the number trespassing would be forfeited. This, how-ever, proves a never-failing source of quarrels and contentions between the occupiers of land and those who may be called graziers, that is, the propri-etors of the Merino stock who, under the sanction of a peculiar code, claim the privilege of feeding, not only in the common pasture, but even in the plantations of olives. The murders consequent on these quarrels have been more than two hundred in the space of a few years; and the litigations have cost the contending parties more than the value both of their sheep and of their olives. The Council of Castile interfered, in the year 1570, to prohibit this; but the great sheep-masters plead their privilege, as granted by the *Mesta* code, and support their claim by force.

When we arrived [in Ecija, in Andalusia], we found everyone engaged in talking over a defeat which the king's troops had suffered the preceding day from the smugglers, near one hundred of whom, well armed, entering the city, had driven away the military, had killed one man, and had then, un-molested, sold their snuff to the inhabitants. This violence was more than usual, and proceeded from the bad policy of government; in raising the price of tobacco from thirty to forty *reales* the pound whilst the illicit trader pur-chased the same commodity in Portugal for eight, with such encouragement for defrauding the revenue, it will never be possible to prevent this trade; and whilst men have such powerful inducements to violate the laws, no gov-ernment, however strenuous its exertions, and how cruel the punishment inflicted on offenders, will ever be able to maintain a good police. In Spain, unless it be accompanied with murder, the penalty for smuggling is com-monly a confinement for seven or ten years to hard labor in the presidios, where, by communication with profligate and hardened villains, . . . they are prepared for the perpetration of the most atrocious crimes; and thus qualified, they are turned loose upon the public. Previous to this part of his education, the smuggler seldom robs on the highway.

56. Gaspar Melchor de Jovellanos, In Praise of Charles III (1788)

Gaspar Melchor de Jovellanos (1744–1811) was among the most brilliant of Spain's Enlightenment authors and government ministers. Just before the death of Charles III (reigned 1759–1788), he gave this speech before the Royal Society of Madrid, offering an idealized portrait of the king's accomplishments, but also presenting a catalog of Enlightenment ideas and aspirations, as well as a revealing glimpse of existing perceptions of Spain's past and present.

SOURCE: Gaspar Melchor de Jovellanos, *Elogio de Carlos tercero: leído a la Real Sociedad de Madrid por el socio D. Gaspar Melchor de Jovellanos en la junta plena del sábado 8 de noviembre de 1788* (Madrid: Imprenta de la Viuda de Ibarra, 1789).

The praise of Charles III pronounced in this center of patriotism must not be an offering of adulation, but rather a tribute of recognition. . . .

Oh, princes, you were placed by the Omnipotent in the midst of nations to bring them abundance and prosperity. You should see this as your primary obligation. . . . It seems that this precept of philosophy resonated in the heart of Charles III when he came from Naples to Madrid, brought by Providence to occupy the throne of his forefathers. Long experience in the art of reigning had taught him that a sovereign's greatest glory is that which rests on the love of his subjects, and that this love is never more sincere, more lasting, more glorious than when it is inspired by gratitude. . . .

The listing of those benefits and efforts with which this benevolent sovereign won our love and gratitude has already been the subject of other, more eloquent speeches. Here I can merely allude to them. The creation of new agricultural settlements; the distribution of the commons [lands that villages owned communally]; the reduction of privileges for livestock herders; the abolition of the *tasa* [a price control] and the freeing of the trade in grain, by which he improved agriculture; the promotion of industrial education; the reform of guild policies; the proliferation of industrial establishments and the generous profusion of exemptions and privileges for the arts and crafts, for the benefit of industry; the breaking of the ancient chains on national commerce; the opening of new points for exportation; peace in the Mediterranean; more regular correspondence and freer communication with our overseas colonies, for the sake of commerce; the reestablishment of the representation of the people, to improve municipal government, and of the sacred power of the father, to improve the home; the opening of centers of charity in a thousand places, the true recipients of public charity having been distinguished from those who are simply lazy . . . ; and above all, the creation of these patriotic bodies, models for public institutions. . . . What an ample and glorious basis for praising Charles III and assuring him the title of father of his vassals! . . .

You, gentlemen, you who cooperate with such zeal in the accomplishment of his paternal designs, must not be unaware how much the nation was lacking in the proper spirit. Useful sciences, economic principles, a general spirit of enlightenment; these are what Spain will owe to the reign of Charles III.

If you doubt that the happiness of a state can be measured in these things, turn your eyes once again to those sad times [in the Middle Ages] when Spain lived in superstition and ignorance. What a spectacle of horror and sadness! Religion, sent from the heavens to enlighten and console man, but forced by interested parties to sadden and deceive him; anarchy established in place of order; the head of the state either a tyrant or a victim of the nobility; the people, like so many sheep, delivered to the greed of their lords; those in poverty burdened with taxes; the wealthy entirely exempt from these [taxes] and authorized to increase their burden [on the poor]; laws openly resisted or insolently trampled upon; the judicial system disrespected, the restraint of customs broken. . . .

Spain took several centuries to come out of this abyss, but when the sixteenth century began, sovereignty had recovered its authority, the nobility having suffered the reduction of its prerogatives and the people having been assured their representation as the courts made the voice of the laws and the action of justice respected, while agriculture, industry, and commerce prospered amid the protection of order. What human power would have been able to topple Spain from that apex of grandeur to which it had ascended if the spirit of true enlightenment had already taught it to keep what it had so rapidly acquired?

No, Spain did not disdain learning; rather, it also aspired to fame by that path. Ah, but what are the useful truths it gathered through the efforts of its scholars? What did religious studies do for Spain, once the subtleties of scholasticism took away all the attention that should have been paid to morality and doctrine? What did jurisprudence do, on the one hand, stubbornly multiplying the number of laws, and on the other hand, submitting their meaning to the arbitrary will of their interpreters? What did the natural sciences do, only being known for the ridiculous abuse they made of astrology and alchemy? What good did mathematics do, cultivated only speculatively and never converted or applied for the benefit of men? . . .

Among so many fields of study, there was no place then for civil economy [economics], a science that teaches one to govern, and one whose principles have not yet been corrupted by self-interest, like those of politics, and whose progress is owed entirely to the philosophy of the present time. Public miseries should have awoken the patriotic spirit, leading to the investigation of their causes and the remedy of so many evils; but this period was still very far away. While the abandonment of the countryside, the ruin of the workshops, and the discouragement of commerce troubled men's hearts, foreign wars, the luxuries of the royal court, the greed of the ministry, and the insatiable appetite of the royal treasury aborted numerous plans for reform, reducing to a system the art of crushing the people and causing the work of many generations to be consumed during the reign of two kings [1621–1700].

So at that time the specter of misery, flying over uncultivated fields, over deserted workshops, and over helpless villages, spread horror and sadness everywhere; it was then that patriotism inspired the zeal of several generous Spaniards, who thought so much about public problems and clamored so vigorously for reforms; it was then that people first saw that there was a science that taught one to govern men and make them happy; it was then, finally, that in the very heart of ignorance and disorder, the study of civil economy was born.

But what was the sum of truth and knowledge that our economic science had at that time? Can we really honor it with that name? Vacillating in its principles, absurd in its conclusions, mistaken in its calculations, and so confused in its knowledge of the evils and the choice of solutions, it hardly offered clear maxims of good governance. Each economist formed his own system, each derived from a different source, never coming together on basic elements. . . . There was no evil, no vice, no abuse that did not have its own particular accuser. The wealth of the Church, the poverty and the excessive numbers of monks and nuns, . . . the various taxes, the lack of discipline in people's clothing: everything was examined, calculated, reconsidered, but nothing was solved. Effects were mistaken for causes; no one managed to find the source of the problem, no one sought to bring the remedy to the roots of the problem; and while [wars in] Germany, Flanders, and Italy buried men, swallowed up the treasures, and consumed the resources of the state, the nation agonized in the arms of the doctors. . . .

Poor analysis had reduced our fatherland to such a sad and horrible state when the Austrian dynasty ended with the seventeenth century. The heavens had reserved for the Bourbon dynasty the restoration of Spain's splendor and force. At the beginning of the eighteenth century, the first of the Bourbon kings crossed the Pyrenees, and during the horrors of a war as just as it was bloody, he turned his eyes from time to time toward the people, who were struggling valiantly to defend their rights. Philip [V, 1700–1746], knowing that he could not make them happy if he did not educate them, founded academies, built seminaries, established libraries, protected letters and the educated, and, in a reign of almost a half century, taught them to know what education is worth.

Ferdinand [VI, 1746–1759], in a shorter but more flourishing and peaceful period, followed in his father's footsteps; he created the navy, promoted industry, favored internal commerce, supported and rewarded the fine arts, protected talents and . . . sent many outstanding young people throughout Europe in search of precious merchandise, [and] welcomed artists and foreign scholars to Spain, paying for their enlightenment with awards and salaries. In this way, the paths that Charles III later took so gloriously were prepared.

This pious sovereign, having decided to let light enter his kingdom, began removing the obstacles that could block its progress. This was his first concern. Ignorance continued to defend its trenches, but Charles ended up overrunning them. Truth fought alongside him, and all darkness disappeared at the sight of him. . . .

The teaching of ethics, of natural and public law, established by Charles III, improved the field of jurisprudence. . . . But Charles did not content himself with guiding his subjects to the knowledge of the higher truths that are the object of that field. Although worthy of his attention because of its influence on the beliefs, customs, and tranquility of the citizen, he knew that there are other truths, less sublime, certainly, but upon which the prosperity of peoples depends more directly. . . .

Man, condemned by Providence to work, is born ignorant and weak. Without enlightenment, without strength, he does not know how to direct his desires or where to apply his physical efforts. It took the passage of many centuries and the accumulation of a multitude of observations to bring together a scant amount of useful knowledge to guide labor, and it was to these few truths that the world owed the first multiplication of its inhabitants.

Nevertheless, the Creator had placed in the spirit of man a great supplement to the weakness of his physical constitution. Capable of simultaneously understanding the extension of the earth, the depth of the seas, the height and immensity of the heavens; capable of penetrating the most obscure mysteries of nature once placed under his observation, he only needed to study nature and to gather together and organize his ideas in order to subject the universe to his dominion. Finally growing tired of being lost in the darkness of metaphysical investigation, . . . he changed direction, contemplated nature, created the sciences that focus on nature, improved himself, came to realize all the vigor of his mind, and made happiness a product of his will.

Charles, wishing to carry out this kind of regeneration in his kingdom, began promoting the teaching of the exact sciences. . . . Madrid, Seville, Salamanca, and Alcalá saw their ancient schools of mathematics reborn. Barcelona, Valencia, Zaragoza, Santiago, and almost all of the universities also saw them reestablished. The force of demonstration replaced the subtleties of the syllogism [i.e., empirical observation replaced theoretical speculation]. The study of physics, now supported by experiments and calculation, was improved, and the other sciences related to it were also born: chemistry, mineralogy and metallurgy, natural history, and botany. And while the observer of nature was investigating and discovering the primary elements of physical bodies, . . . the man of politics was studying the relations that the wisdom of the Creator placed in them to assure the multiplication and the happiness of the human race.

Yet another science was still necessary to allow for a truly profitable outcome. Its goal is to take advantage of this knowledge, to distribute its effects usefully, to make it available for the common good, and, in a word, to apply it, based on certain and constant principles, to the government of peoples. This is the true science of the state, the science of the public official. Charles turned his gaze toward this science, and civil economy once again appeared in his kingdom. . . .

[Jovellanos then reviews the accomplishments of several scholars.]

It was up to Charles III to take advantage of the rays of light that these worthy citizens had cast with their works. The pleasure of diffusing them throughout his kingdom and the glory of converting his vassals to the study of the economy was reserved for him. . . . The sanctuary of the sciences is only opened to a small portion of the citizens, devoted to investigating in silence the mysteries of nature, only to declare them to the nation. Yours is the duty of gathering their oracles, yours the duty of passing on the light of their investigations, yours the duty of applying them for the benefit of your subjects. Economic science belongs exclusively to you and the holders of your authority. The ministers who surround your throne, . . . the high officials, who must make that will known to the people and make their rights and needs known to you; those who preside over the domestic government of your kingdom, those who watch over your provinces, those who directly guide your vassals must study that science, must know it, or else descend into the classes destined to work and obey. Your decrees must emanate from your principles, and those who execute them must respect them. . . . There is no evil in them, there is no vice, there is no abuse that does not derive from some violation of these principles. An error, a bit of carelessness, a false calculation in matters of the economy fills the provinces with confusion and the peoples with tears, and keeps happiness away from them forever. . . .

Charles had barely ascended to the throne when the spirit of inquiry and reform touched all matters of public economy. The government's action awoke the citizens' curiosity. The study of this science was then reborn, a science that was then occupying most of the attention of philosophy. Spain read its most famous writers, examined their principles, analyzed their works; people spoke, debated, and wrote, and the nation began to have economists. . . .

It is to you, oh good Charles, to you that the greatest part of this glory and our gratitude is owed. Without your protection, without your generosity, without the ardent love that you profess for your peoples, these precious seeds would have perished. Sown on an infertile land, the vice of contradiction would have suffocated them in their bed. You saw to it that the tender plants that germinated were respected; you are going to harvest their fruit, and this fruit of enlightenment and truth will be the most certain proof of the happiness of your people. Yes, Spaniards, behold the greatest of all the benefits that Charles III brought to you. He brought to the nation the rays of light that have enlightened you and cleared for you the paths of knowledge.

57. Pedro Rodríguez de Campomanes, On the Political Economy of Spain (1789)

Few writers or government ministers expressed the spirit of enlightened absolutism in Spain better than Pedro Rodríguez de Campomanes (1723–1803). As
head of the Council of Castile for many years, Campomanes had the opportunity to enact many of the kinds of reforms mentioned in these letters written to
a colleague, the count of Lerena.

SOURCE: Antonio Rodríguez Villa, ed., *Cartas político-económicas al conde de
Lerena* (Madrid: Librería de M. Murillo, 1878), 161–62, 202–8, 210–11, 213–18,
221–23, 227–28.

It is true that foreign trade brings great wealth, but it is also true that it is
exposed to great risks. We can scarcely find examples in history of commercial nations remaining prosperous for long, or of commercial enterprises
remaining wealthy for more than two generations. The domestic economy
of a republic is an eternal treasure. Spain finds itself forced to view its foreign
trade as a great chain binding it to its vast overseas territories; but Spain,
having greater wealth at home than in the Americas, must pay greater attention to these certain sources of wealth than to those, which are exposed to
great risks. We lost Flanders, we lost Italy, so why could we not lose Mexico
and Peru? And if that happens, what role will we play in the world?

The peninsula is the basis of our power, and so it should be the prime
object of our attention. Little Prussia has given the world a surprising example of what a medium-sized kingdom can do; and the emperor has earned
more glory for the war he has waged against bad government in his own
states than for any he has fought against the Turk. . . .

Good order in a family generally depends on proper divisions within
the household, and a poorly divided kingdom will never be well ordered.
The provinces, in their current state, were not formed for economic purposes, but rather by the accidents of war. . . . In those unfortunate times,
when the furors of war demanded more strong points from which to fight
the enemy than fertile places from which to make the vassals happy, when
the study of political economy was scarcely known, when the sword and the
lance were solely responsible for the glory of a king, when artisans and farmers were thought of like slaves or cattle, and when the ferocity and roughness
of the soldier was the model for administration, one showed little concern
for proportions in civil government.

The map of the peninsula is full of such ridiculous things as provinces
that are enclaves of others, highly irregular angles everywhere, capitals situ-
ated at the edges of their provinces, very large and very small intendancies,

bishoprics of four leagues in length and others of seventy, tribunals whose jurisdiction barely reaches beyond the walls of a city and others that comprise two or three kingdoms; in sum, everything that brings with it disorder and confusion. . . . Natural proportion in the limbs is the principle for the perfect organization of the human body, and of its health and robustness. If one leg is long and the other short, the mind will tire itself endlessly trying to dictate rules for equality in walking, for the legs will always inevitably limp; the same is true for a political body. . . . Equality in the division of the provinces is the foundation for proper economic, civil, and military administration; it is the great foundation for precision in the art of calculation, and it is the only one that can allow us to reform this giant body of the monarchy. The administration of justice is the first step toward happiness, which depends on the establishment and convenient location of the courts. The immense jurisdiction of the two chancelleries of Valladolid and Granada causes more damage than one can imagine. Bringing suit before these two tribunals causes unbearable expenses, even for the most trivial matter. . . . The . . . delays experienced in the resolution of matters is a powerful incentive for those who have less justice on their side to try to stall forever, which is easy to do if one has money. The multitude of clerks, scribes, attorneys, and officials have their ties of personal interest among themselves, and they work together against others, without judges being able to prevent these intrigues. . . . The poor, in spite of the laws, suffer without even the small consolation of being able to have their complaints heard. . . . Judicial robberies are punished with fines; if those on the highways were punished the same way, no one would dare go outside. I have never heard of a judge being hanged, nor of a scribe having his hand cut off. . . . The laws, which are so hard on poor robbers of money, seem to have been softened for the fortunate robbers of rights and even of the lives of the citizens. Our criminal code is perhaps the least defective of the ancient codes of Europe, but all the same it does not fail to show the spirit of the despotism and tyranny of the barbaric ages. . . .

The greatest support for the laws is the image of impartiality and honesty that the lawgiver manages to create; especially in monarchies, in which the people have no part of legislative authority, it is necessary to inform them even of the minor circumstances that are motives for a law, and of the evils it seeks to avoid and the benefits it seeks to provide. . . . Laws, like gold, have their touchstone that determines their value, and this is the equality of the citizens [before the law]. . . .

A prince's orders will encounter fewer obstacles when there are fewer powerful organized bodies in his kingdom. . . . We should think of Spain as being made up of various confederated republics under the government and protection of our kings. Each town should be seen as a little kingdom, and the whole kingdom as a big town. As long as complete harmony is not established among the parts and the whole, it will be impossible to simplify government. . . .

A wise lawgiver must take the greatest possible care to make the people's customs as uniform as possible. The schools, public entertainments, popular songs, even children's games deserve the attention of philosophy, deriving advantages from everything, as the Greeks did, seeking to create virtue and even heroism among the lower classes. A brief political catechism, a few epigrams posted in public places, certain ceremonies for admission to the status of citizenship . . . are things that cost nothing and are worth much. . . .

Human passions can be compared to a stringed instrument, which is tempered by the will of the musician. The same legislation should produce the same effects in any part of the world, being weaker or stronger depending on those who must observe it. The system of our hereditary nobility, of our coats of arms and our military orders, would have caused the same quixotism in China as it did in Spain. . . .

Hierarchical order of command is indispensable among men, otherwise one will condemn them to a perpetual and destructive anarchy; but hierarchies of families are an extremely damaging illusion, albeit one consecrated by the vanity and greed of the powerful. . . . It makes sense that rewards and punishments, as recompense for personal actions, should not pass beyond the persons who earned them. The inheritability of dignities and positions is only just for kings, given the need to avoid the extremely grave problems that a republic would suffer if kings were elected; for others it is not only unjust, but also extremely damaging. Every citizen must have free access to the paths that lead to the temple of immortality, and only those who have overcome the difficulties of the ascent through their own efforts should be admitted to it. God distributes great souls among the lower classes and upper classes alike, and a great general or a great minister can just as easily come from the chisel and the hammer as from gold and purple. Education is the only thing that influences us, giving us clear or twisted ideas of things. Honor and dishonor derive their content from popular whims or conceptions, having no more reality than that which men's ways of thinking give them. Therefore, one of the greatest concerns of education must be to imprint an advantageous notion of these great checks on human action on minds from the outset. Honor and virtue must be considered synonymous. I am well aware that honor is the reward for virtue and is not virtue itself, but these philosophical fine points are not for the common people. If the honor of offices be made to correspond to the greater or lesser utility that each one brings to society, we would undoubtedly promote useful actions and be done with the superfluous ones.

Industry must take its principal incentive from men's self-interest. The desirability that men see in things moves them to want them and to acquire them. . . . As long as people do not see rewards in the mechanical arts, the government will try in vain to make them value them. The laws can declare that it is not dishonorable to be a shoemaker, a tailor, etc., but as long as they do not declare it dishonorable to be idle, there will always be hidalgos who consider idleness an inseparable companion of nobility. . . .

Entailed estates . . . inevitably perpetuate inequality in inheritable fortunes, and they are sources of public calamity, along with such fantasies as nobility and honor. If there is no such thing as a family of heroes, why should there be families that enjoy the fruits of rewards intended for heroes? If my father having been a hero does not prove that I am as well, why should I base my vanity on someone else's virtue? . . .

To achieve great things it is necessary to take advantage even of men's fanaticism. Among our populace, the idea that the king is the absolute lord over lives, property, and honor is so widely accepted that it seems a kind of sacrilege even to call it into question, and here we have the key to reform. I am well aware that absolute power in a monarch exposes monarchy to the most terrible evils, but I also know that the ancient evils of our land can only be cured with absolute power.

Great reforms in states have rarely been carried out through combinations of forces. An assertion of the power of one of the parts that make up the state has imposed its will on the others and has established the constitution. Happy is the kingdom whose ruler is ruled by the maxims of wisdom; if he uses his force to correct stubborn problems, he uses justice to temper his authority. . . . One can see that the solidity of a monarchy consists in the balance of sovereign authority with civil liberty; that the happiness of the king requires the happiness of his vassals; that a long lifespan of empires cannot be reconciled with oppression; that mutual confidence and unity are the foundations of happiness, but that such relations are not possible between slaves and masters. . . . So the work of a prudent lawgiver demands all the maturity and profound reflection of philosophy. . . . Absolute power demands absolute wisdom for its use, and that, as I said elsewhere, is not found among men. . . .   In favor of absolute power or no?

These are the ends I propose to achieve with my system of revenues: to fully meet the needs of the person of the king and those of the state; to equalize the tax payments of the vassals, so that each one pays in proportion to the goods one enjoys in society; to leave domestic commerce and exchange in perfect liberty; to oblige men to be industrious, attracting them gradually to the countryside and to agriculture; to decrease the number of privileged persons, and to increase the number of those who contribute to the common good; to oppress vanity, the basis of idleness and the source of infinite evils; to prevent the powerful from entailing their property, and to force the division of the latter, to the benefit of the great landowners themselves; to promote arts and crafts, increasing the number of hands by inducing sedentary women to work; to make the whims of fashion and foreign luxury unbearable; to simplify the administration of the royal treasury, . . . and above all to rid the interior of the kingdom of the enormous burden of smugglers and guards.

58. Gaspar Melchor de Jovellanos, On Spectacles and Public Entertainments (1790)

Enlightenment ideas about the common people often showed a profound ambivalence. On the one hand, upper-class reformers had severe doubts about how enlightened most of their poorer compatriots were, or even about how enlightened they could ever become. Yet they also believed in a range of universal rights derived from nature as well as every human being's ability to reason, and they took up the cause of common people oppressed by the powerful. Such ambivalence can be seen in the following essay, in which Jovellanos mixes observation of various aspects of popular culture in Spain with recommendations on how governments should deal with traditional popular activities and pastimes.

SOURCE: Gaspar Melchor de Jovellanos, *Obras publicadas e inéditas de Gaspar Melchor de Jovellanos*, Biblioteca de autores españoles 46 (Madrid: Real Academia Española, 1858; reprint, Madrid: Real Academia Española, 1963), 486–87, 491–500.

To expound my ideas with great clarity and precision, I will divide the people into two classes: one that works and another that is leisured. . . .

The people who work . . . need entertainment, but not spectacles. They do not need the government to entertain them, but only to allow them to entertain themselves. In the few days, in the brief hours, that they can devote to their relaxation and recreation they will seek out and invent their entertainments; it is enough for them to be given liberty and protection to enjoy them. A clear and calm day of rest, in which they can freely stroll, run, . . . play ball games, . . . bowl, picnic, drink, dance, and frolic in the countryside, will satisfy their desires and will offer them the most fulfilling entertainment and pleasure. . . .

So why is it that most people in Spain are not entertained in any way at all? Anyone who has traveled throughout our provinces will have made this painful observation. On the main holidays, in place of the joy and bustle that should indicate the happiness of the inhabitants, a lazy inactivity reigns in the streets and plazas, a sad silence, which cannot be observed without wonder and regret. If some people come out of their houses, it seems that tedium and sluggishness force them to do so and drag them to the commons, to the roadside shrine, to the plaza, or to the gate of the church, where, concealed in their capes, or perhaps loitering or sitting at some street corner or wandering here and there, without any fixed purpose, they sadly pass the hours and entire afternoons without finding amusement or entertainment. And if one adds to this the dryness and filthiness of these places, the poverty and slovenliness of their neighbors, the sad and silent atmosphere, the idleness and the lack of unity and movement that is notable everywhere, who can fail to be surprised and disheartened at such a strange phenomenon?

This is not the place to describe all the causes that come together to produce this situation; whatever they may be, one can be sure that they all originate in the laws. But . . . one of the most ordinary and familiar of these causes is the bad policing of many towns. The untempered zeal of more than a few judges leads them to think that the greatest perfection of a town government is measured in the subjection of its people, so that the height of good order consists of the inhabitants jumping to the commands of the voice of justice, and no one dares to move or to hesitate upon hearing one's name called. Consequently, any disturbance, any uproar or disorder is called an uprising and a riot; any quarrel or scuffle is the object of criminal proceedings, bringing with it investigations and lawsuits and imprisonment and fines, and all the trouble and bother of the judicial system. Under such rigid policing, the people become cowardly and sad, and, sacrificing their pleasure to their security, they renounce public and innocent, though dangerous, entertainment, preferring solitude and inaction. . . .

In some places music and tin-pan serenades are prohibited, while in others evening events and dances are. In some, the inhabitants are required to remain in their houses for a curfew, and in others not to go outside without a lamp, or not to loiter on the street corners, or not to hang around and gossip, and other such privations. The passion for giving orders and sometimes the greed of the judge have extended to the most pitiful little villages regulations that the confusion of the capital can barely justify; and the poor farmhand, who has drenched the fields with his sweat and slept on the threshing floor all week cannot cry out freely in the plaza or sing a romantic song at his sweetheart's door on Saturday night.

Even the province where I live, despite its being so famous for being so hardworking and for its natural happiness and the innocence of its customs, has been unable to free itself from such regulations. And the displeasure with which they are received . . . suggests these reflections to me. The dispersal of its population neither calls for nor even allows for municipal policing, which was invented for more urban populations. But ours do come together to entertain themselves in pilgrimages, but even there police regulations pursue them and beset them. Regulations have prohibited the use of walking sticks, which the unevenness of the land . . . makes necessary here. Men's dances have been banned, and women's dances have to stop in the middle of the afternoon, and finally, pilgrimages, which are the only form of diversion for these hardworking and innocent people, have to break up before the time for prayer. How could they be happy and content amid such annoying policing?

Some will say that people put up with all of this, and that is true: everything is put up with, but reluctantly. People put up with everything, but who will not fear the consequences of such long and forced suffering? The state of liberty is a situation of peace, comfort, and happiness; the state of subjection is one of agitation, violence, and unhappiness; consequently the first is durable, the second susceptible to changes. So it is not enough for people to be calm; they must also be content, and only in insensitive hearts or in minds empty of any sense of humanity and even of political sense can one consider the idea of hoping for the former without the latter.

Those who look upon this issue with indifference either do not see the relationship that exists between the liberty and the prosperity of a people, or at least do not care about that, and both are equally bad. Nevertheless this relationship is quite clear and quite worthy of the attention of a just and sensitive administration. A free and happy people will be active and hardworking, and being so, will be . . . obedient to justice. The more fun they have, the more they will like the government under which they live, and the more they will obey it, and the more willingly they will rush to support and defend it. The more fun they have, the more they will have to lose, the more they will fear disorder, and the more they will respect authorities whose job is to keep them under control. This people will be more anxious to grow wealthy, because they will know that their pleasures will grow along with their riches. In a word, they will aspire all the more to be happy. . . .

Men who frequently gather to relax and enjoy themselves together will always be a united and affectionate people; they will see the general interest, and they will be all the more reluctant to sacrifice it for personal interest. They will have a loftier spirit, being freer. . . . Respecting the hierarchy and the order established by the constitution, they will live according to it, will love it, and will defend it vigorously, believing that they are defending themselves. . . .

Do not conclude from this that I consider it useless or oppressive for a justice system to watch out for public tranquility. . . . Liberty itself needs protection, for license tends to threaten it when there are no checks that restrain those who would go beyond its limits. But this is where those indiscreet judges who confuse vigilance with oppression go wrong. . . . To judge by appearances, it seems that they try only to establish their authority upon the subjects' fear, or to secure tranquility at the price of their liberty and pleasure. This is in vain: the public cannot entertain itself as long as it lacks the proper freedom to do so, because amid rounds and patrols, amid . . . soldiers, amid clubs and bayonets, liberty takes fright, and timid and innocent happiness flees and disappears.

That is certainly not the way to attain the goals for which a public justice system has been created. If one can compare the humble with the lofty, its vigilance should resemble that of the Supreme Being; being firm and continual, but invisible; being known by all without being perceived by anyone; . . . in a word, to be a restraint for the bad and the protector and shield of the good. . . .

These are our ideas on popular enjoyments. There is no province, there is no district, there is no town or place that does not have certain forms of enjoyment and entertainment, habitual or periodical, established by custom. Tests of force, skill, agility, or litheness; public dances, bonfires, or light refreshments, strolls, races, masquerades or masked dances; whatever they may be, all must be good or innocent as long as they are public. The good governor should protect the people engaged in such pastimes, should set aside and adorn the places intended for them, and should keep away anything that could disturb them. . . . In sum, never forget that people who work, as we have seen, do not need the government to entertain them, but only [need] to be allowed to entertain themselves.

Bullfighting

The laws of the [Siete] Partidas [the medieval Castilian law code] count this among those public spectacles or games . . . that clergymen should not attend. Another law . . . gives grounds for believing that this art was already being practiced by people of low status, for it places [bullfighters] among the infamous people who fight wild beasts for money. And if my memory serves me well, by another law or ordinance of the *fuero* of Zamora one must deduce that toward the end of the thirteenth century there was in that city, and consequently in others, a plaza or site destined for such festivals.

Be that as it may, we cannot doubt that this was also one of the exercises of skill and courage that the nobles of the medieval era took on for training. . . . As time went on, and when the renewal of studies began introducing more enlightenment in people's ideas and more humanity in customs, bullfighting began to be seen by some as a bloody and barbaric form of entertainment. Gonzalo Fernández de Oviedo pondered the horror with which the pious and magnificent Isabella the Catholic viewed one of these festivals, perhaps in Medina del Campo. As this good lady was thinking of prohibiting such a wild spectacle, the desire to preserve it suggested to some courtiers a decree to lessen her displeasure. They told her that by wrapping the bull's horns in a kind of sheath, in order to soften the blow, one could prevent penetrating injuries. The measure was applauded and embraced at that time; but because no witness assures us of the continuation of that practice, we may believe that the courtiers . . . returned to enjoying [bull-fighting] in all its fierceness.

The fondness [for bullfighting] of the following centuries, making it more common and frequent, also gave it a more regular and stable form. It was established in various capitals, . . . in plazas constructed for that purpose, [and] its proceeds began to be devoted to certain civil and pious institutions. And this, removing it from the sphere of a voluntary and free form of entertainment for the nobility, summoned to the arena a certain kind of daring men, who, taught by experience and motivated by interest, made a lucrative profession of this exercise, and finally made an art form out of the daring of courage and the arduousness of skill. . . .

And so went the fate of this spectacle, more or less popular or famous according to its level of pomp, and also according to the tastes and spirit of the provinces that adopted it, without the greatest applause ever being enough to free it from ecclesiastical condemnation, and even less from that which reason and humanity brought together. But the clamor of its critics, far from lessening, increased the fondness of its fans and seemed to spur them even more to support it, until the enlightened zeal of the pious Charles III generally outlawed it. . . .

Bullfighting has never been a pastime that was either held daily or widely attended by all the towns of Spain, nor has it been generally sought out and applauded. In many provinces it has never been known, while in others it has been limited to the capital cities. . . . We can thus calculate that of all the people of Spain, scarcely one-hundredth can have ever seen this spectacle. So how can it have been claimed to be the national pastime?

But if it is called that because it has been known among us since ancient times; because it has always been well attended and held to great applause; because the cult of Europa [a Greek goddess who rode across the sea on the back of a bull] has not been preserved in any other country; who can deny this glory to the Spaniards who desire it? Nevertheless, to believe that the daring and skill of a dozen men, brought up from childhood in this trade, familiarized with the risks, and who end up being killed or maimed by it, can be presented to Europe as an argument for Spain's courage and strangeness would be absurd. And it is an illusion to argue that banning these festivals, which elsewhere could produce great political benefits, would create a risk that the nation might suffer some significant loss, either in the moral or the civil realm. . . . It is thus clear that the government was right to prohibit this spectacle, and that when it finishes carrying out such a praise-worthy project, it will be very deserving of the esteem and the praise of good and sensible people.

59. José Marchena,
To the Spanish Nation (1792)

Although not one whose views were common at the time, José Marchena was one Spaniard who openly embraced the French Revolution. Marchena wrote this piece shortly after arriving in the French town of Bayonne (just across the border from the Basque region of Spain), where he had fled, he said, from the Inquisition. The revolutionary Jacobin Club of Bayonne, interested in spreading the revolution to Spain, had Marchena's address printed and smuggled into Spain. Although it is unlikely that more than a handful of copies actually made it past Spanish censors and customs officials, the essay casts light on Spanish reactions to the French Revolution.

SOURCE: Fernando Díaz-Plaja, ed., *Historia de España en sus documentos: Siglo XVIII* (Madrid: Cátedra, 1986), 299–302; the text also appears in Alfonso García-Gallo, ed., *Manual de historia del derecho Español*, 3rd ed., vol. 2 (Madrid: A.G.E.S.A., 1967), 1021–23.

Spaniards: The time has come to offer the truth to all peoples; tyranny tries in vain to smother their cries. The country of liberty [France], where the people are king, offers asylum to philosophers and the defenders of humanity, who are safe from any worry in the heart of France, which is scattering the fertile seeds that will one day produce happiness for all men. This sublime revolution, which has solemnly proclaimed the eternal rights of humanity and which has toppled superstition and tyranny from their golden throne in order to place equality and reason on it, will not limit its beneficial influence to the narrow terrain of the French nation. Who can stop the progress of an immense bonfire surrounded by combustible materials? Nature did not intend men to be slaves of other men; superstition can temporarily lull a people to sleep behind the bars of slavery. But if reason awakens that people, may hypocrites and oppressors beware.

Who will believe that the Spanish people consider the French nation to be like those cannibals who wage a cruel war, like the enemies of God and of laws? Ah, Spaniards, . . . a nation that under the intolerable weight of religious and political despotism still produces great souls who take offense at the yoke that strangles your necks; open your eyes and learn to hate those infamous impostors who deceive you in order to enslave you. The French, enemies of God? . . . They, who have sworn fraternity and reciprocal tolerance before the heavens! In France the Jew comes to the aid of the Christian, the Protestant embraces the Catholic; religious hatreds are unknown, and the decent man is loved and respected by all, while the wicked man is disdained and detested. If the religion of Jesus is the system of peace and universal charity, who are the real Christians? [The French] who come to the aid of all men, who look upon them as their brothers, or you, who perse-cute, who arrest, who kill all those who do not adopt your ideas? You call yourselves Christians; why don't you follow the maxims of your lawgiver? Jesus did not come armed with the power to inculcate his religion with the force of the sword; he preached his doctrine without forcing men to follow it. Defenders of the cause of heaven: who entrusted you with its vengeance? Does the Omnipotent One need to use your weak hands to destroy his enemies? Couldn't he unleash lightning bolts against those who offend him, and annihilate them with a single breath? . . . The terrifying dungeons of the Inquisition will open for the unfortunate ones who have incurred the indig-nation of the priests and the hypocrites. Spain is ten thousand miles from Europe, and ten centuries from the eighteenth century. . . .

The mere name of the Inquisition makes my hair stand on end. . . . Tell me if your Inquisition has not pursued to the death men of talent from Barto-lomé Carranza to Fray Luis de León and even [Pablo] Olavide y Bails. . . . Other nations have made enormous progress in matters of learning, and you, the homeland of Seneca, of Lucan, of Quintilian, of Columela, of Silius [ancient Romans Marchena contends were born in Spain], where is your ancient glory? Brilliance has prepared to take flight, and the torch of the Inquisition has burned its wings. . . .

Isn't it time for the nation finally to shake off the intolerable yoke of the oppression of thought? Isn't it time for the government to suppress a tribu-nal of darkness that dishonors even despotism? Why make men into mere automatons? . . . The first step in any progress is to destroy the Inquisition to its very foundations. Let's not slander the people; the wicked may deceive them, but when they are presented with good they embrace it enthusiasti-cally. . . . All wish to see the Inquisition abolished, but some have suggested to me that there are men of ill will who pretend to believe that the nation, deceived, could oppose this measure. Opposition of the Spanish people? There the monarch is all-powerful, but enlightenment, despite all the pre-cautions taken, has spread more than people realize! Tyrants should tremble in fear of the oppressed people everywhere breaking free in a terrible explo-sion, destroying all hypocrites and oppressors.

Equality, humanity, fraternity, tolerance; Spaniards, this is, in four words, the system of the philosophers that a few wicked men portray to you as monsters. . . . You have but one means remaining, Spaniards, of destroy-ing religious despotism, and that is to convoke a meeting of your Cortes. Do not waste a single moment. "Cortes, Cortes" must be the universal cry. What moment could be more opportune for you? The electric spark of liberty is spreading from one end of Europe to the other and is inflaming all the victims of tyranny in a holy indignation against the oppressors.

Spaniards, the deficit of your treasury increases while your taxes also increase; your country, which nature endowed with everything, is lacking everything, because a flawed constitution and a ravenous government are devouring your purest substance. . . .

In vain will the ignorant or those of ill will try to scare you with the example of France. The Estates General of that country did not have clear rules or rigid limits, but your Cortes do, and they are well known. France needed a revolution; Spain needs only rejuvenation. Only the political charlatans who know nothing can contest this truth, that the Cortes of Aragon and Catalonia were the best political model of a justly balanced government. . . . The French have written their constitution with the goal of being happy, and not with that of making others unhappy. They cannot be happy, any more than anyone else can, without acquiring liberty, which the Creator of all things gave them as the most precious patrimony; therefore they do not wish to conquer anyone; they do not wish to take over any property, but only to destroy tyrants, who, while not working, seek to use other people's property, and to live off the work of the poor, taking advantage of it to fulfill their infamous pleasures, [while] calling them, to deceive them, "beloved children" and "vassals."

Peace and war the French bring with them—peace for men and war for tyrannical kings. If France's troops cause any damage, France swears and promises to pay for it as it has done in Belgium and Germany.

60. Charles IV,
Declaration of War on France (1793)

When the French Revolution began in 1789, Spain's rulers watched warily and used all available means to keep word of events in France from crossing the border into Spain. In August 1792, however, a crowd in Paris invaded the royal palace and imprisoned King Louis XVI, who was a blood relative of Spain's king, Charles IV. After months of debate among the French revolutionaries, the French government decided to execute Louis XVI, beheading him on January 21, 1793. Amid the deteriorating relations between the two countries, France declared war on Spain, prompting Charles to issue the following public statement on March 25, 1793.

SOURCE: Fernando Díaz-Plaja, *Historia de España en sus documentos: Siglo XVIII* (Madrid: Cátedra, 1986), 290–91.

Among the principal objectives I have pursued since my ascension to the throne, one I have regarded as supremely important has been that of seeking to maintain tranquility in Europe. This is a matter in which, in contributing to the general good of humanity, I have given my faithful and beloved vassals special proof of the paternal vigilance I constantly use in everything that can contribute to the happiness I so strongly desire for them. . . . The moderation with which I have proceeded in dealing with France ever since the moment when it began to show the beginnings of disorder, of impiety, and of anarchy . . . is so well known that it would be pointless to demonstrate it. It will therefore be enough for me to limit myself to what has happened in these last months, without mentioning the horrendous and repeated events I wish to keep out of my mind and those of my beloved vassals, though I will indicate the most atrocious of them, since that is indispensable.

My principal aims were limited to finding out if it would be feasible to reduce the French to a national party that would contain its excessive ambitions, avoiding a general war in Europe, while we simply sought the freedom of the deeply Christian king Louis XVI and his august family, prisoners in a tower, and exposed daily to the greatest insults and dangers. To achieve these ends, so useful to universal calm, so much in accordance with the laws of humanity, so consistent with the obligations that blood ties impose, and so necessary for the maintenance of the luster of the Crown, I acceded to the repeated requests of the French Ministry, having two notes sent in which neutrality and the reciprocal withdrawal of troops were stipulated. When it appeared following negotiations that both points would be accepted, the clause concerning the withdrawal of troops was disputed, as they proposed to leave some of theirs on the outskirts of Bayonne, under the specious pretext of fearing an invasion by the English; but in reality the point was to gain advantages by keeping themselves in a fearful state, and one that would be costly for us given the need we would face of leaving equal forces on our border, if we did not wish to be exposed to a surprise attack by undisciplined and disobedient people. Nor did they fail to speak repeatedly and ostentatiously (in that same note) in the name of the "French Republic," and they did this intending for us to recognize that status by accepting that document.

I had ordered that in presenting the notes referred to here in Paris, one should make the most effective efforts possible in favor of King Louis XVI and his unfortunate family, and if I did not specifically make an improvement in the fate of those princes a condition of neutrality and disarmament, it was because I feared that doing so might worsen their situation. . . . But I was convinced that unless there was a complete lack of good faith on the part of the Ministry of France, the latter could not fail to see that such a strong recommendation and intervention, made at the time of the delivery of the notes, had such a strong tacit link, that they had to have known it was not feasible to determine the one if the other was not observed, and that not expressing it was purely a matter of being diplomatic and circumspect, so that the French Ministry, in having to deal with the various parties into which France was and is divided, would have some leeway in achieving the good we believed was appropriate. [The French Ministry's] bad faith was soon made evident, for as misunderstanding arose regarding the suggestions and interventions of a sovereign who is at the head of a great and generous nation, it insisted that the notes be amended; each instance was accompanied by threats that if these amendments were not accepted, then their representatives would be withdrawn from the negotiations. While these demands continued, mixed with threats, they were carrying out the cruel and unimaginable murder of their sovereign. When my heart and those of all the Spaniards found themselves burdened, horrified, and outraged by such an atrocious crime, even then they sought to continue negotiations, no longer, certainly, in the belief that they would be likely to succeed, but rather to outrage my honor and that of my vassals. For they knew well that in such circumstances each demand was a kind of irony and a taunt to which one could not listen without abandoning one's dignity and decorum. Their envoy asked for passports, which were given; at the same time a French ship was pursuing a Spanish one near the coast of Catalonia, through which the commanding general ordered a reprisal; and at the same time news arrived that other prisoners had been taken, and that in Marseilles and other French ports our ships were being detained and blockaded.

Finally, on the seventh day of this month they declared war on us, which they had already been waging (though without having announced it) at least since February 26, for that is the date when the interference with our ships of war and commerce began. . . .

As a consequence, then, of such conduct and of the hostilities begun by France, even before its declaration of war, I have sent orders, by my royal decree of the twenty-third day of this month, communicated to my Supreme Council of War, to take all measures to detain, rebuff, or attack the enemy on land or sea, given the opportunities that present themselves. I have resolved that from the moment when this is declared and published in this court, measures and steps appropriate for the defense of my dominions and vassals, and for the harm of the enemy, should be taken against France, its possessions, and inhabitants, without any delay. [We] prohibit . . . all commerce, dealings, and communication between them and us, under the grave penalties expressed in the Pragmatic Laws and Royal Certificates released with such motives, which all of my vassals and inhabitants of these kingdoms and territories, without exception for anyone, no matter how privileged, [must obey]. It is my royal will that this declaration of war should be made known to my vassals as quickly as possible, so that they can guard their interests and persons from the insults of the French, and so that they can devote themselves to hampering them by means of arms, and by all other means that the laws of war permit. Toward the same end, the captains and commanding generals should have this decree promulgated in the capitals, . . . in the plazas, ports, and other towns under their respective commands by the commanders or officers or the judicial officials, where there are no officers.

61. Gaspar Melchor de Jovellanos, Letter on the French Revolution (1794)

Given that Spain's Enlightenment reformers had always looked to France for ideas and inspiration, the advent of the French Revolution in 1789 put them in a difficult situation—which only grew more difficult as that revolution turned increasingly violent and radical. There are relatively few examples of the reformers' statements about the revolution, in part because of the Spanish government's rigid policy of public silence about events in France, and in part because of the reformers' own discomfort at their association with French ideas. One exception is the following letter that Jovellanos wrote to a friend, Alexander Jardine, the English consul in the northwestern town of La Coruña. Although most British officials were hostile to the French Revolution, Jardine generally supported it and was a friend of the revolutionary leader Georges Danton.

SOURCE: Gaspar Melchor de Jovellanos, *Obras completas*, vol. 2 (Oviedo: Centro de Estudios del Siglo XVIII, 1985), 634–37; the text also appears in Biblioteca de autores españoles 50 (Madrid: Real Academia Española, 1952), 366–67.

My dear friend,

[José] Hermida finally arrived and delivered your two letters of April 3 and 26 to me; he also delivered the one included by Lord F. Cornide. I have read all three carefully and completely. . . . I cannot fail to offer a warning: that you write with some caution. It is not necessary in regard to me (as long as the letters come by secure means); but it is in regard to others whose spirits are not mature enough to face great truths. You explain yourself very openly in relation to the Inquisition; I am of the same sentiments on that point, and I believe that there are many, very many, who agree with us. But how far we are from that opinion being general! As long as it is not, this abuse cannot be attacked frontally; all would be lost. The same thing would happen as on other occasions: [it would] consolidate its foundations more and more and make its system more cruel and insidious. What is the solution? I can only find one. To begin by taking away its right to prohibit books, and to give it solely to the council in general, and to the bishops in matters of dogma; to destroy one authority with another. You cannot imagine how much would be gained by this.

It is true that the council members are as superstitious as the Inquisitors; but enlightenment will be introduced among them more quickly. . . . Even among the bishops there are better ideas. Ecclesiastical studies have improved greatly. Within a few years Salamanca will be much better than it is now, and though it is now worth little, it is worth more than it was twenty years ago. I am sure you will say that these remedies are slow in coming. This is true, but there are no others; and if there are, I will not be for them.

I have already said this: I will never consent to sacrificing the present generation to improve future ones. You approve of the spirit of rebellion, but I do not: I disapprove of it openly, and I am very far from believing that it bears the seal of merit. Let us understand each other. I praise those who have the courage to speak the truth, those who sacrifice themselves for it, but not those who sacrifice other innocent beings to their opinions, which generally are nothing but their own personal desires, whether good or bad. I believe that a nation that becomes enlightened can carry out great reforms without bloodshed, and I think that to become enlightened rebellion is not necessary. I reject the opinion of Mably,[1] which authorizes civil war, whatever it may bring; I detest it, and the French will make all sensible men detest it. This is its situation. The Vendée, Lyon, Toulon, Marseilles, etc. [where rebellions against the revolutionary government had broken out] prove this, as if Paris was not a theater of this two years ago. I compare their proscriptions of September 1792 through April 5 of last year with those of Rome, and I find them more ferocious, more prolonged and durable, and more unworthy. . . . [Jovellanos is arguing that the measures the Catholic Church takes against its opponents are milder and more reasoned than those the French revolutionaries use; his reference to September 1792, for example, concerns the "September Massacres," when a revolutionary mob in Paris stormed a prison and slaughtered the revolutionary government's political prisoners.]

Let us reduce our disagreements to specific and precise points, and let us devote one or more letters to each one, and I will tell you some of my ideas.

1. Offering as the object of the present work the most perfect end, that is, the system of Godwin,[2] I believe that we will distance ourselves more from him. If the human spirit is progressive, as I believe (although this truth itself merits a separate discussion), it is clear that one cannot pass from the first to the last idea. Progress supposes a gradual chain, and the way will be pointed out by the order of its links. The rest will not be called progress, but rather something else. It would not be improving, but rather going around; not moving along a line, but rather moving inside a circle. France proves

1. Gabriel Bonnot de Mably (1709–1785) was a French philosopher and political writer who advocated a bold and confrontational approach to political change in the decades before the French Revolution.

2. William Godwin, author of *Enquiry Concerning Political Justice* (London, 1793). Godwin, whose ideas helped create the concept of anarchism, opposed the existence of private property and governments, trusting in the power of reason to allow people to live in self-sufficient communities.

this to us. Liberty, equality, republic, federalism, anarchy . . . and who knows what else will follow, but certainly they will not proceed to our goal, or else my vision is very poor. It is, then, necessary to pursue progress gradually.

2. The moral state of nations is not uniform, but rather as diverse as their governments. So all cannot propose the same end in their improvements. Following the natural progress of ideas, each one must look for that which is closest to its state, to pass from that to a better one. England, for example, has less to do than we do (let us not speak of France until we see where it ends up . . .). Does it seem to you that it would be unfortunate for us to become like England, to know representation, political and civil liberty, and, supposing the division of property, a legislation more protective of it? Certainly it would be great, given that in being in that situation we would have grounds to aspire not to Godwin's system, but rather, for example, to a constitution like the one that Louis XVI swore to in 1791.[3] Do you see the immense distance that there is between the two, between the [1791 constitution] and that of [17]93? And perhaps the latter touches upon the link forged by Godwin? Can there not be many other intermediate steps? I believe so.

3. To bring nations closer to each other, that fortunate communication of ideas that you and I both desire is necessary; but this communication requires a general peace. If this is possible, it will only be so through the means of the unity of ideas, and that unity must be the effect, as it is the goal of that communication. . . . You must admit that each nation has its own means, which is that of improving its education; to improve it, it is necessary to remove the obstacles that block the progress of enlightenment; but only education can reveal them and can produce a determination to remove them. Here we have another circle. It is, then, impossible to take on this project other than slowly and, so to speak, obliquely, improving educational institutions, guiding them toward knowledge that helps approach the goal, steering them away from ideas that are contrary to them. . . .

4. In the meantime it is appropriate that each nation work to improve its own system, even if it is flawed, in order to bring itself closer to another that is better or less flawed. For example, if in working on our agrarian policies one should wish to establish communal property, one would commit a great blunder. If Godwin himself, instead of forming a theory, sought real improvements, he would have to leave his system for the meditation of the

---

3. The first constitution of the French Revolution featured a separation of powers, with a king acting as head of the executive and governing alongside an elected legislature—a system that would have represented a major liberalization if adopted in Spain. By 1792, however, a growing republican movement in France demanded the replacement of the 1791 constitution with a more radical document.

scholars and propose another one that was realistic; to have as few laws as possible; to allow as much individual land ownership and labor as possible, to let personal interest continue, and to seek in it the stimulus that is foolishly hoped for in laws and regulations; to diffuse the knowledge upon which the perfection of all the useful arts and particularly that of agriculture, the first and most important of all, depends; and in place of grants and privileges and partial systems of protection, to promote it through roads, irrigation canals, the removal of tolls for river crossings, the draining of lakes, the distribution of uncultivated public lands. This, in sum, is my system. . . .

Jovellanos wrote the following notes in his diary, referring to another letter to Jardine (now lost).

Letter to Jardine for tomorrow's mail: that nothing good can be hoped for from revolutions of government, and everything good from the improvement of ideas; that consequently they must derive from general opinion. . . . The example of France will corrupt the human species: proof in Poland, which now has its revolutionary tribunal. That the idea of communal property must only be proposed as a theory. That the effect of the war will be: first, France will remain a republic, but weak, turbulent, exposed to military tyranny, and if it is victorious, it will later recover its splendor; second, England, wise and ambitious, will increase its power with colonies; its government will be disturbed and bloody out of the necessity of preserving them, and its grandeur will always remain precarious; third, the other powers [will be] weakened, but if, being chastised, they prefer peace and protect the peaceful arts, and above all agriculture (the only one that can consolidate their powers), they will avoid ruin.

Bibliography

GENERAL HISTORIES (IN ENGLISH)

Carr, Raymond, ed. *Spain: A History*. Oxford: Oxford University Press, 2000.
Elliott, J. H. *Imperial Spain, 1469–1716*. London: Penguin Books, 1990.
Herr, Richard. *A Historical Essay on Modern Spain*. Berkeley: University of California Press, 1971.
Kamen, Henry. *Spain, 1469–1714: A Society of Conflict*. London: Longman, 1983.
Lynch, John. *Spain Under the Habsburgs*. 2nd ed. 2 vols. New York: New York University Press, 1984.
Payne, Stanley G. *A History of Spain and Portugal*. 2 vols. Madison: University of Wisconsin Press, 1973.
Pierson, Peter. *The History of Spain*. Westport, Conn.: Greenwood Press, 1999.
Vicens Vives, Jaime. *Approaches to the History of Spain*. 2nd ed. Trans. Joan Connelly Ullman. Berkeley: University of California Press, 1970.

COLLECTIONS OF HISTORICAL DOCUMENTS
(IN SPANISH AND ENGLISH)

Colección de documentos inéditos para la historia de España. 112 vols. Madrid: Imprenta de la Viuda de Calero, 1842–1895.
Díaz-Plaja, Fernando, ed. *Historia de España en sus documentos: Siglo XV*. Madrid: Cátedra, 1984.
——, ed. *Historia de España en sus documentos: Siglo XVI*. Madrid: Cátedra, 1988.
——, ed. *Historia de España en sus documentos: Siglo XVII*. Madrid: Cátedra, 1987.
——, ed. *Historia de España en sus documentos: Siglo XVIII*. Madrid: Cátedra, 1986.
García-Gallo, Alfonso, ed. *Manual de historia del derecho español*, 3rd ed. 2 vols. Madrid: A.G.E.S.A., 1967.
Hargreaves-Mawdsley, W. N., ed. and trans. *Spain Under the Bourbons, 1700–1833: A Collection of Documents*. Columbia: University of South Carolina Press, 1973.

SPECIALIZED STUDIES IN ENGLISH

Balcells, Albert. *Catalan Nationalism: Past and Present*. Ed. Geoffrey Walker, trans. Jacqueline Hall and Geoffrey Walker. New York: St. Martin's Press, 1996.
Beinart, Haim. *The Expulsion of the Jews from Spain*. Trans. Jeffrey M. Green. Portland: Littman Library of Jewish Civilization, 2002.
Bethell, Leslie, ed. *Colonial Spanish America*. Cambridge: Cambridge University Press, 1987.

——, ed. *The Independence of Latin America*. Cambridge: Cambridge University Press, 1987.

Boyden, James M. *The Courtier and the King: Ruy Gómez de Silva, Philip II, and the Court of Spain*. Berkeley: University of California Press, 1995.

Brown, Jonathan. *Painting in Spain, 1500–1700*. New Haven, Conn.: Yale University Press, 1999.

Callahan, William J. *Church, Politics, and Society in Spain, 1750–1874*. Cambridge, Mass.: Harvard University Press, 1984.

Casey, James. *Early Modern Spain: A Social History*. London: Routledge, 1999.

Christian, William A., Jr. *Local Religion in Sixteenth-Century Spain*. Princeton, N.J.: Princeton University Press, 1981.

Corteguera, Luis R. *For the Common Good: Popular Politics in Barcelona, 1580–1640*. Ithaca, N.Y.: Cornell University Press, 2002.

Defourneaux, Marcelin. *Daily Life in Spain in the Golden Age*. Trans. Newton Branch. Stanford, Calif.: Stanford University Press, 1970.

Dopico Black, Georgina. *Perfect Wives, Other Women: Adultery and Inquisition in Early Modern Spain*. Durham, N.C.: Duke University Press, 2001.

Elliott, J. H. *The Count-Duke of Olivares: The Statesman in an Age of Decline*. New Haven, Conn.: Yale University Press, 1986.

——. *Revolt of the Catalans*. Cambridge: Cambridge University Press, 1963.

——. *Spain and Its World, 1500–1700*. New Haven, Conn.: Yale University Press, 1989.

Feros, Antonio. *Kingship and Favoritism in the Spain of Philip III, 1598–1621*. Cambridge: Cambridge University Press, 2000.

Gibson, Charles. *Spain in America*. New York: Harper and Row, 1966.

Greenblatt, Stephen. *Marvelous Possessions: The Wonder of the New World*. Chicago: University of Chicago Press, 1991.

Haliczer, Stephen. *The Comuneros of Castile: The Forging of a Revolution, 1475–1521*. Madison: University of Wisconsin Press, 1981.

Herr, Richard. *The Eighteenth-Century Revolution in Spain*. Princeton, N.J.: Princeton University Press, 1958.

——. *Rural Change and Royal Finances in Spain at the End of the Old Regime*. Berkeley: University of California Press, 1989.

Kagan, Richard L. *Lucrecia's Dreams: Politics and Prophecy in Sixteenth-Century Spain*. Berkeley: University of California Press, 1990.

Kamen, Henry. *Philip of Spain*. New Haven, Conn.: Yale University Press, 1997.

——. *The Spanish Inquisition: A Historical Revision*. New Haven, Conn.: Yale University Press, 1998.

Lewis, James E. *The American Union and the Problem of Neighborhood: The United States and the Collapse of the Spanish Empire, 1783–1829*. Chapel Hill: University of North Carolina Press, 1998.

Liss, Peggy K. *Isabel the Queen: Life and Times*. Oxford: Oxford University Press, 1992.

Lynch, John. *The Spanish American Revolutions, 1808–1826*. 2nd ed. New York: W.W. Norton, 1986.

Mackay, Ruth. *The Limits of Royal Authority: Resistance and Obedience in Seventeenth-Century Castile*. Cambridge: Cambridge University Press, 1999.

Martin, Colin, and Geoffrey Parker. *The Spanish Armada*. Manchester: Manchester University Press, 1999.

Mattingly, Garrett. *The Armada*. Boston: Houghton Mifflin, 1974.

Nader, Helen. *Liberty in Absolutist Spain: The Habsburg Sale of Towns, 1516–1700*. Baltimore: Johns Hopkins University Press, 1990.

Nalle, Sara T. *God in La Mancha: Religious Reform and the People of Cuenca, 1500–1650*. Baltimore: Johns Hopkins University Press, 1992.

Pagden, Anthony. *European Encounters with the New World: From Renaissance to Romanticism*. New Haven, Conn.: Yale University Press, 1993.

———. *The Fall of Natural Man: The American Indian and the Origins of Comparative Ethnology*. Cambridge: Cambridge University Press, 1982.

———. *Lords of All the World: Ideologies of Empire in Spain, Britain, and France, c. 1500– c. 1800*. New Haven, Conn.: Yale University Press, 1995.

———. *Spanish Imperialism and the Political Imagination*. New Haven, Conn.: Yale University Press, 1998.

Parker, Geoffrey. *The Army of Flanders and the Spanish Road, 1567–1659*. Cambridge: Cambridge University Press, 1972.

———. *The Dutch Revolt*. Ithaca, N.Y.: Cornell University Press, 1977.

———. *The Grand Strategy of Philip II*. New Haven, Conn.: Yale University Press, 1998.

———. *Philip II*. Chicago: Open Court, 1995.

———. *Spain and the Netherlands, 1559–1659: Ten Studies*. London: Collins, 1979.

Payne, Stanley G. *Spanish Catholicism: An Historical Overview*. Madison: University of Wisconsin Press, 1984.

Phillips, Carla Rahn and William D. Phillips, Jr. *Spain's Golden Fleece: Wool Production and the Wool Trade from the Middle Ages to the Nineteenth Century*. Baltimore: Johns Hopkins University Press, 1997.

Phillips, William D., Jr. and Carla Rahn Phillips. *The Worlds of Christopher Columbus*. Cambridge: Cambridge University Press, 1992.

Rawlings, Helen. *Church, Religion, and Society in Early Modern Spain*. Houndmills: Palgrave, 2002.

Ringrose, David R. *Spain, Europe, and the "Spanish Miracle," 1700–1900*. Cambridge: Cambridge University Press, 1996.

Roth, Norman. *Conversos, Inquisition, and the Expulsion of the Jews from Spain*. Madison: University of Wisconsin Press, 1995.

Rubin, Nancy. *Isabella of Castile: The First Renaissance Queen*. New York: St. Martin's Press, 1991.

Ruiz, Teofilo. *Spanish Society, 1400–1600*. Harlow: Longman, 2001.

Shubert, Adrian. *Death and Money in the Afternoon: A History of the Spanish Bullfight*. New York: Oxford University Press, 1999.

Thompson, I. A. A. *Crown and Cortes: Government, Institutions, and Representation in Early-Modern Castile*. Aldershot: Variorum; Brookfield, Vt.: Ashgate, 1993.

———. *War and Society in Habsburg Spain*. Aldershot: Variorum; Brookfield, Vt.: Ashgate, 1992.

Thompson, I. A. A., and Bartolomé Yun Casalilla, eds. *The Castilian Crisis of the Seventeenth Century: New Perspectives on the Economic and Social History of Seventeenth-Century Spain*. Cambridge: Cambridge University Press, 1994.

Tomlinson, Janis. *From El Greco to Goya: Painting in Spain, 1561–1828*. New York: H.N. Abrams, 1997.

Walker, Geoffrey J. *Spanish Politics and Imperial Trade, 1700–1789*. Bloomington: Indiana University Press, 1979.

Index

Boldface indicates readings.